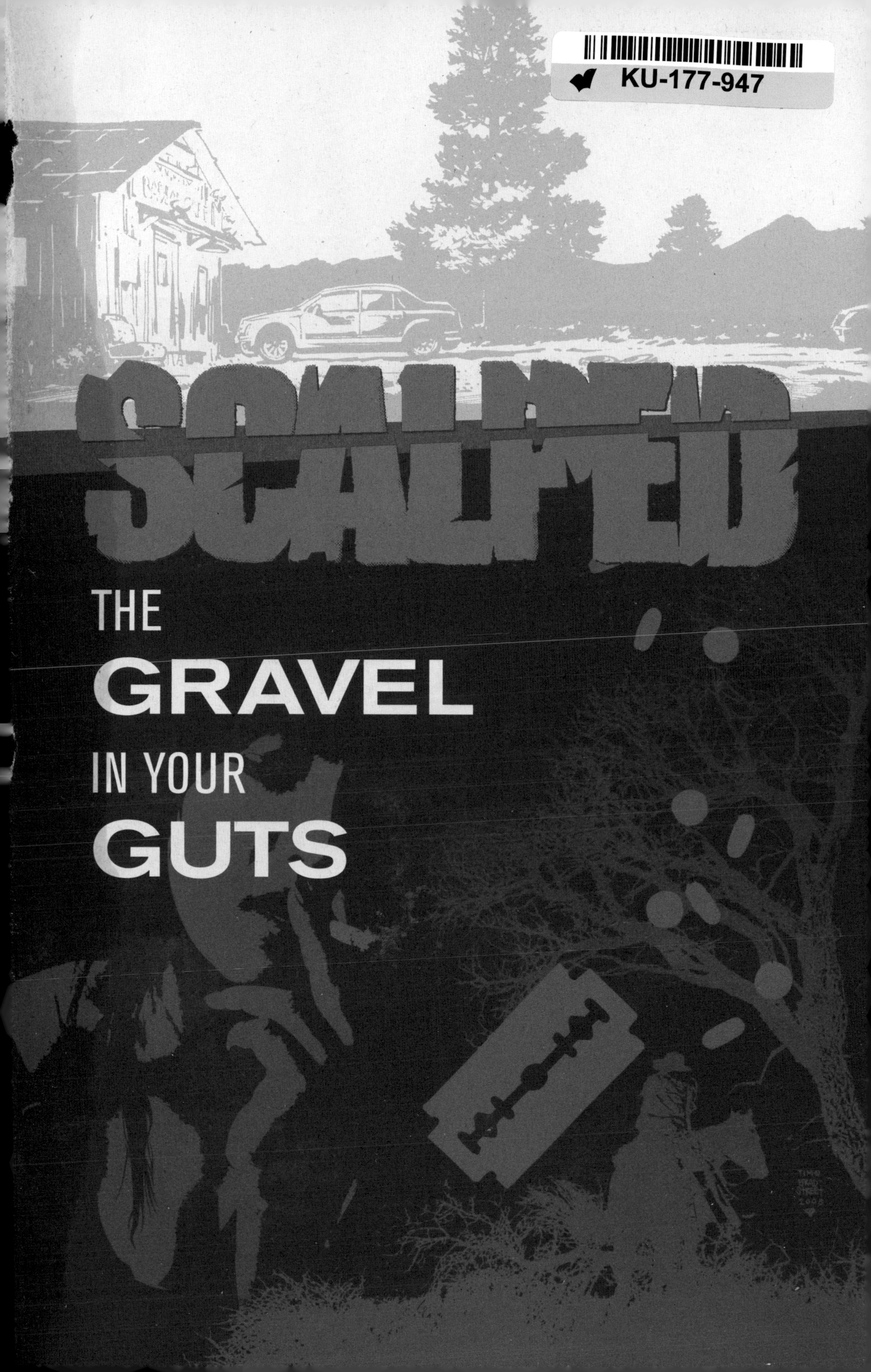
SCALPED
THE GRAVEL IN YOUR GUTS

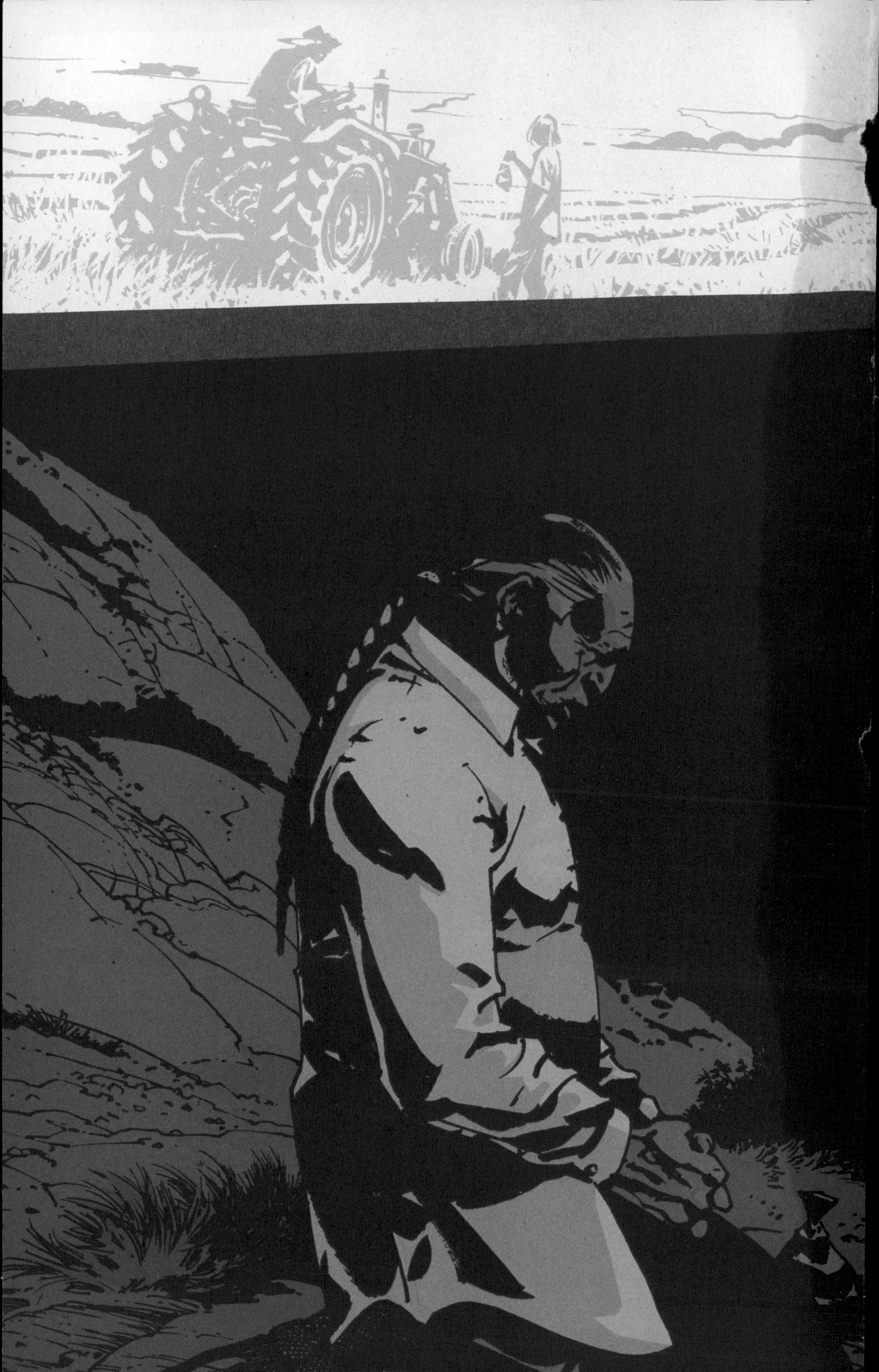

SCALPED

JASON AARON

WRITER

DAVIDE FURNÒ

THE BOUDOIR STOMP

ARTIST

R.M. GUÉRA

THE GRAVEL IN YOUR GUTS

ARTIST

GIULIA BRUSCO

COLORIST

STEVE WANDS

LETTERER

INTRODUCTION BY

ED BRUBAKER

THE GRAVEL IN YOUR GUTS

SCALPED created by

JASON AARON and R.M. GUÉRA

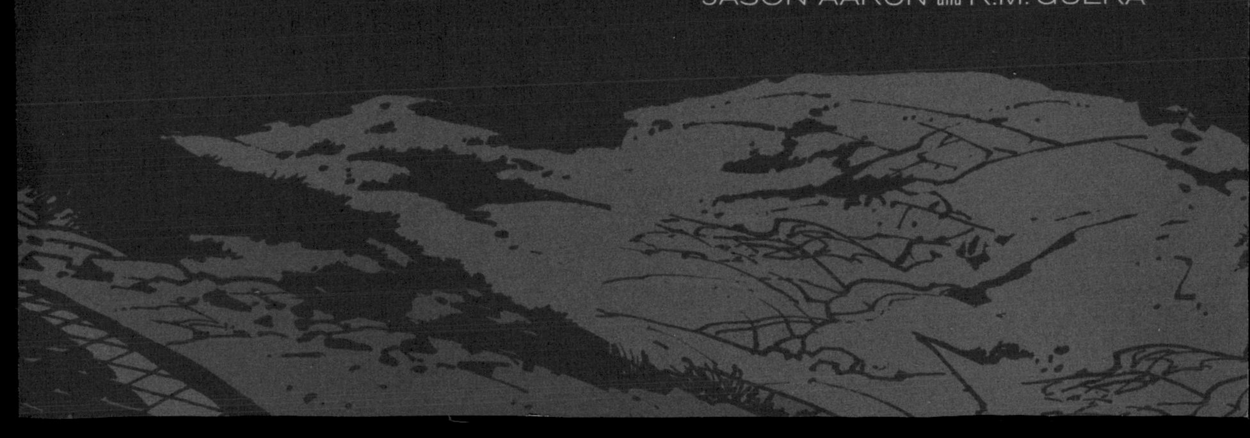

KAREN BERGER
Senior VP-Executive Editor

WILL DENNIS
Editor-original series

CASEY SEIJAS
MARK DOYLE
Assistant Editors-original series

BOB HARRAS
Editor-collected edition

ROBBIN BROSTERMAN
Senior Art Director

PAUL LEVITZ
President & Publisher

GEORG BREWER
VP-Design & DC Direct Creative

RICHARD BRUNING
Senior VP-Creative Director

PATRICK CALDON
Executive VP-Finance & Operations

CHRIS CARAMALIS
VP-Finance

JOHN CUNNINGHAM
VP-Marketing

TERRI CUNNINGHAM
VP-Managing Editor

AMY GENKINS
Senior VP-Business & Legal Affairs

ALISON GILL
VP-Manufacturing

DAVID HYDE
VP-Publicity

HANK KANALZ
VP-General Manager, WildStorm

JIM LEE
Editorial Director-WildStorm

GREGORY NOVECK
Senior VP-Creative Affairs

SUE POHJA
VP-Book Trade Sales

STEVE ROTTERDAM
Senior VP-Sales & Marketing

CHERYL RUBIN
Senior VP-Brand Management

ALYSSE SOLL
VP-Advertising & Custom Publishing

JEFF TROJAN
VP-Business Development, DC Direct

BOB WAYNE
VP-Sales

Cover illustration and logo design by JOCK

SCALPED
THE GRAVEL IN YOUR GUTS
Published by DC Comics. Cover, introduction and compilation
Copyright © 2009 DC Comics. All Rights Reserved.

Originally published in single magazine form as SCALPED
19-24. Copyright © 2008, 2009 Jason Aaron and Raijko
Milosevic. All Rights Reserved. VERTIGO and all characters,
their distinctive likenesses and related elements featured in
this publication are trademarks of DC Comics. The stories,
characters and incidents featured in this publication are
entirely fictional. DC Comics does not read or accept
unsolicited submissions of ideas, stories or artwork.

DC Comics, 1700 Broadway, New York, NY 10019
A Warner Bros. Entertainment Company.
Printed in Canada. Second Printing.
ISBN: 978-1-4012-2179-9

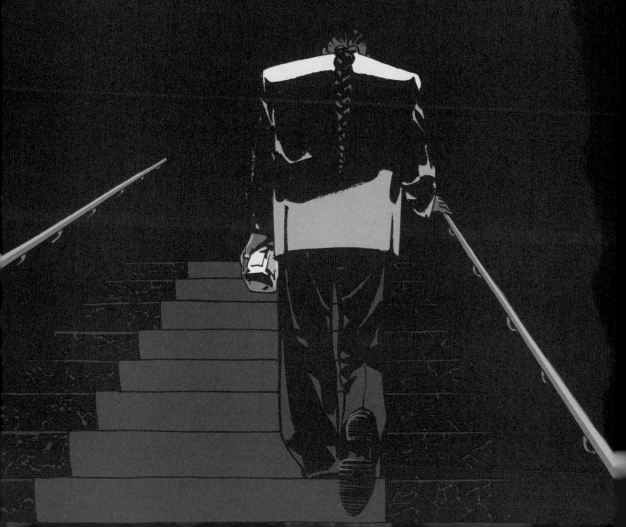

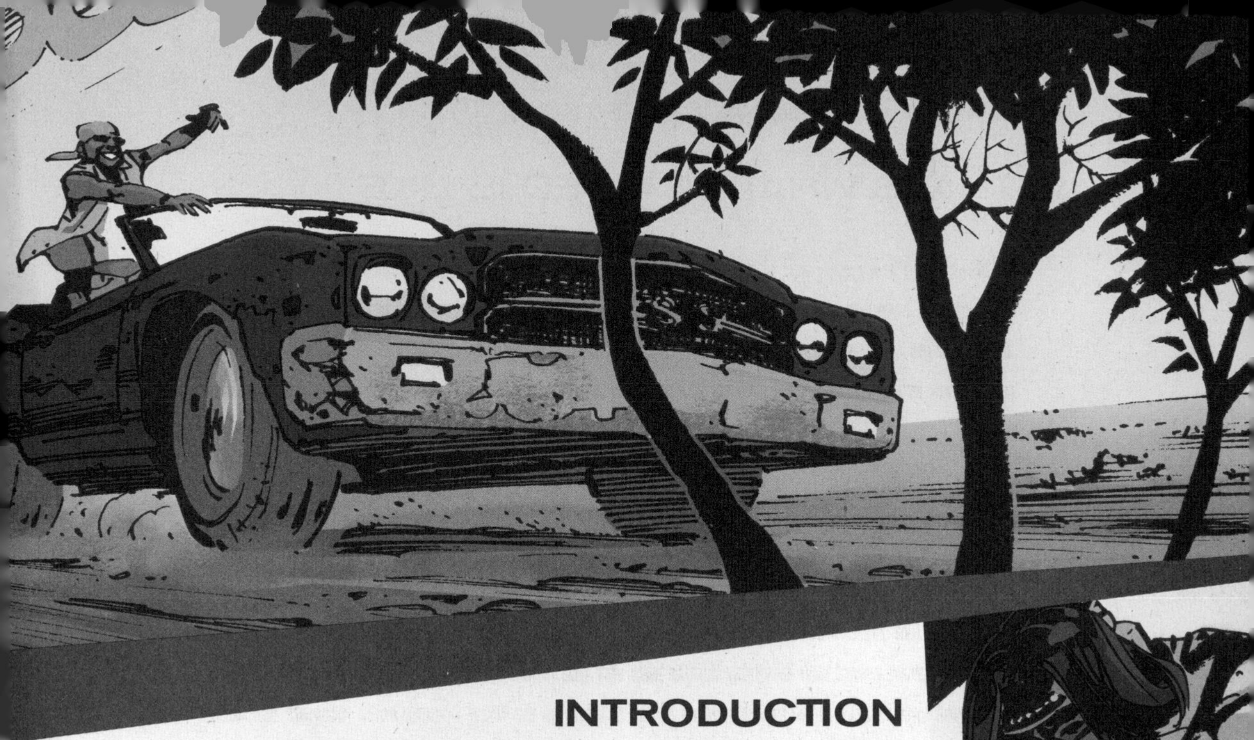

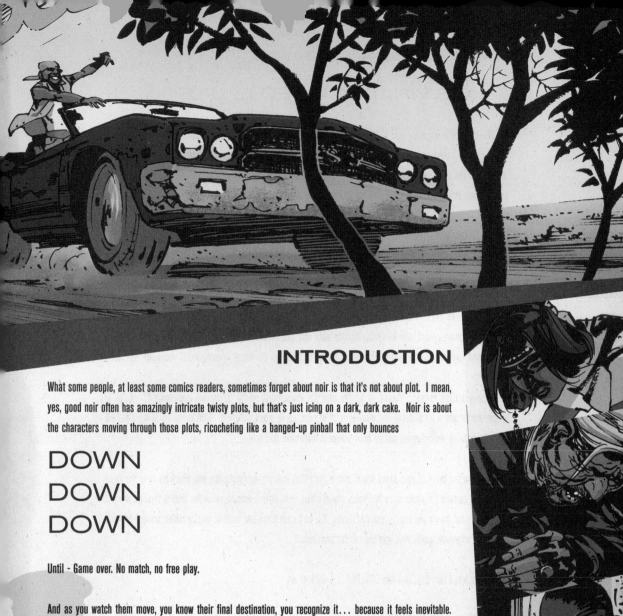

INTRODUCTION

What some people, at least some comics readers, sometimes forget about noir is that it's not about plot. I mean, yes, good noir often has amazingly intricate twisty plots, but that's just icing on a dark, dark cake. Noir is about the characters moving through those plots, ricocheting like a banged-up pinball that only bounces

DOWN
DOWN
DOWN

Until - Game over. No match, no free play.

And as you watch them move, you know their final destination, you recognize it... because it feels inevitable. To me, that's the heart of what noir is, inevitability. Noir is the entropy to society's order, the inevitable decay of us all.

When you're reading a good noir, the shocks and twists have a way of feeling déjà vu-like, as if you saw them coming, but hoped the characters would take a left turn... not answer that phone, not sleep with that woman, not sell drugs to those cops... but you knew they would. It would have been wrong if they didn't, and the real surprise can be that you care about someone you know is in for hell. You relate to them, even when their hell is so much bigger than your own. But we're all going to die, and we all make mistakes.

The best noir stories make you forget plot entirely by giving you characters that feel so well-realized you can't look away as they

FALL
FALL
FALL

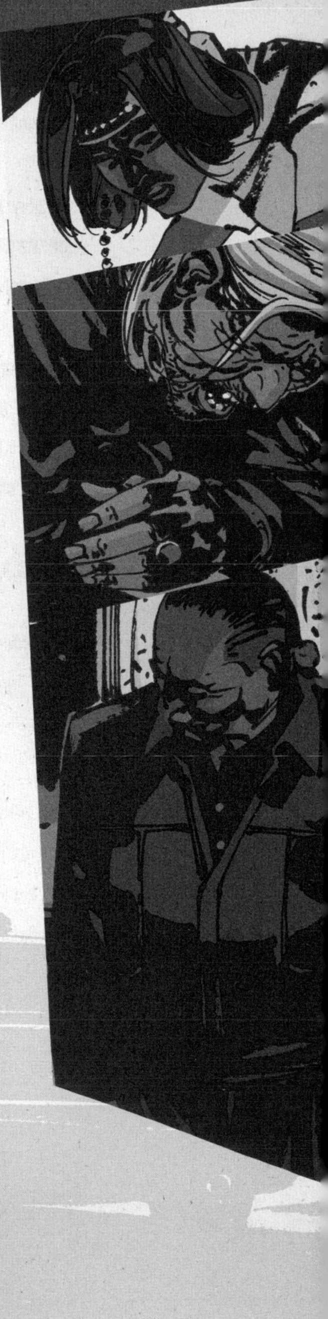

And setups that feel so real that you want to run from them screaming.

THAT'S WHAT SCALPED IS LIKE.

For three years in the early part of this decade, my wife and I lived on a farm in Mendocino County in a valley that had once been entirely Indian land. About half the valley was still a Reservation, and the town was split up among Indians and cowboys — it had its fair share of farmers and ranchers and hippies and pot growers, but it really came down to cowboys and Indians at the end of the day. So I know a bit about Indian life in modern America.

I've done ridealongs in sheriff's cars and listened to stories of abuse and self-hatred and fear. And I've seen their celebrations and listened to stories of proud history and magic.

And it feels like Jason Aaron has, too. I know he's making this all up, but his depiction of this once-proud people staggering toward their inevitable demise feels very real to me. And I think the guys on the Rez, from the drunks and speed-freaks at the car graveyards, to the activists on the Tribal Council, would recognize that, too.

The valley I lived in was referred to by the sheriff's department as "a target-rich environment." A lot of desperate people, a lot of drugs and alcohol, a lot of guns, all in close proximity. That is the world of SCALPED. It's a target-rich environment, and no book proves it more than this one.

Tapping into the heart of noir, Jason Aaron tells a story that is really many stories, and which all have the same ending. It doesn't get much more inevitable (there's that word again) than knowing the ending through most of the book — but here's the key... you don't care. You turn each page just as fast, maybe faster, wanting to know how each character winds their way toward that conclusion.

And that's why I love noir, and why SCALPED is a work of art.

ED BRUBAKER
January 2009

A one-time cartoonist, Ed Brubaker has been working as a writer since the early 1990s, and in that time his work has won several awards, including both the Harvey and Eisner Awards for Best Writer in 2007, and has been translated around the world. His comics credits include BATMAN, CATWOMAN, GOTHAM CENTRAL and SLEEPER for DC/WildStorm and *Daredevil*, *Captain America* and *Criminal* for Marvel. He recently created and scripted the online movie "Angel of Death" for Sony. Brubaker lives and works in Seattle, Washington with his wife, Melanie, and many pets.

THE BOUDOIR STOMP PART 1

COVER ART BY TIM BRADSTREET

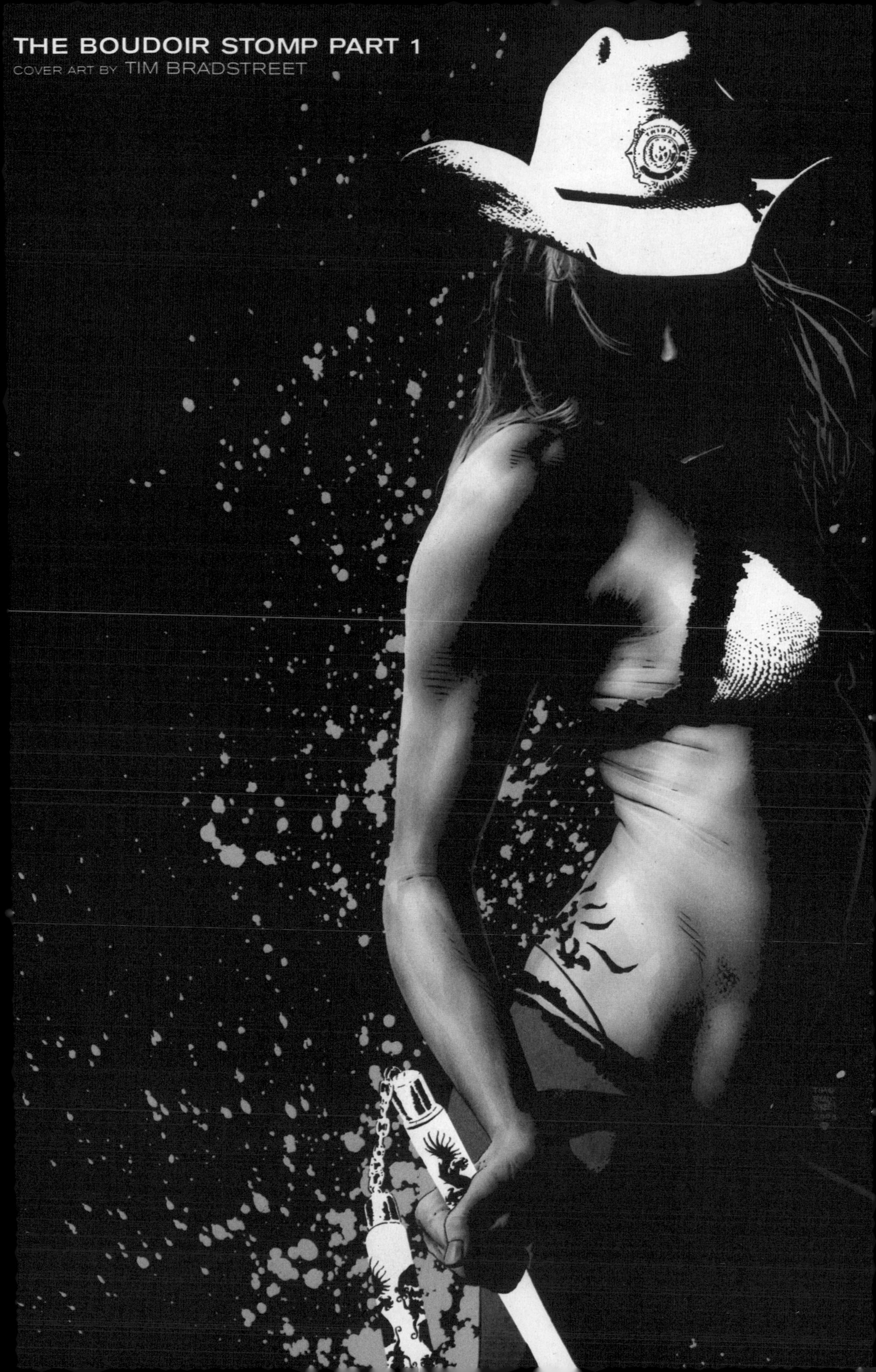

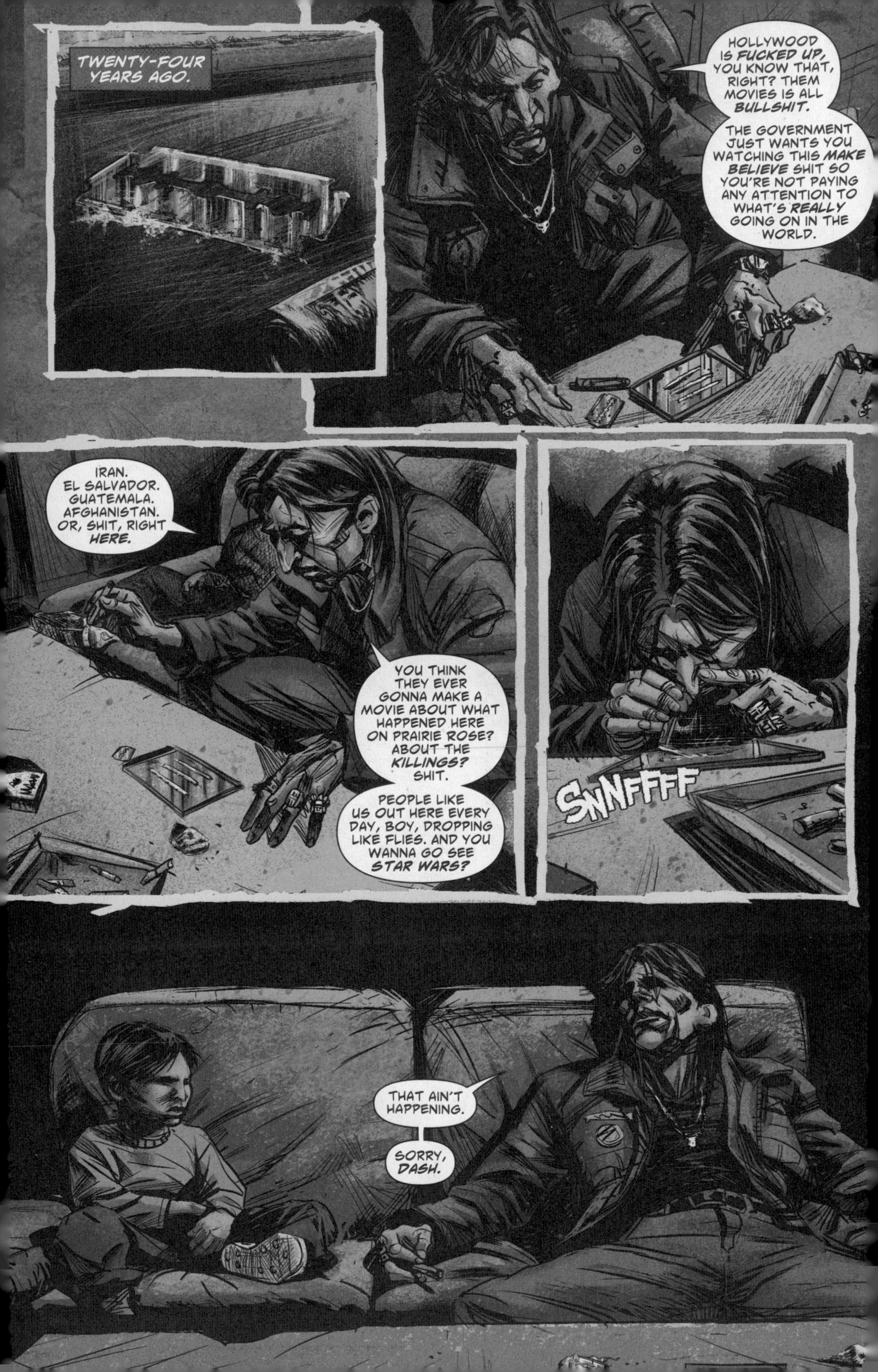
TWENTY-FOUR YEARS AGO.
HOLLYWOOD IS FUCKED UP, YOU KNOW THAT, RIGHT? THEM MOVIES IS ALL BULLSHIT.
THE GOVERNMENT JUST WANTS YOU WATCHING THIS MAKE BELIEVE SHIT SO YOU'RE NOT PAYING ANY ATTENTION TO WHAT'S REALLY GOING ON IN THE WORLD.
IRAN. EL SALVADOR. GUATEMALA. AFGHANISTAN. OR, SHIT, RIGHT HERE.
YOU THINK THEY EVER GONNA MAKE A MOVIE ABOUT WHAT HAPPENED HERE ON PRAIRIE ROSE? ABOUT THE KILLINGS? SHIT.
PEOPLE LIKE US OUT HERE EVERY DAY, BOY, DROPPING LIKE FLIES. AND YOU WANNA GO SEE STAR WARS?
SNNFFFF
THAT AIN'T HAPPENING.
SORRY, DASH.

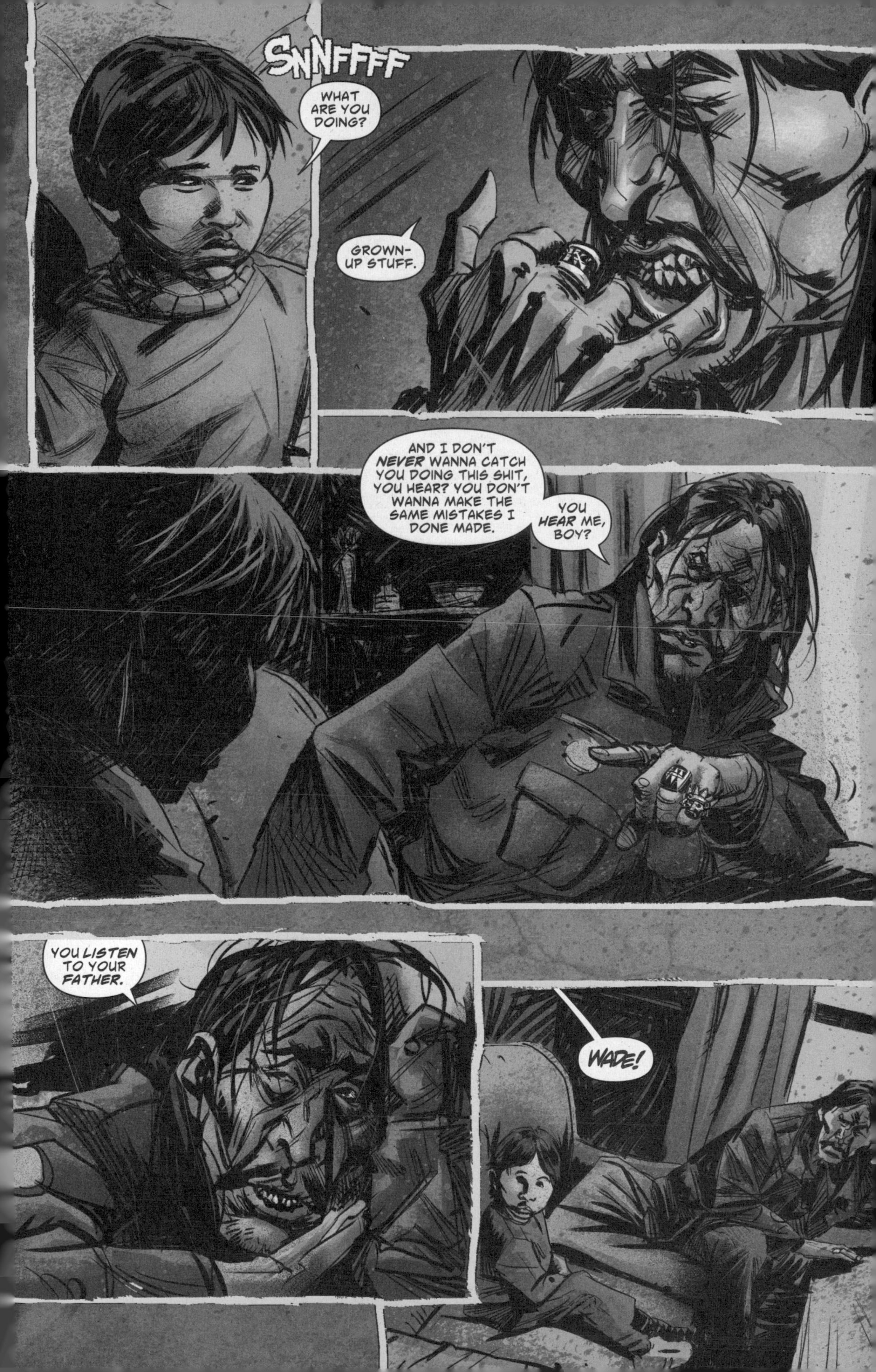
SNNFFFF
WHAT ARE YOU DOING?
GROWN-UP STUFF.
AND I DON'T NEVER WANNA CATCH YOU DOING THIS SHIT, YOU HEAR? YOU DON'T WANNA MAKE THE SAME MISTAKES I DONE MADE.
YOU HEAR ME, BOY?
YOU LISTEN TO YOUR FATHER.
WADE!

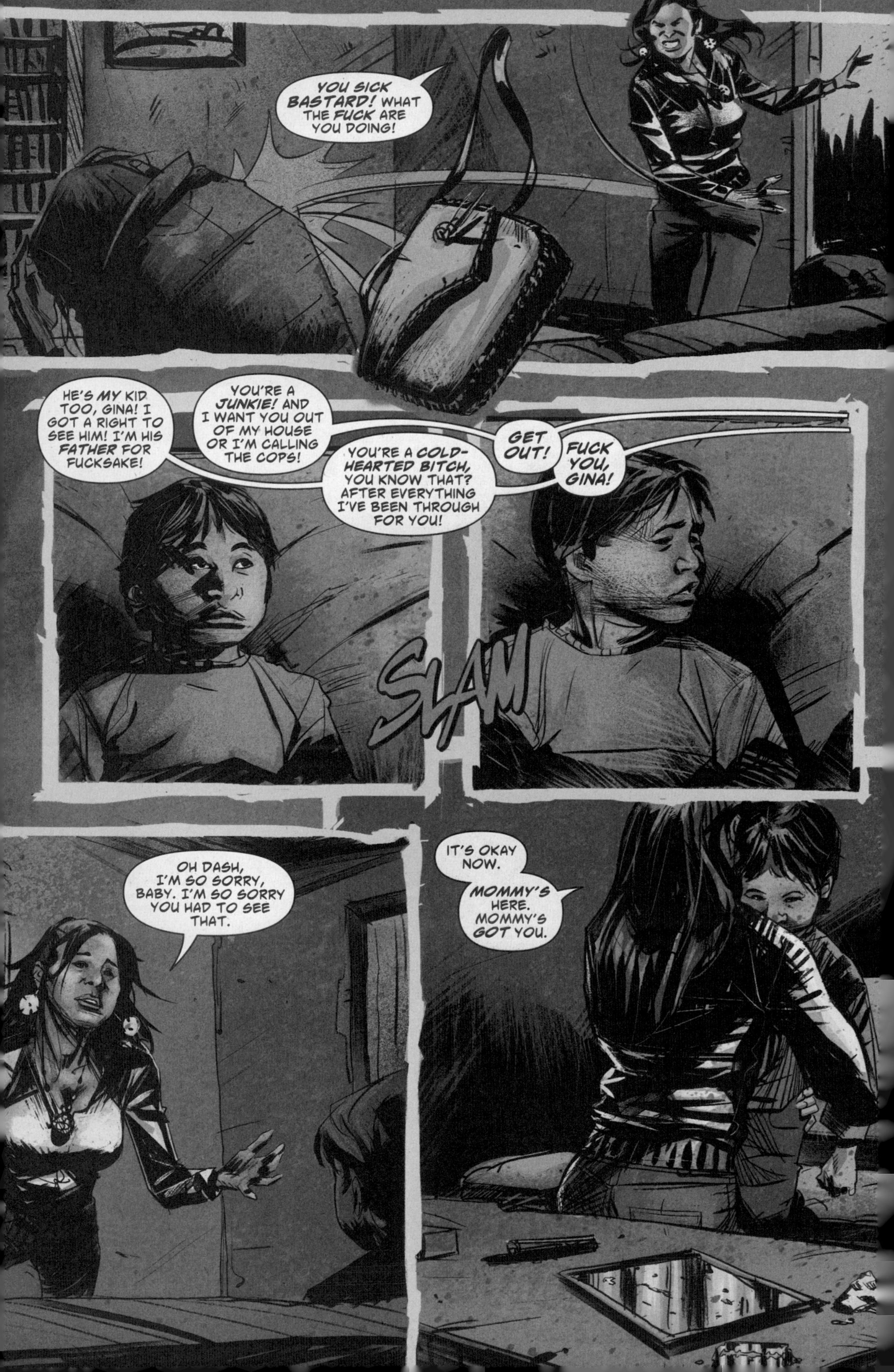
YOU SICK BASTARD! WHAT THE FUCK ARE YOU DOING!
HE'S MY KID TOO, GINA! I GOT A RIGHT TO SEE HIM! I'M HIS FATHER FOR FUCKSAKE!
YOU'RE A JUNKIE! AND I WANT YOU OUT OF MY HOUSE OR I'M CALLING THE COPS!
YOU'RE A COLD-HEARTED BITCH, YOU KNOW THAT? AFTER EVERYTHING I'VE BEEN THROUGH FOR YOU!
GET OUT!
FUCK YOU, GINA!
SLAM
OH DASH, I'M SO SORRY, BABY. I'M SO SORRY YOU HAD TO SEE THAT.
IT'S OKAY NOW.
MOMMY'S HERE. MOMMY'S GOT YOU.

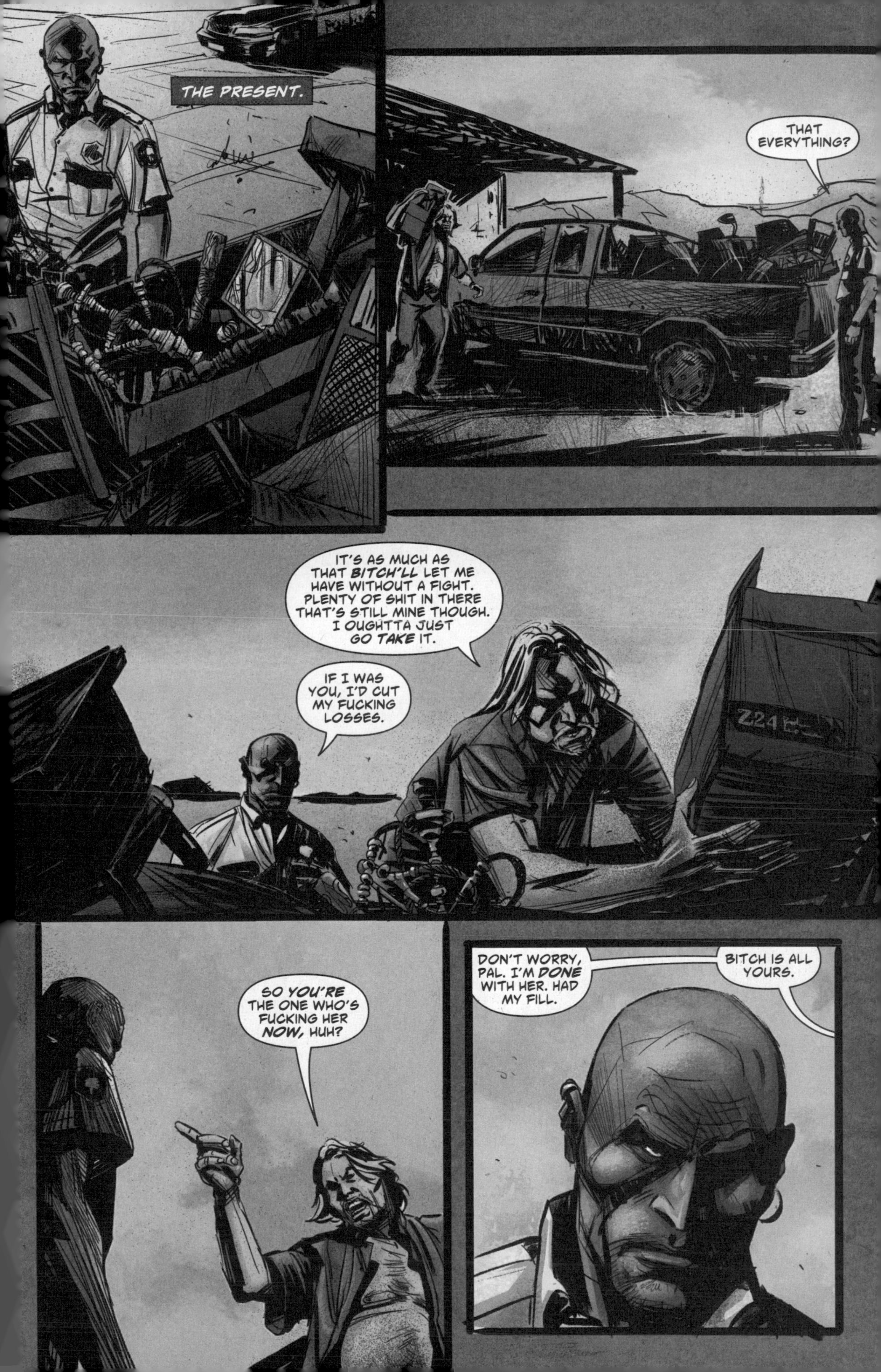
THE PRESENT.
THAT EVERYTHING?
IT'S AS MUCH AS THAT BITCH'LL LET ME HAVE WITHOUT A FIGHT. PLENTY OF SHIT IN THERE THAT'S STILL MINE THOUGH. I OUGHTTA JUST GO TAKE IT.
IF I WAS YOU, I'D CUT MY FUCKING LOSSES.
SO YOU'RE THE ONE WHO'S FUCKING HER NOW, HUH?
DON'T WORRY, PAL. I'M DONE WITH HER. HAD MY FILL.
BITCH IS ALL YOURS.

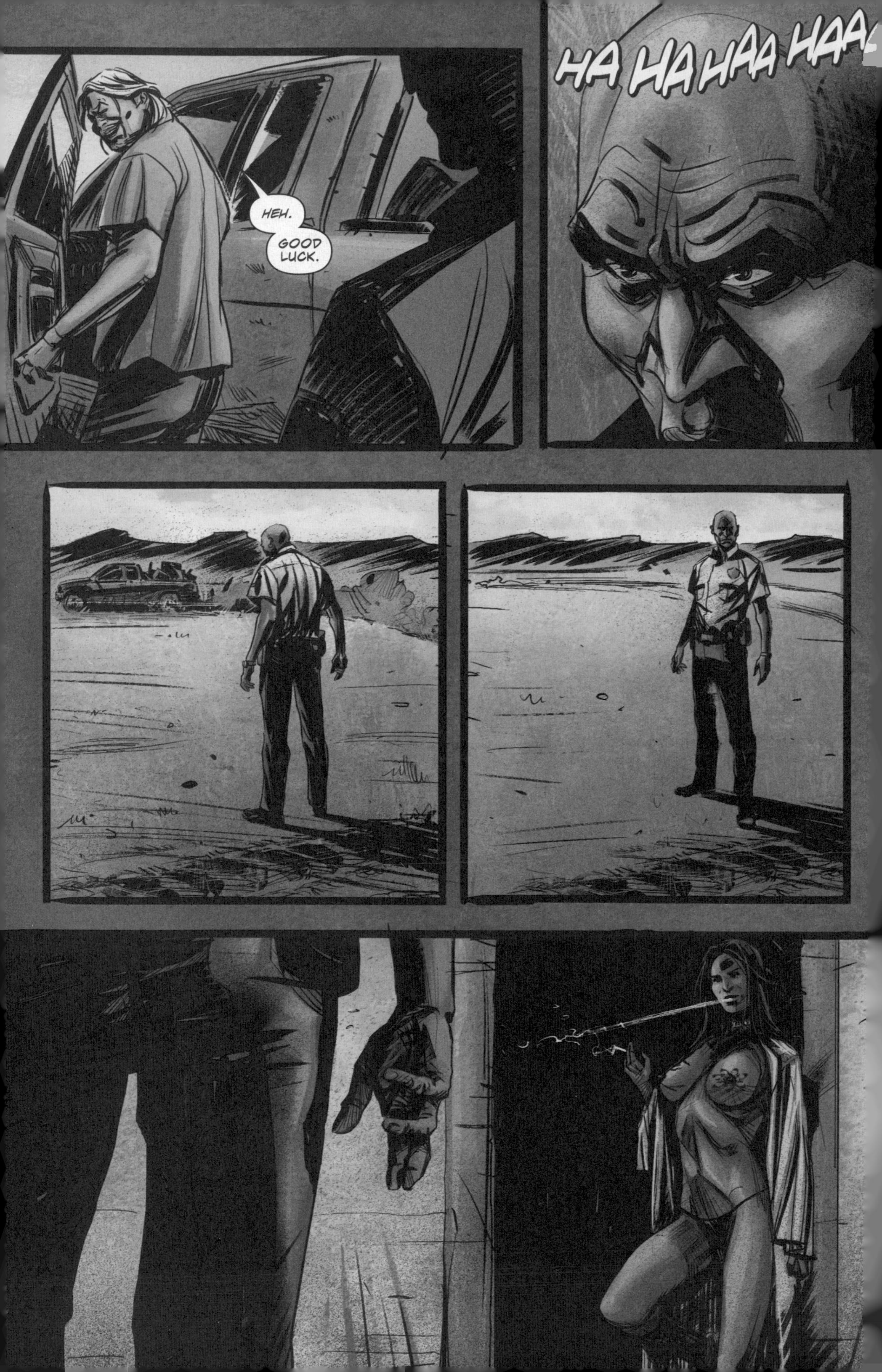
HEH.
GOOD LUCK.
HA HA HAA HAA

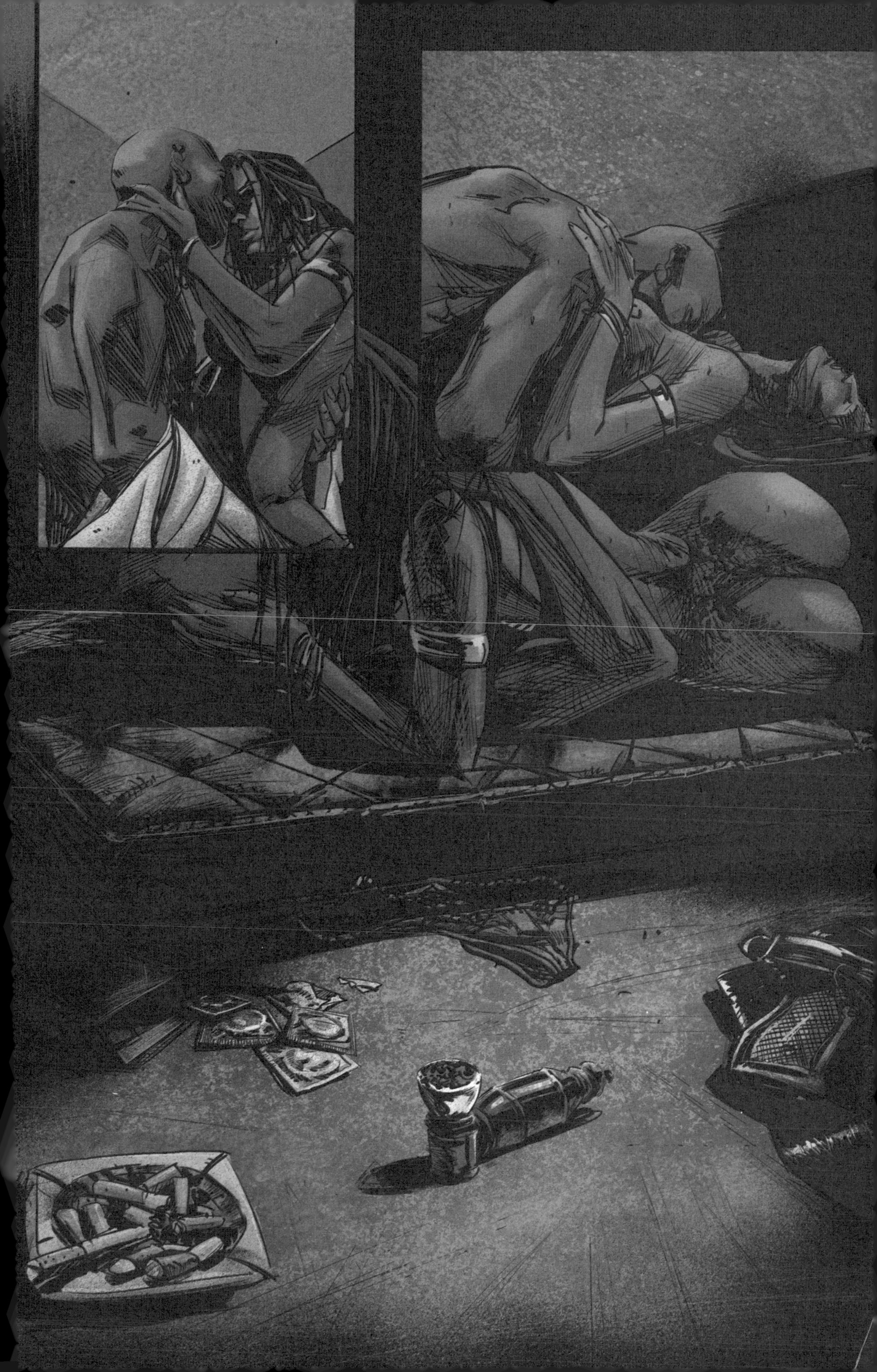

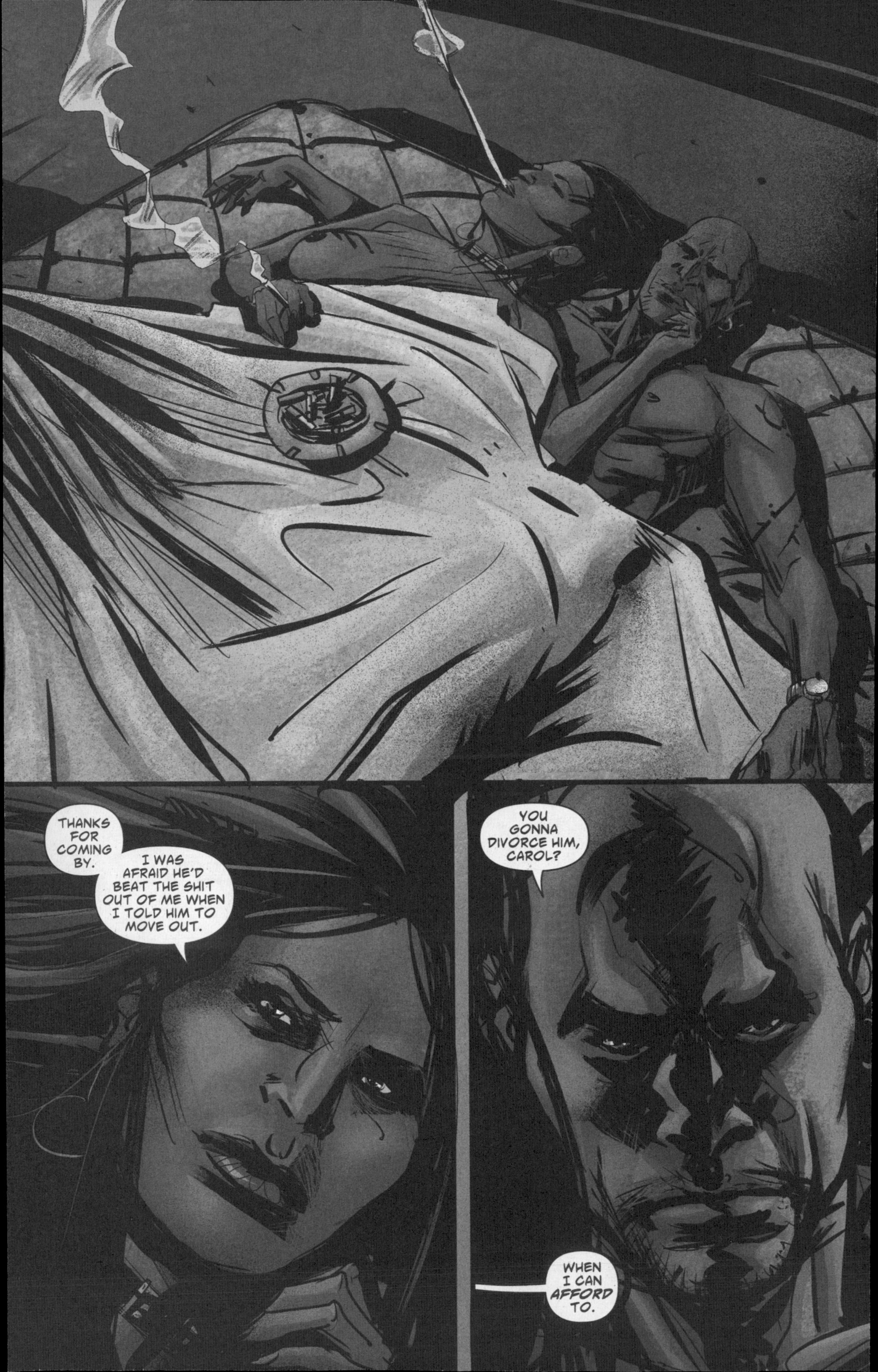
THANKS FOR COMING BY.
I WAS AFRAID HE'D BEAT THE SHIT OUT OF ME WHEN I TOLD HIM TO MOVE OUT.
YOU GONNA DIVORCE HIM, CAROL?
WHEN I CAN *AFFORD* TO.

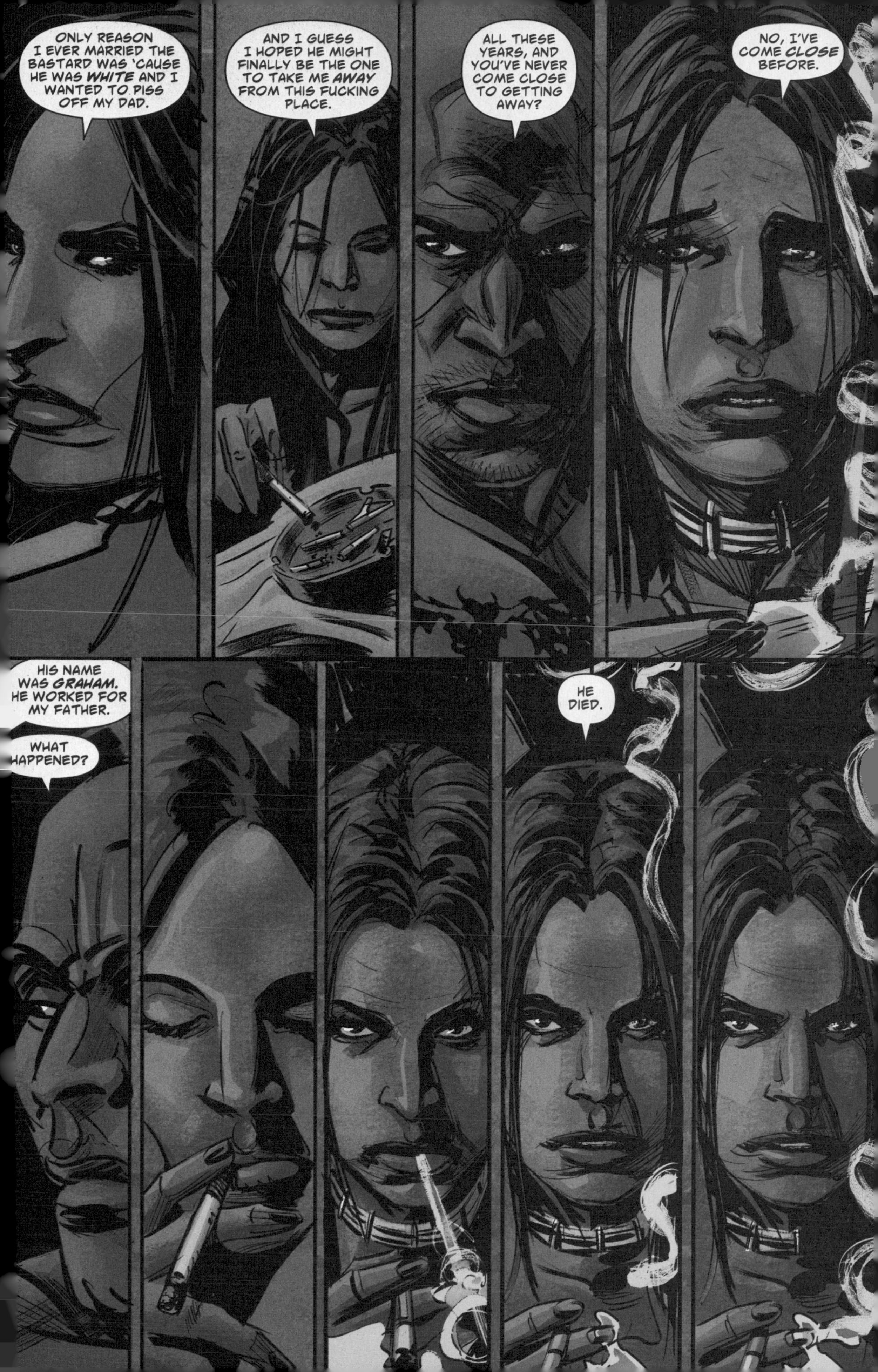
ONLY REASON I EVER MARRIED THE BASTARD WAS 'CAUSE HE WAS WHITE AND I WANTED TO PISS OFF MY DAD.
AND I GUESS I HOPED HE MIGHT FINALLY BE THE ONE TO TAKE ME AWAY FROM THIS FUCKING PLACE.
ALL THESE YEARS, AND YOU'VE NEVER COME CLOSE TO GETTING AWAY?
NO, I'VE COME CLOSE BEFORE.
HIS NAME WAS GRAHAM. HE WORKED FOR MY FATHER.
WHAT HAPPENED?
HE DIED.

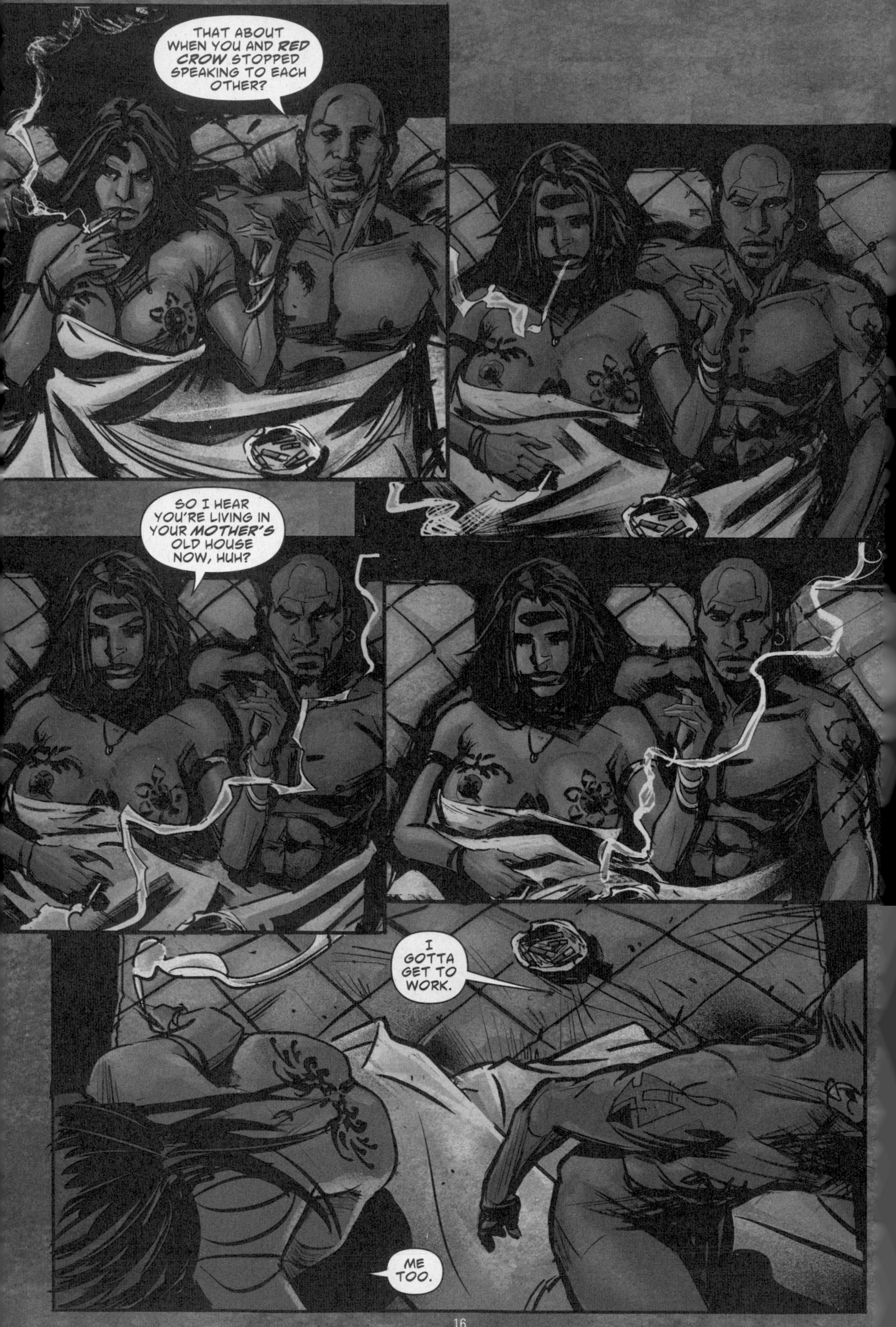
THAT ABOUT WHEN YOU AND RED CROW STOPPED SPEAKING TO EACH OTHER?
SO I HEAR YOU'RE LIVING IN YOUR MOTHER'S OLD HOUSE NOW, HUH?
I GOTTA GET TO WORK.
ME TOO.

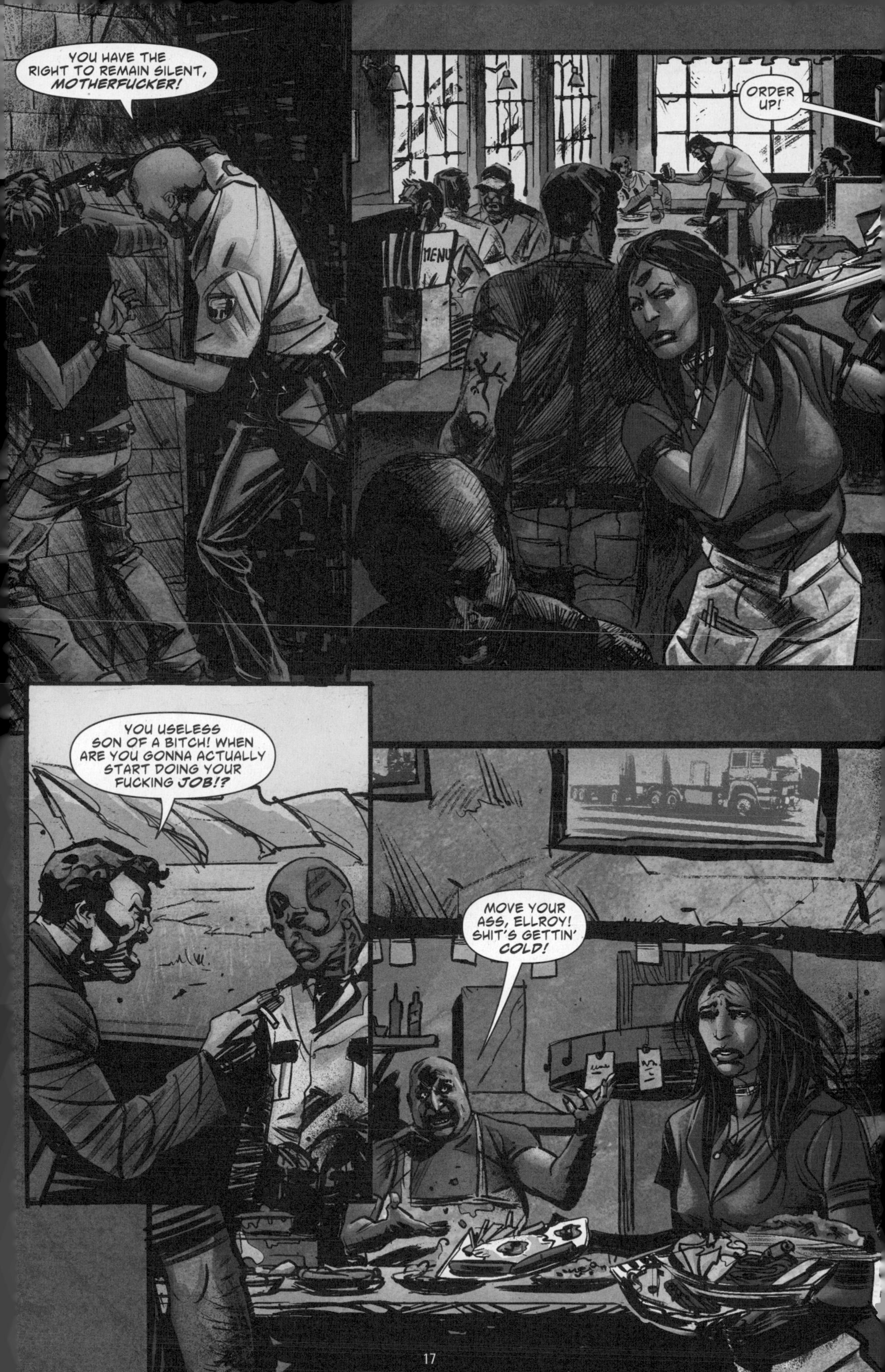
YOU HAVE THE RIGHT TO REMAIN SILENT, *MOTHERFUCKER!*
ORDER UP!
MENU
YOU USELESS SON OF A BITCH! WHEN ARE YOU GONNA ACTUALLY START DOING YOUR FUCKING *JOB!?*
MOVE YOUR ASS, ELLROY! SHIT'S GETTIN' *COLD!*

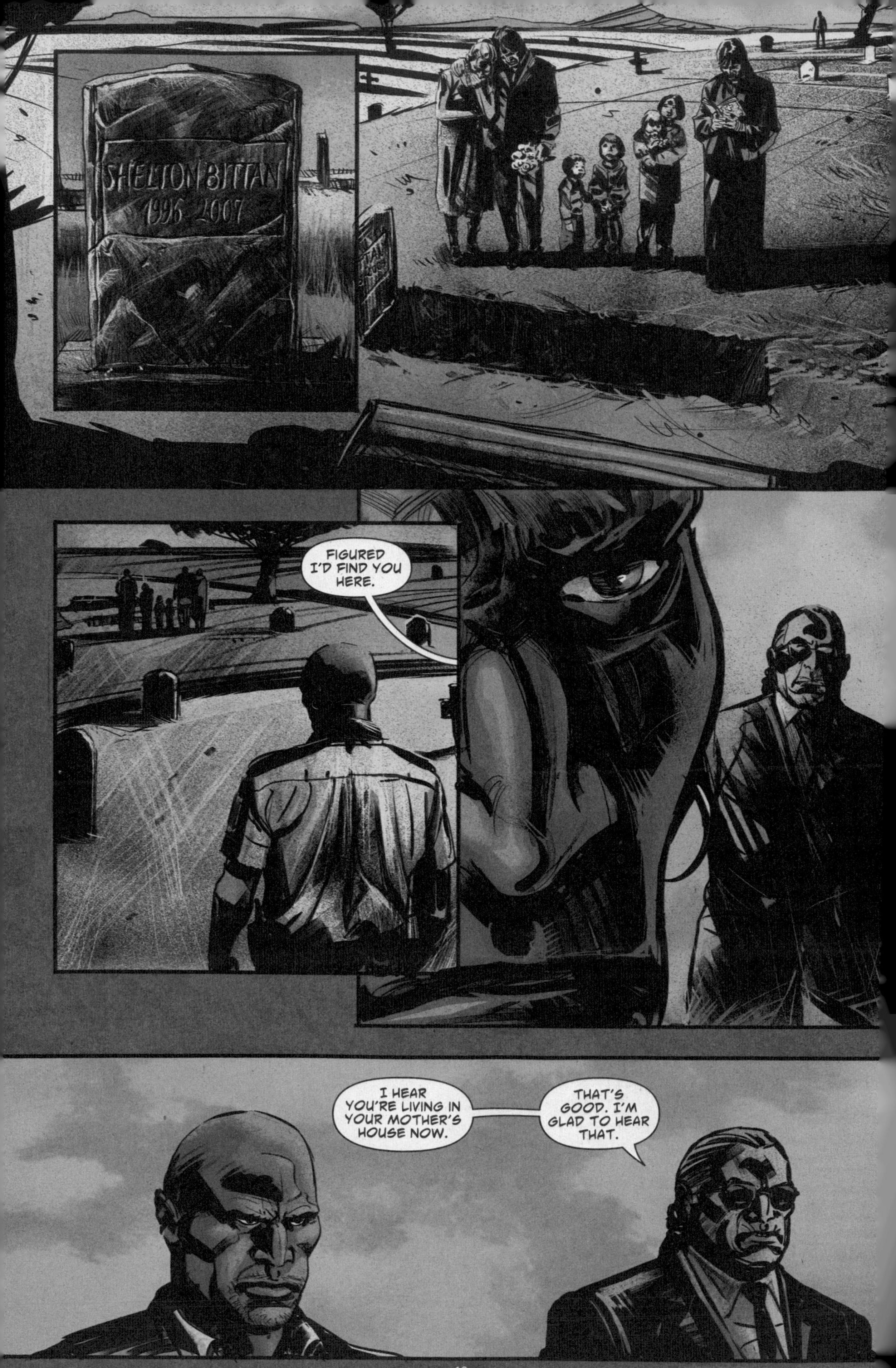
SHELTON BITTAN
1996 2007
FIGURED I'D FIND YOU HERE.
I HEAR YOU'RE LIVING IN YOUR MOTHER'S HOUSE NOW.
THAT'S GOOD. I'M GLAD TO HEAR THAT.

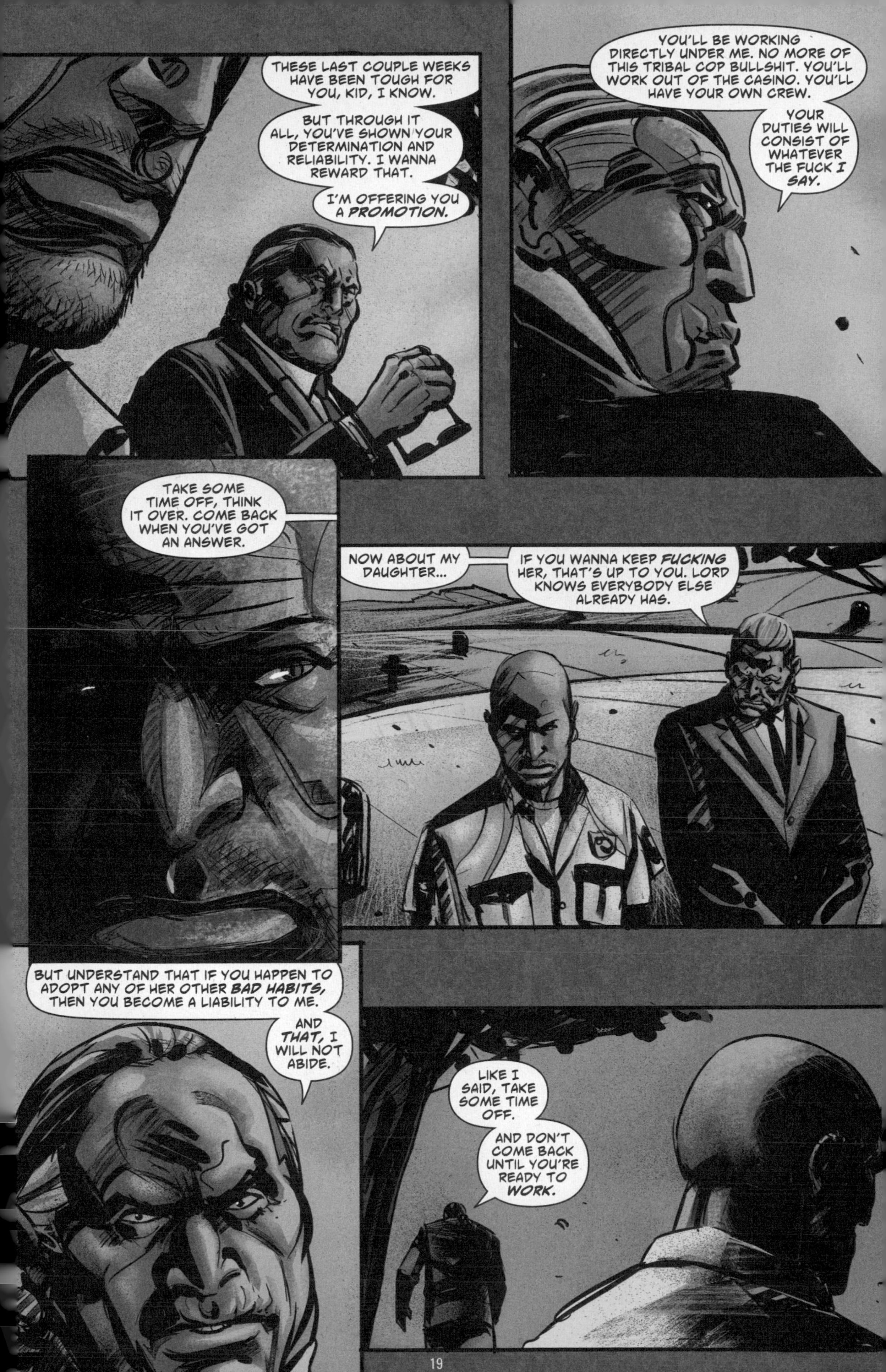
THESE LAST COUPLE WEEKS HAVE BEEN TOUGH FOR YOU, KID, I KNOW.
BUT THROUGH IT ALL, YOU'VE SHOWN YOUR DETERMINATION AND RELIABILITY. I WANNA REWARD THAT.
I'M OFFERING YOU A PROMOTION.
YOU'LL BE WORKING DIRECTLY UNDER ME. NO MORE OF THIS TRIBAL COP BULLSHIT. YOU'LL WORK OUT OF THE CASINO. YOU'LL HAVE YOUR OWN CREW.
YOUR DUTIES WILL CONSIST OF WHATEVER THE FUCK I SAY.
TAKE SOME TIME OFF, THINK IT OVER. COME BACK WHEN YOU'VE GOT AN ANSWER.
NOW ABOUT MY DAUGHTER...
IF YOU WANNA KEEP FUCKING HER, THAT'S UP TO YOU. LORD KNOWS EVERYBODY ELSE ALREADY HAS.
BUT UNDERSTAND THAT IF YOU HAPPEN TO ADOPT ANY OF HER OTHER BAD HABITS, THEN YOU BECOME A LIABILITY TO ME.
AND THAT, I WILL NOT ABIDE.
LIKE I SAID, TAKE SOME TIME OFF.
AND DON'T COME BACK UNTIL YOU'RE READY TO WORK.

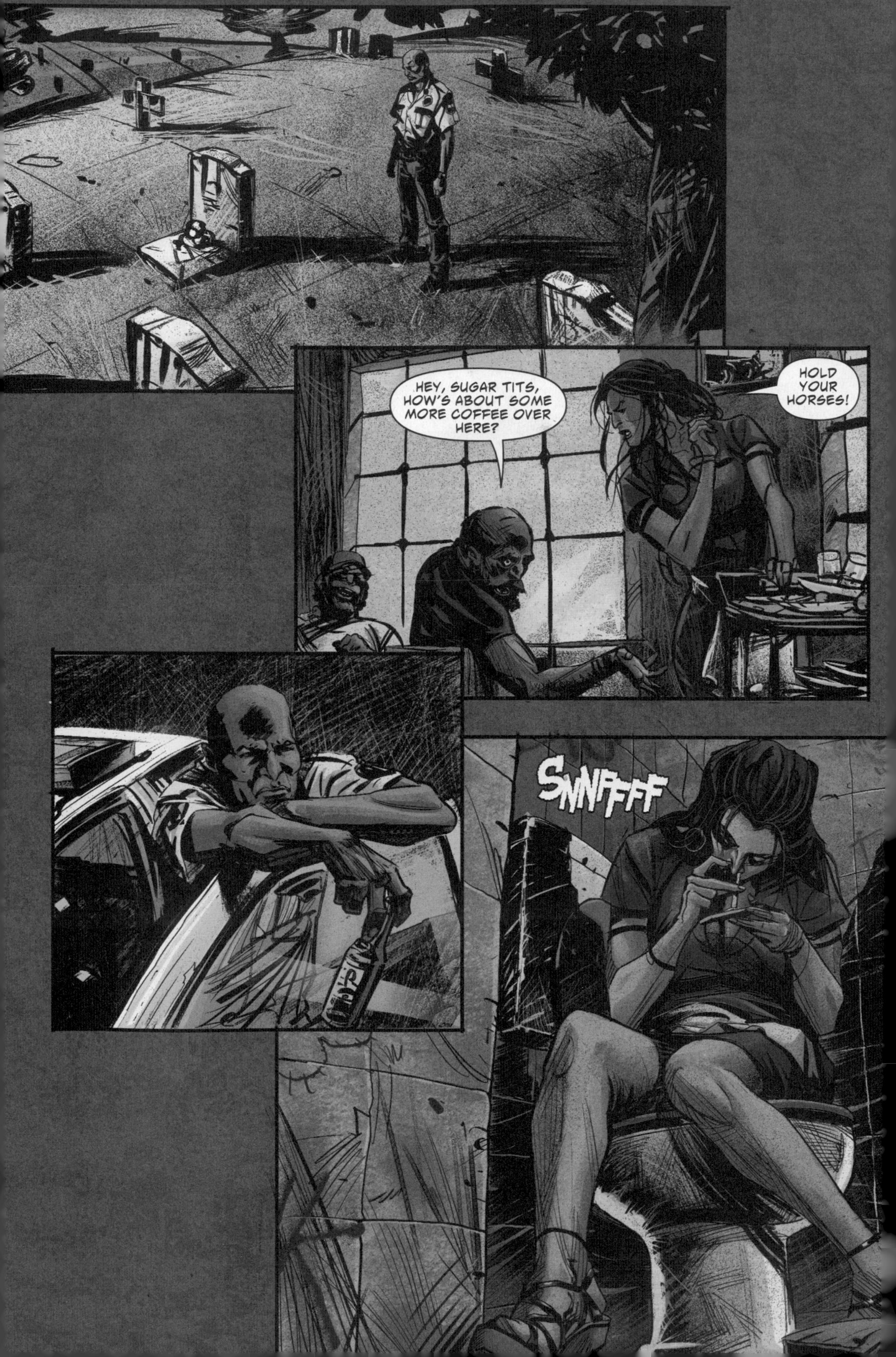
HEY, SUGAR TITS, HOW'S ABOUT SOME MORE COFFEE OVER HERE?
HOLD YOUR HORSES!
SNNFFFF

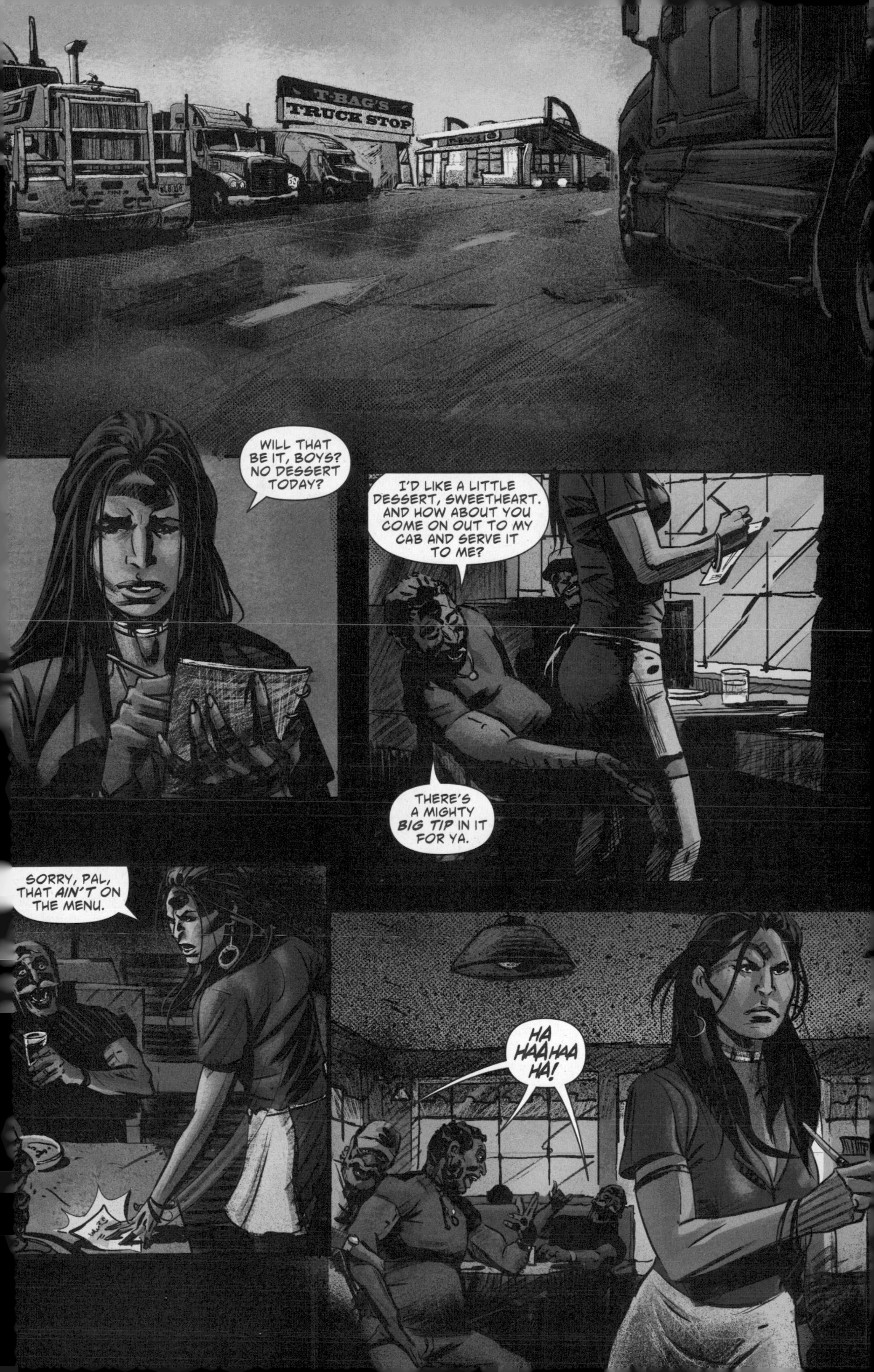
T-BAG'S
TRUCK STOP
T-BAG'S
WILL THAT BE IT, BOYS? NO DESSERT TODAY?
I'D LIKE A LITTLE DESSERT, SWEETHEART. AND HOW ABOUT YOU COME ON OUT TO MY CAB AND SERVE IT TO ME?
THERE'S A MIGHTY *BIG TIP* IN IT FOR YA.
SORRY, PAL, THAT *AIN'T* ON THE MENU.
HA HAAHAA HA!

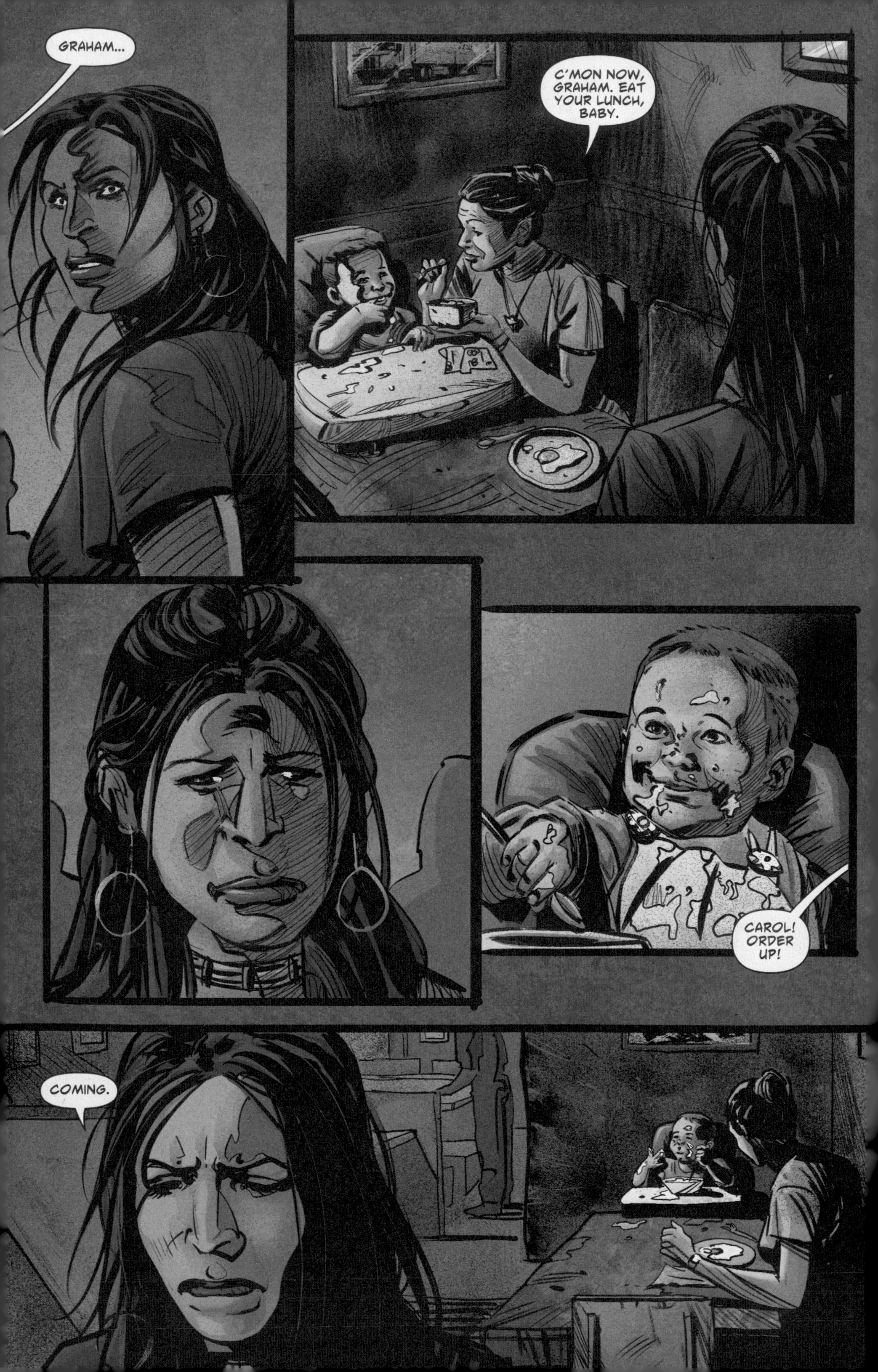
GRAHAM...
C'MON NOW, GRAHAM. EAT YOUR LUNCH, BABY.
CAROL! ORDER UP!
COMING.

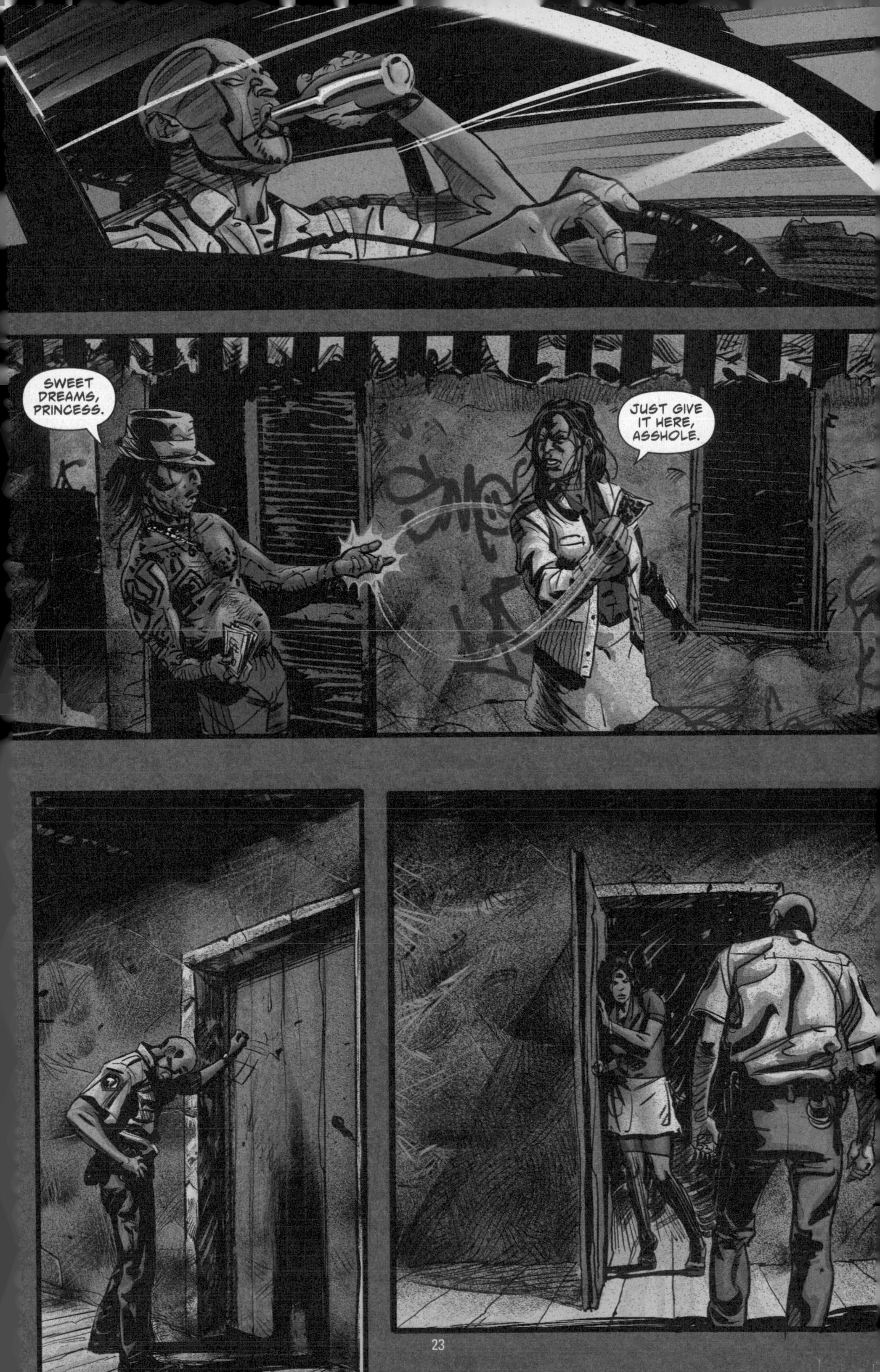
SWEET DREAMS, PRINCESS.
JUST GIVE IT HERE, ASSHOLE.

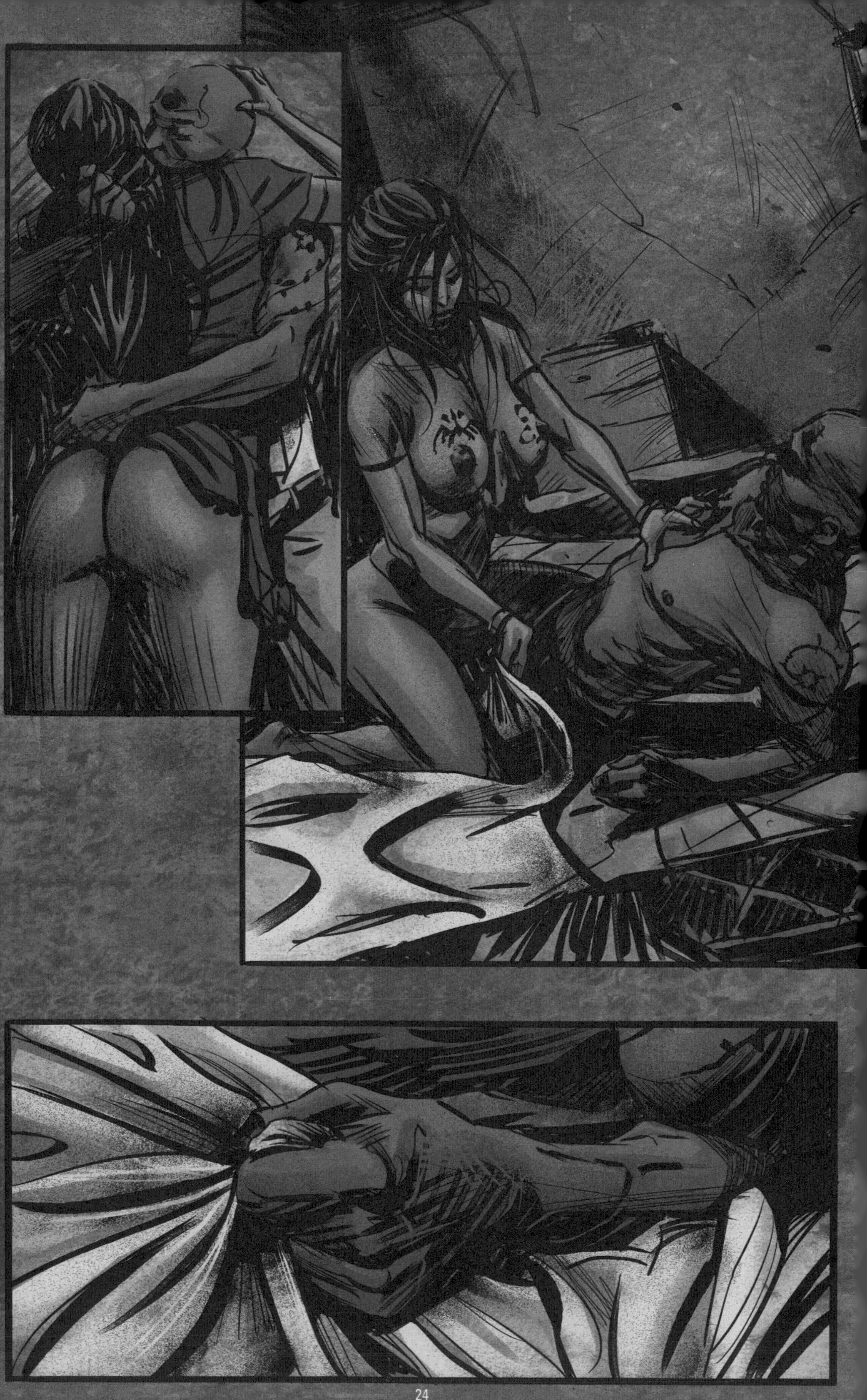

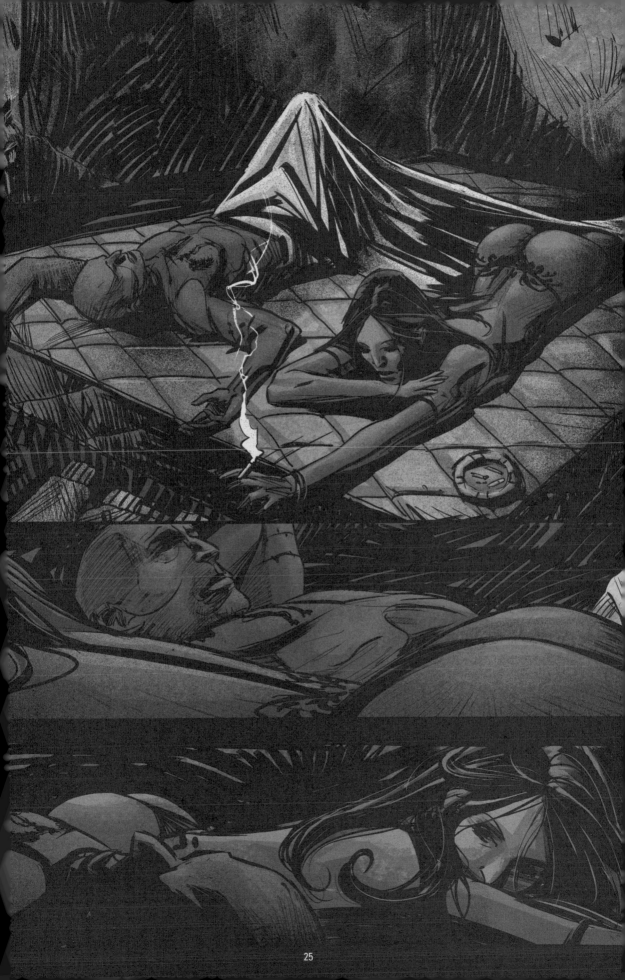

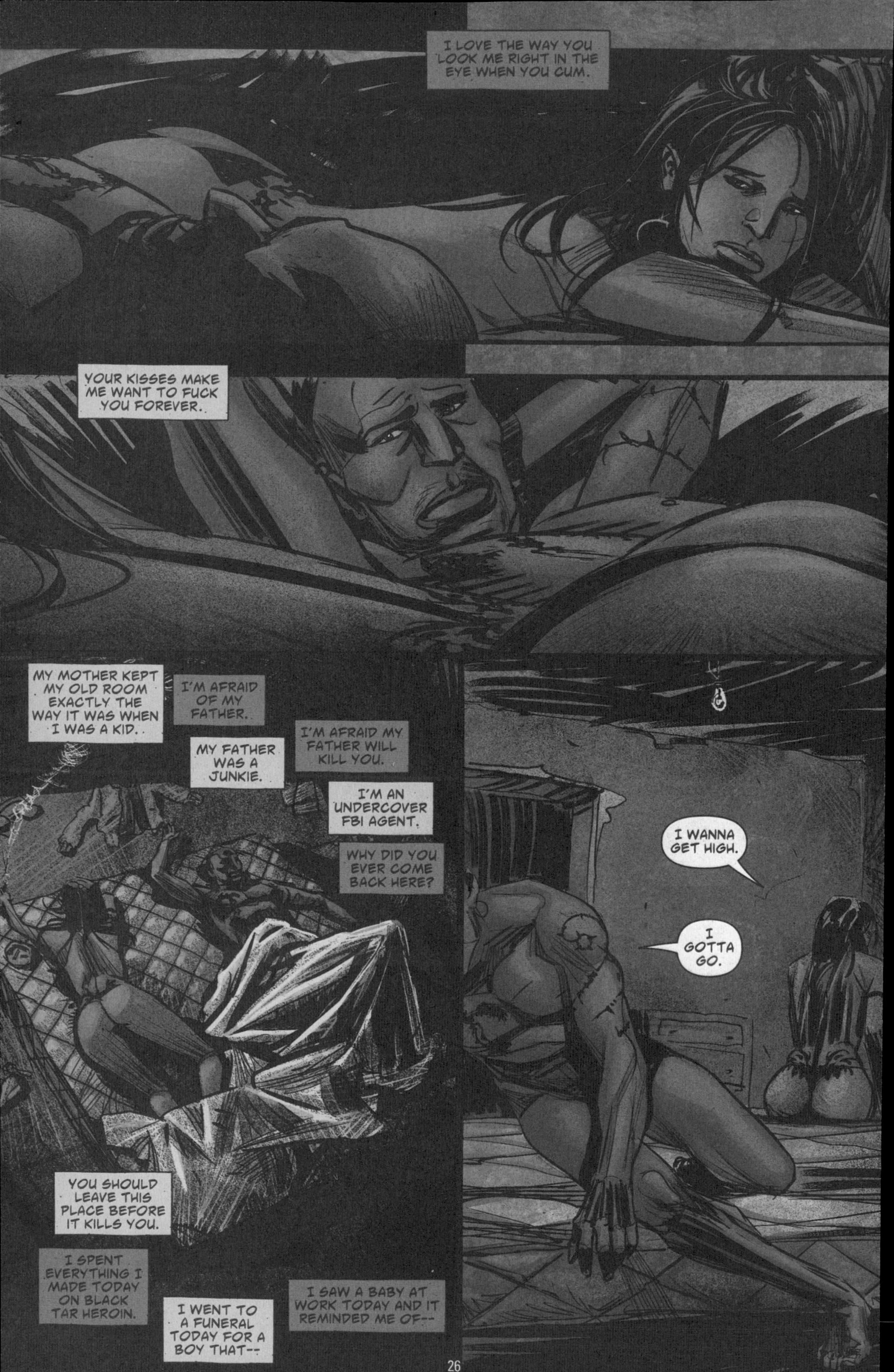
I LOVE THE WAY YOU LOOK ME RIGHT IN THE EYE WHEN YOU CUM.
YOUR KISSES MAKE ME WANT TO FUCK YOU FOREVER.
MY MOTHER KEPT MY OLD ROOM EXACTLY THE WAY IT WAS WHEN I WAS A KID.
I'M AFRAID OF MY FATHER.
MY FATHER WAS A JUNKIE.
I'M AFRAID MY FATHER WILL KILL YOU.
I'M AN UNDERCOVER FBI AGENT.
WHY DID YOU EVER COME BACK HERE?
YOU SHOULD LEAVE THIS PLACE BEFORE IT KILLS YOU.
I SPENT EVERYTHING I MADE TODAY ON BLACK TAR HEROIN.
I WENT TO A FUNERAL TODAY FOR A BOY THAT--
I SAW A BABY AT WORK TODAY AND IT REMINDED ME OF--
I WANNA GET HIGH.
I GOTTA GO.

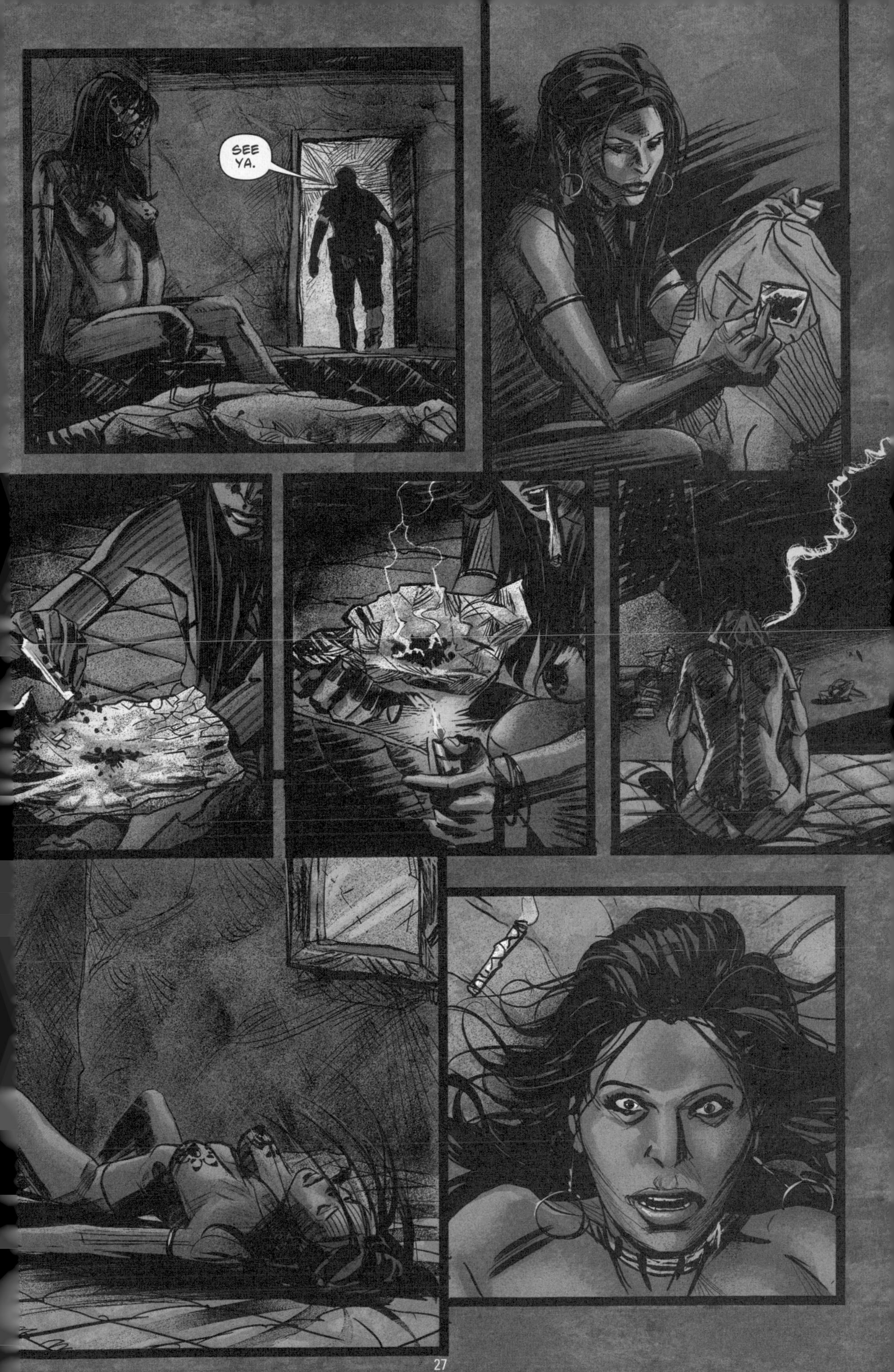
SEE YA.

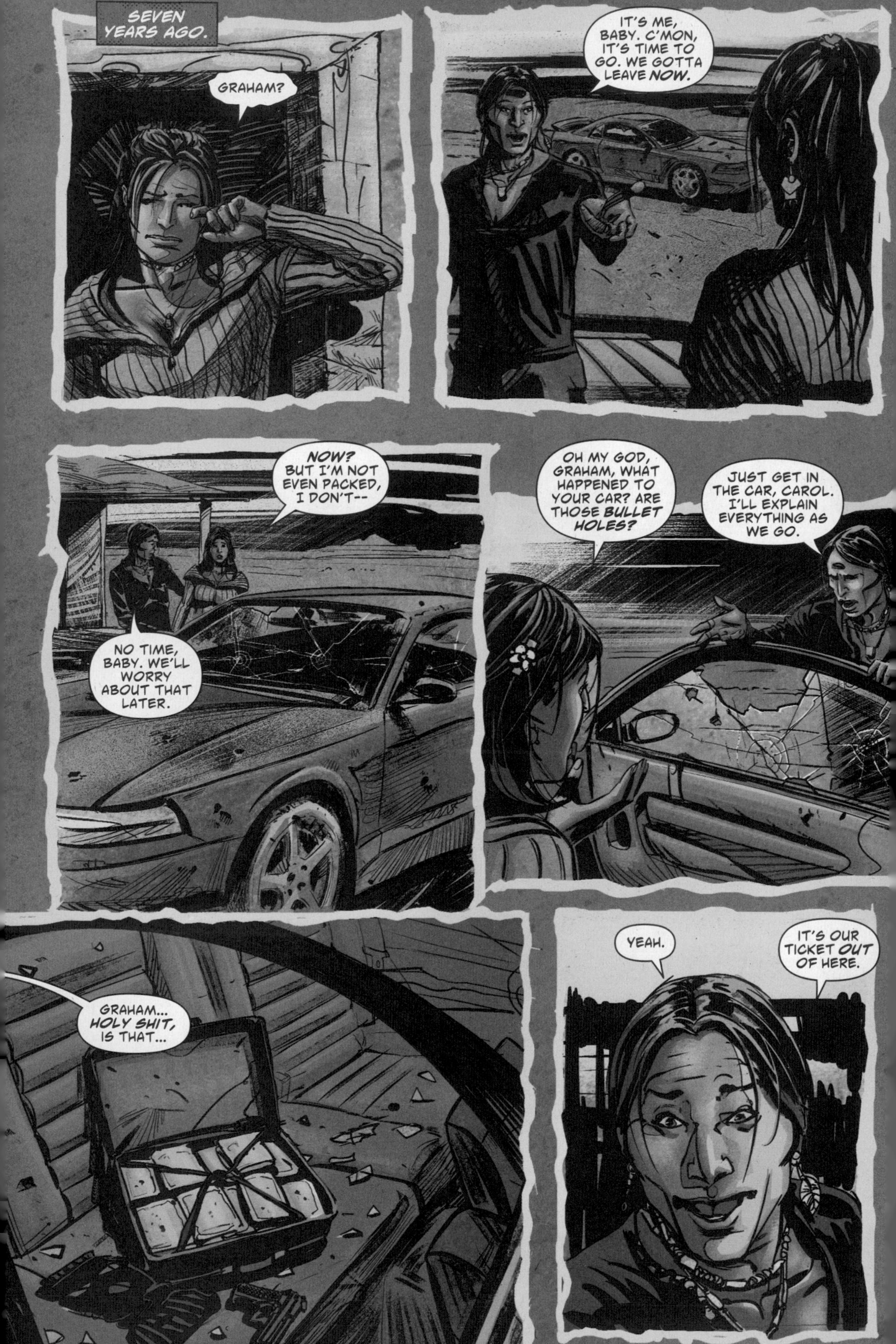
SEVEN YEARS AGO.
GRAHAM?
IT'S ME, BABY. C'MON, IT'S TIME TO GO. WE GOTTA LEAVE NOW.
NOW? BUT I'M NOT EVEN PACKED, I DON'T--
NO TIME, BABY. WE'LL WORRY ABOUT THAT LATER.
OH MY GOD, GRAHAM, WHAT HAPPENED TO YOUR CAR? ARE THOSE BULLET HOLES?
JUST GET IN THE CAR, CAROL. I'LL EXPLAIN EVERYTHING AS WE GO.
GRAHAM... HOLY SHIT, IS THAT...
YEAH.
IT'S OUR TICKET OUT OF HERE.

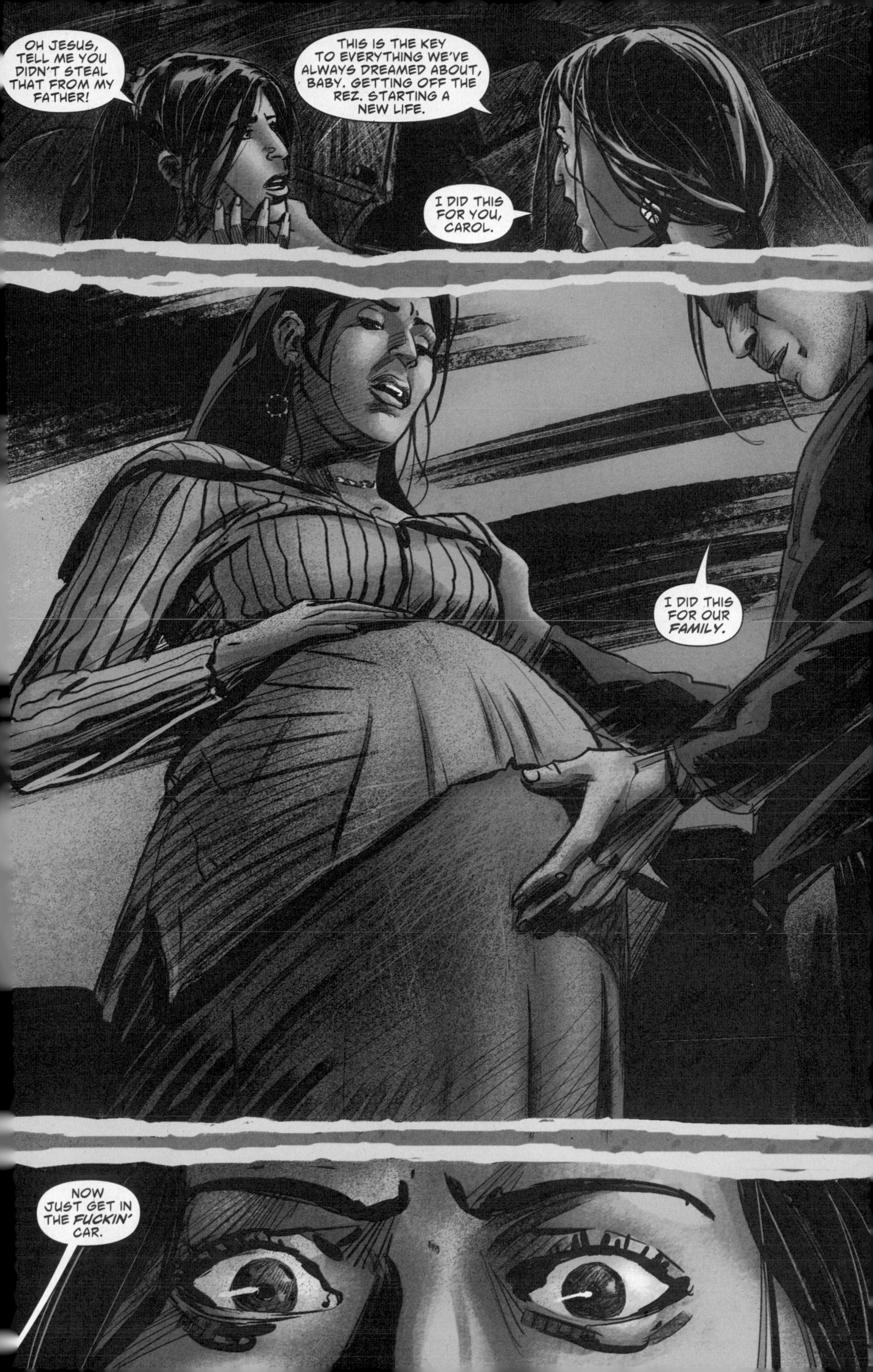
OH JESUS, TELL ME YOU DIDN'T STEAL THAT FROM MY FATHER!
THIS IS THE KEY TO EVERYTHING WE'VE ALWAYS DREAMED ABOUT, BABY. GETTING OFF THE REZ. STARTING A NEW LIFE.
I DID THIS FOR YOU, CAROL.
I DID THIS FOR OUR *FAMILY.*
NOW JUST GET IN THE *FUCKIN'* CAR.

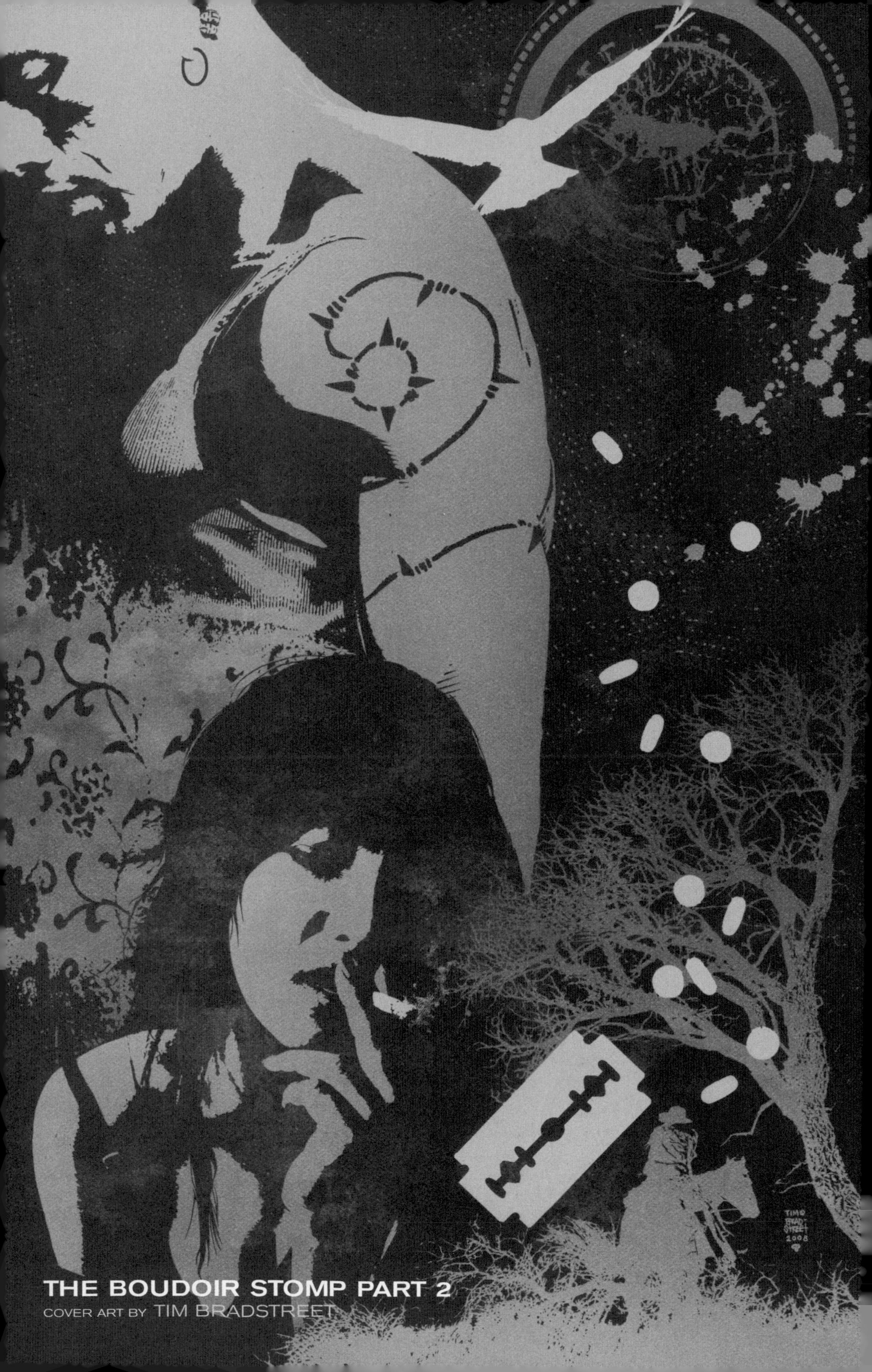

THE BOUDOIR STOMP PART 2
COVER ART BY TIM BRADSTREET

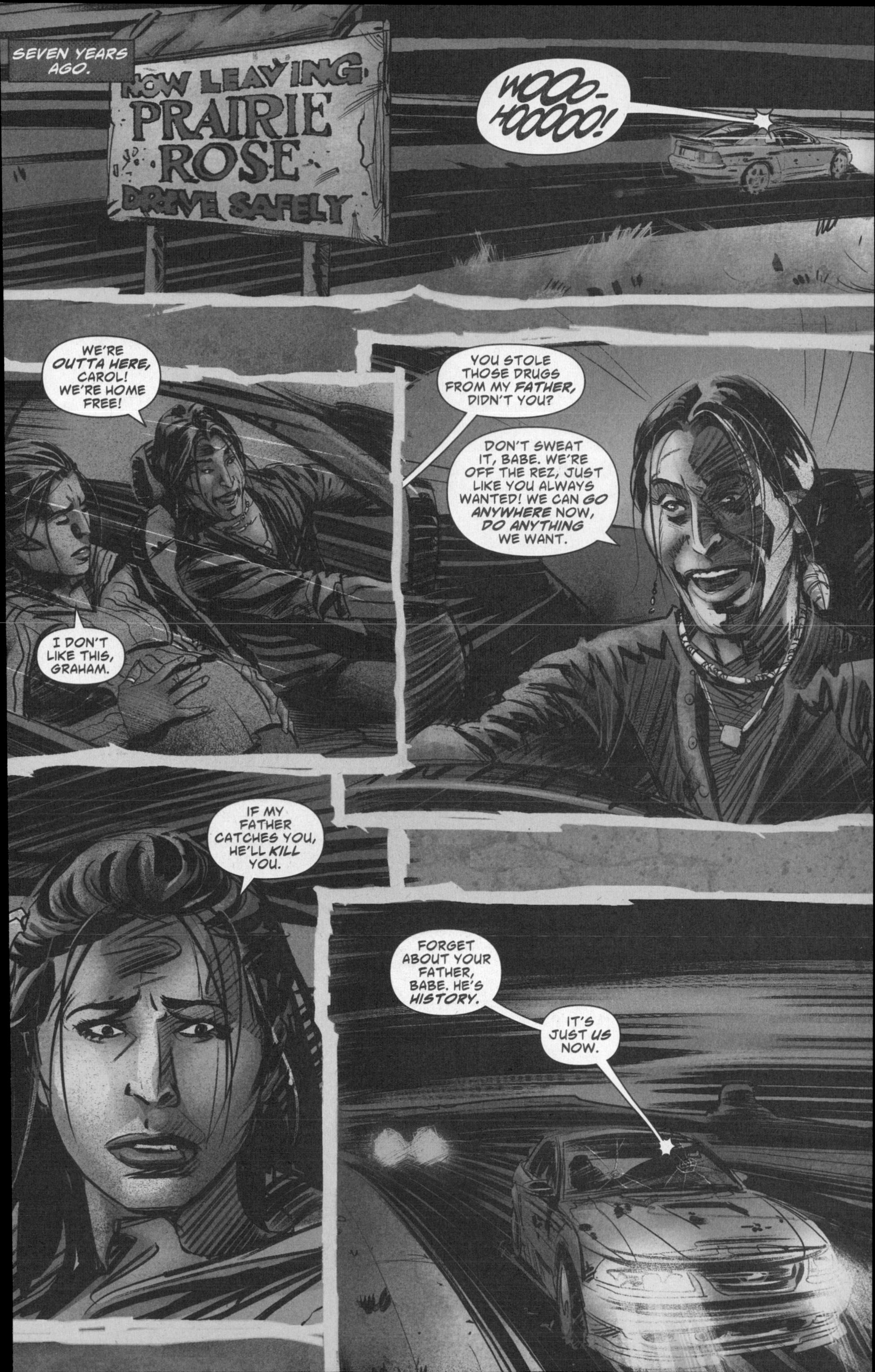
SEVEN YEARS AGO.
NOW LEAVING PRAIRIE ROSE DRIVE SAFELY
WOOO-HOOOOO!
WE'RE OUTTA HERE, CAROL! WE'RE HOME FREE!
I DON'T LIKE THIS, GRAHAM.
YOU STOLE THOSE DRUGS FROM MY FATHER, DIDN'T YOU?
DON'T SWEAT IT, BABE. WE'RE OFF THE REZ, JUST LIKE YOU ALWAYS WANTED! WE CAN GO ANYWHERE NOW, DO ANYTHING WE WANT.
IF MY FATHER CATCHES YOU, HE'LL KILL YOU.
FORGET ABOUT YOUR FATHER, BABE. HE'S HISTORY.
IT'S JUST US NOW.

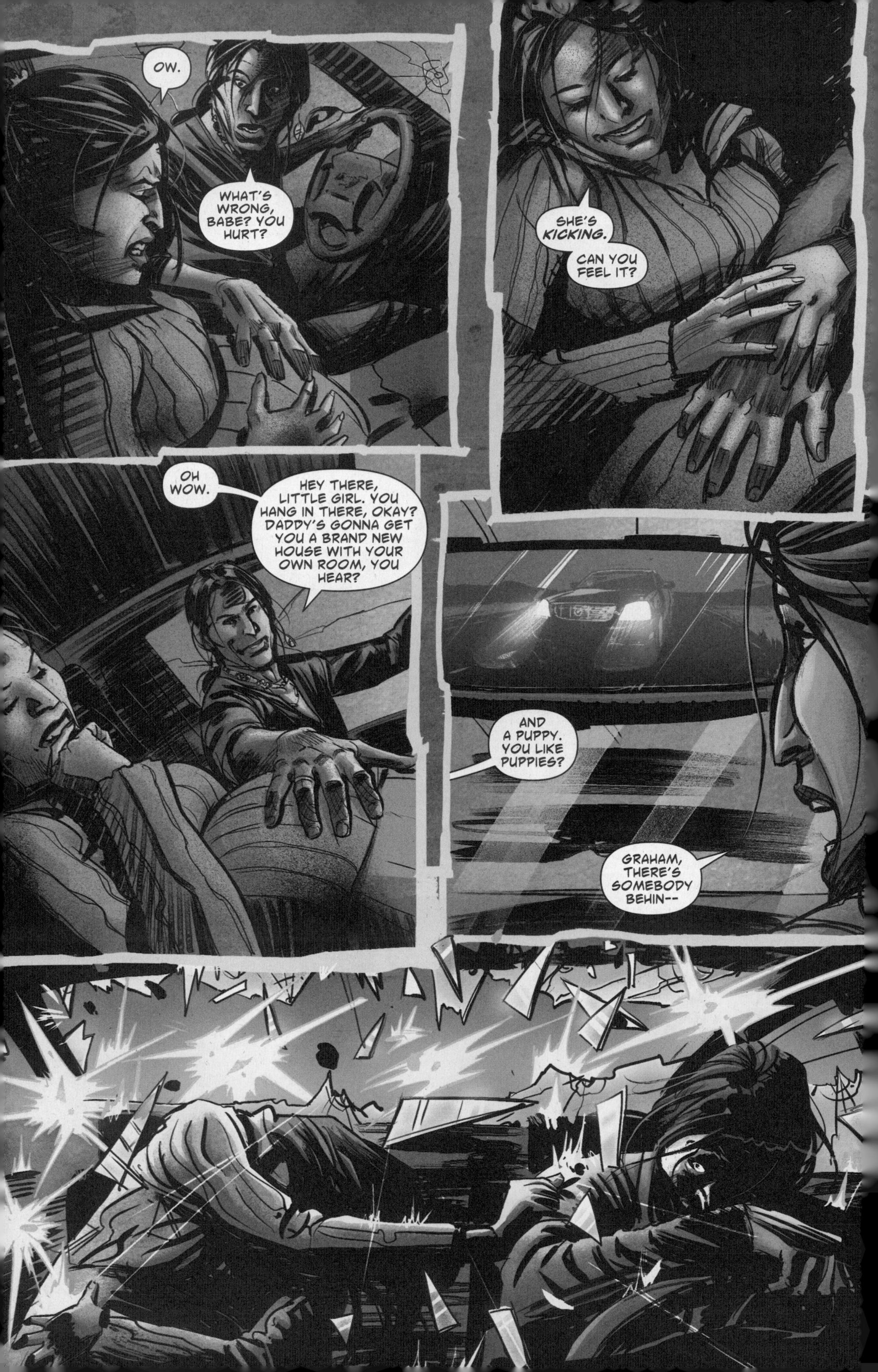
OW.
WHAT'S WRONG, BABE? YOU HURT?
SHE'S *KICKING.*
CAN YOU FEEL IT?
OH WOW.
HEY THERE, LITTLE GIRL. YOU HANG IN THERE, OKAY? DADDY'S GONNA GET YOU A BRAND NEW HOUSE WITH YOUR OWN ROOM, YOU HEAR?
AND A PUPPY. YOU LIKE PUPPIES?
GRAHAM, THERE'S SOMEBODY BEHIN--

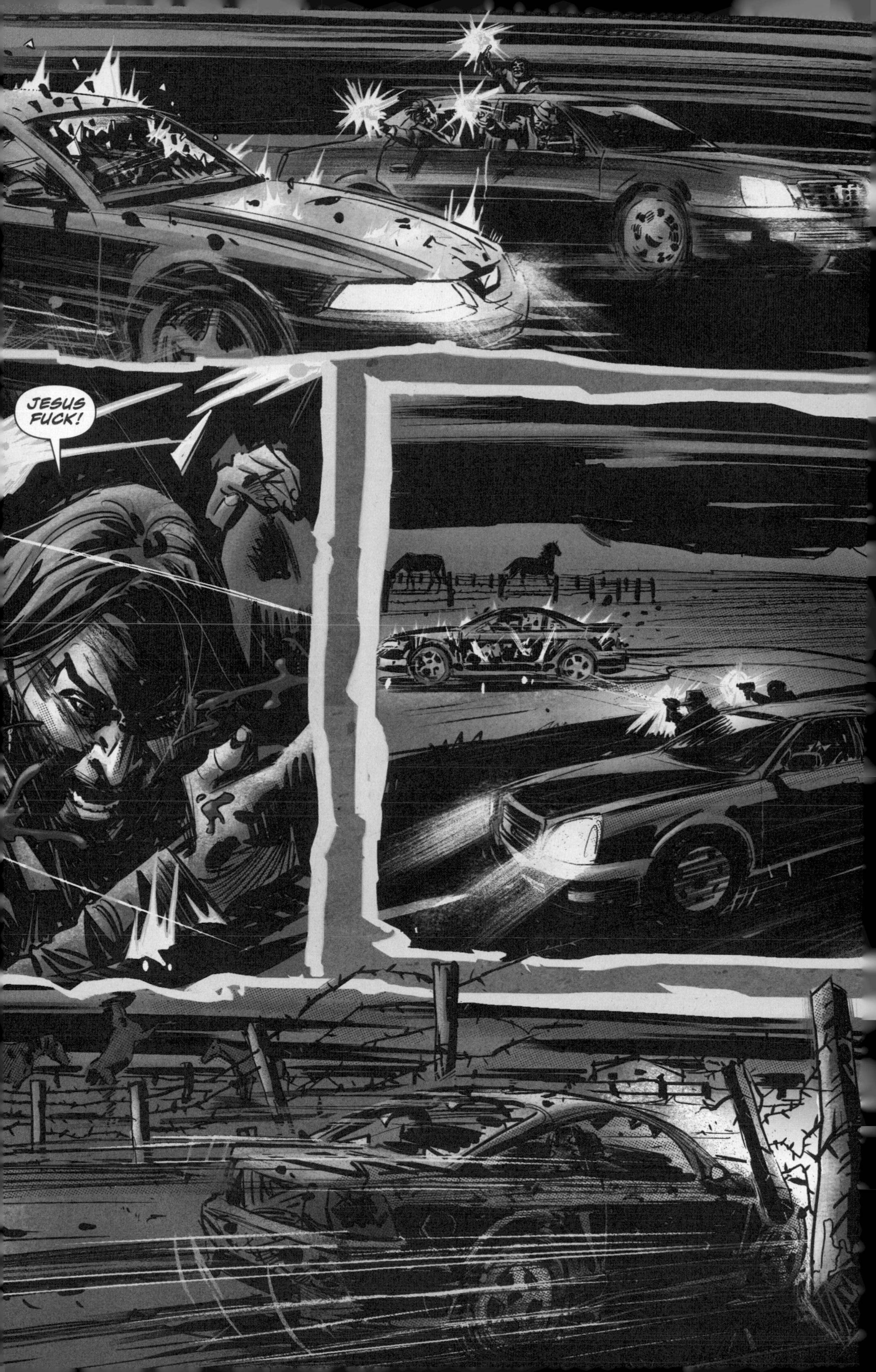
JESUS FUCK!

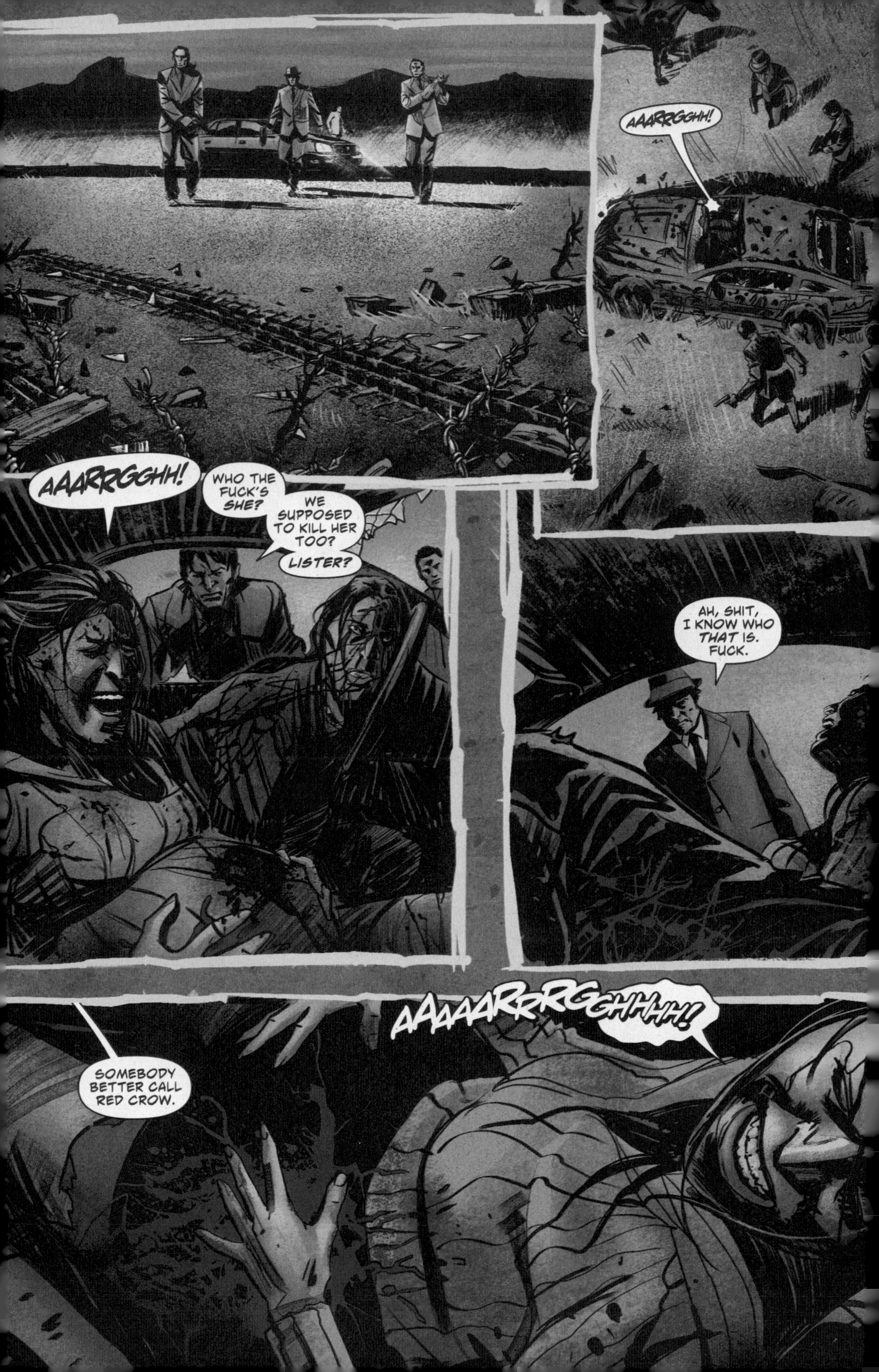
AAARRGGHH!
AAARRGGHH!
WHO THE FUCK'S SHE?
WE SUPPOSED TO KILL HER TOO?
LISTER?
AH, SHIT, I KNOW WHO THAT IS. FUCK.
SOMEBODY BETTER CALL RED CROW.
AAAAARRRGGHHHH!

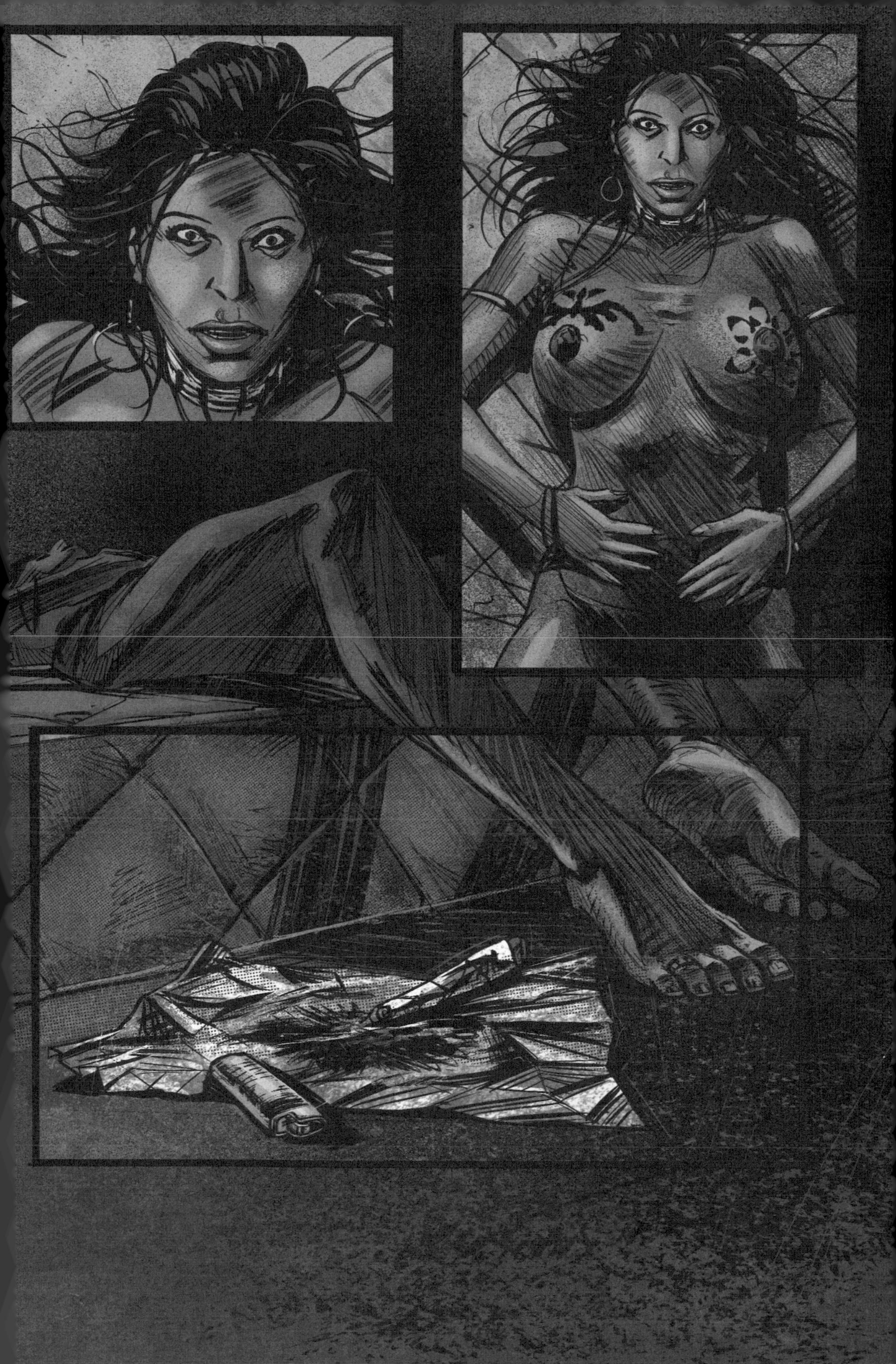

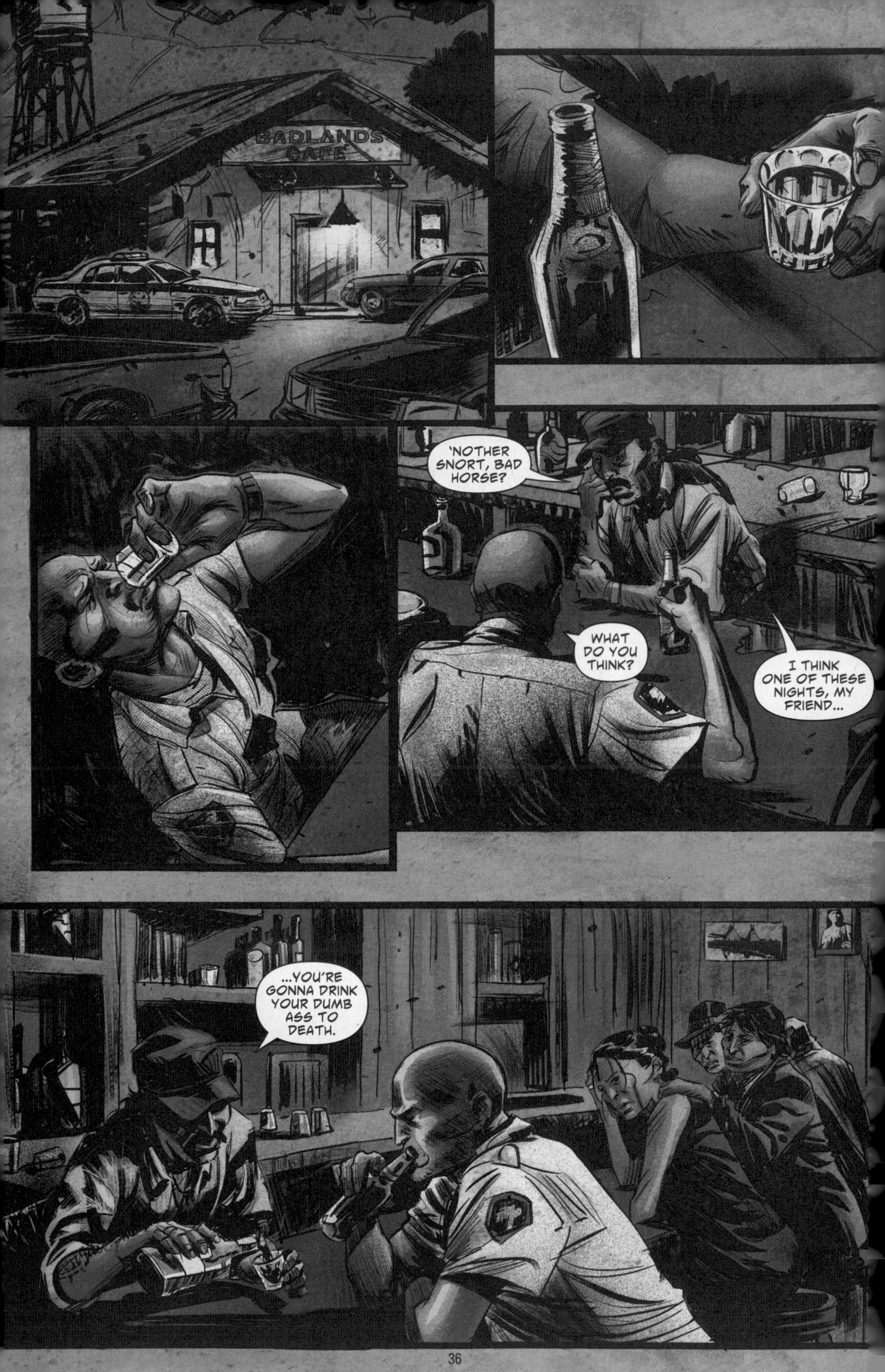
BADLANDS CAFE
'NOTHER SNORT, BAD HORSE?
WHAT DO YOU THINK?
I THINK ONE OF THESE NIGHTS, MY FRIEND...
...YOU'RE GONNA DRINK YOUR DUMB ASS TO DEATH.

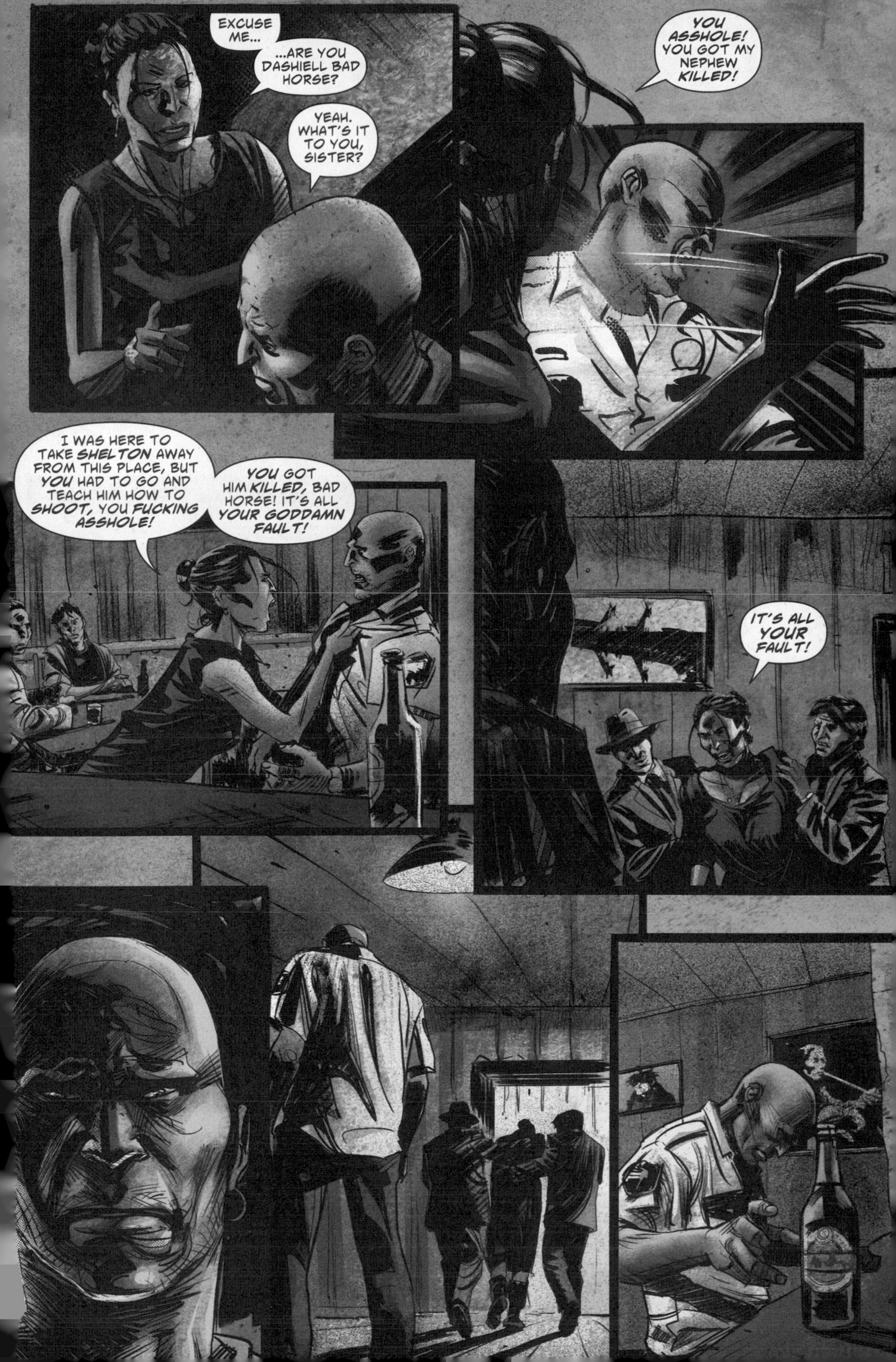
EXCUSE ME...
...ARE YOU DASHIELL BAD HORSE?
YEAH. WHAT'S IT TO YOU, SISTER?
YOU ASSHOLE! YOU GOT MY NEPHEW KILLED!
I WAS HERE TO TAKE SHELTON AWAY FROM THIS PLACE, BUT YOU HAD TO GO AND TEACH HIM HOW TO SHOOT, YOU FUCKING ASSHOLE!
YOU GOT HIM KILLED, BAD HORSE! IT'S ALL YOUR GODDAMN FAULT!
IT'S ALL YOUR FAULT!

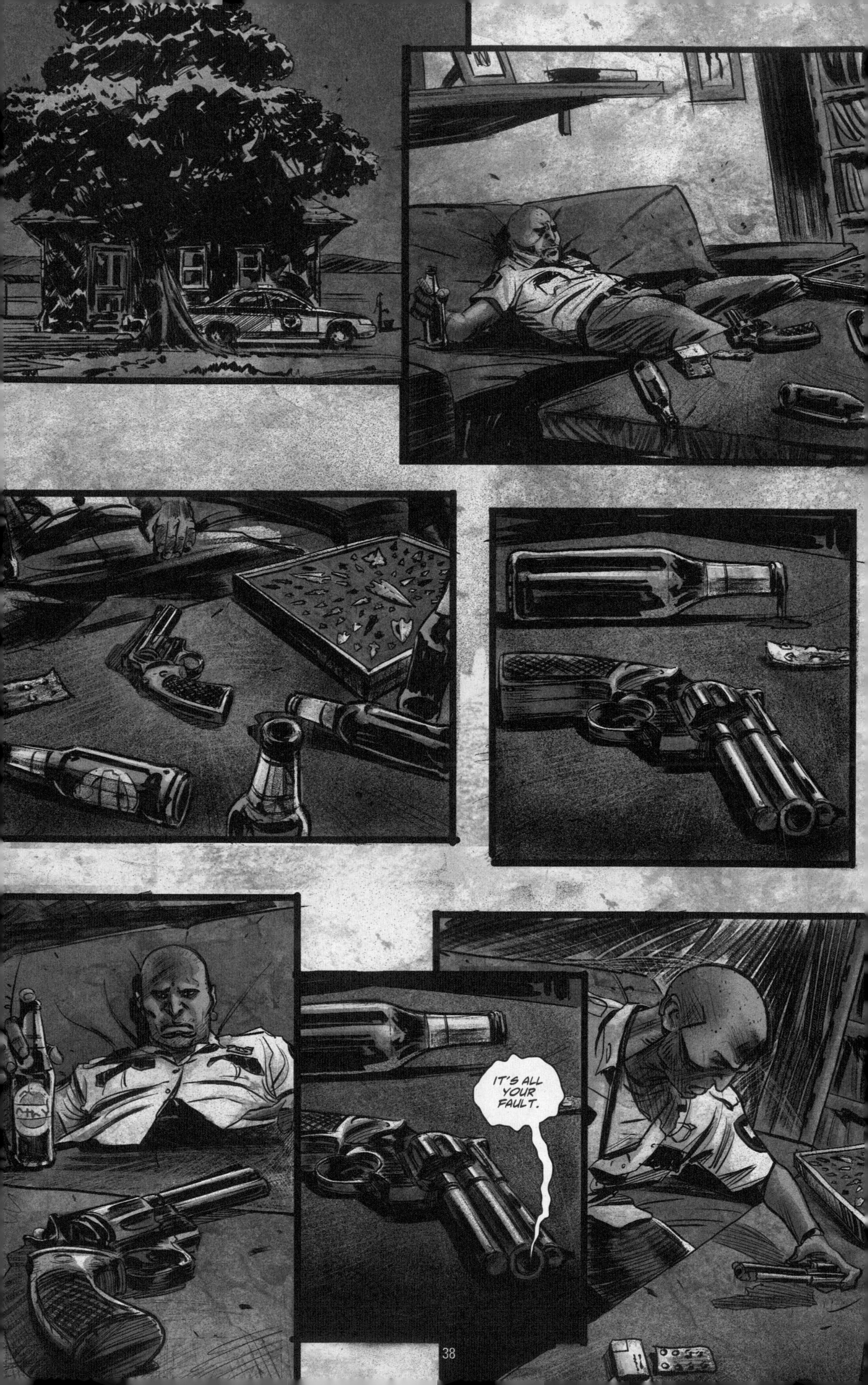
IT'S ALL YOUR FAULT.

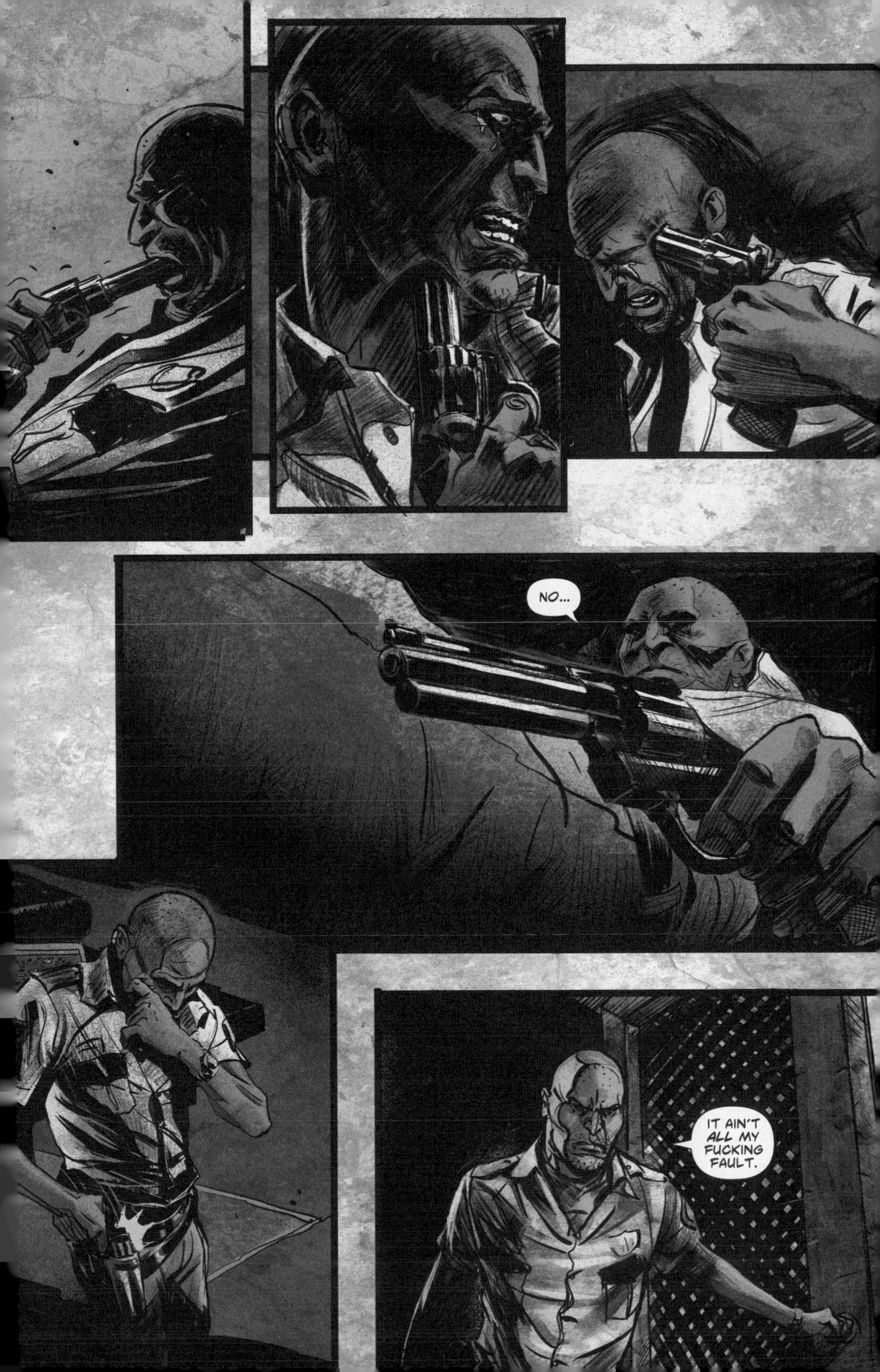
NO...
IT AIN'T ALL MY FUCKING FAULT.

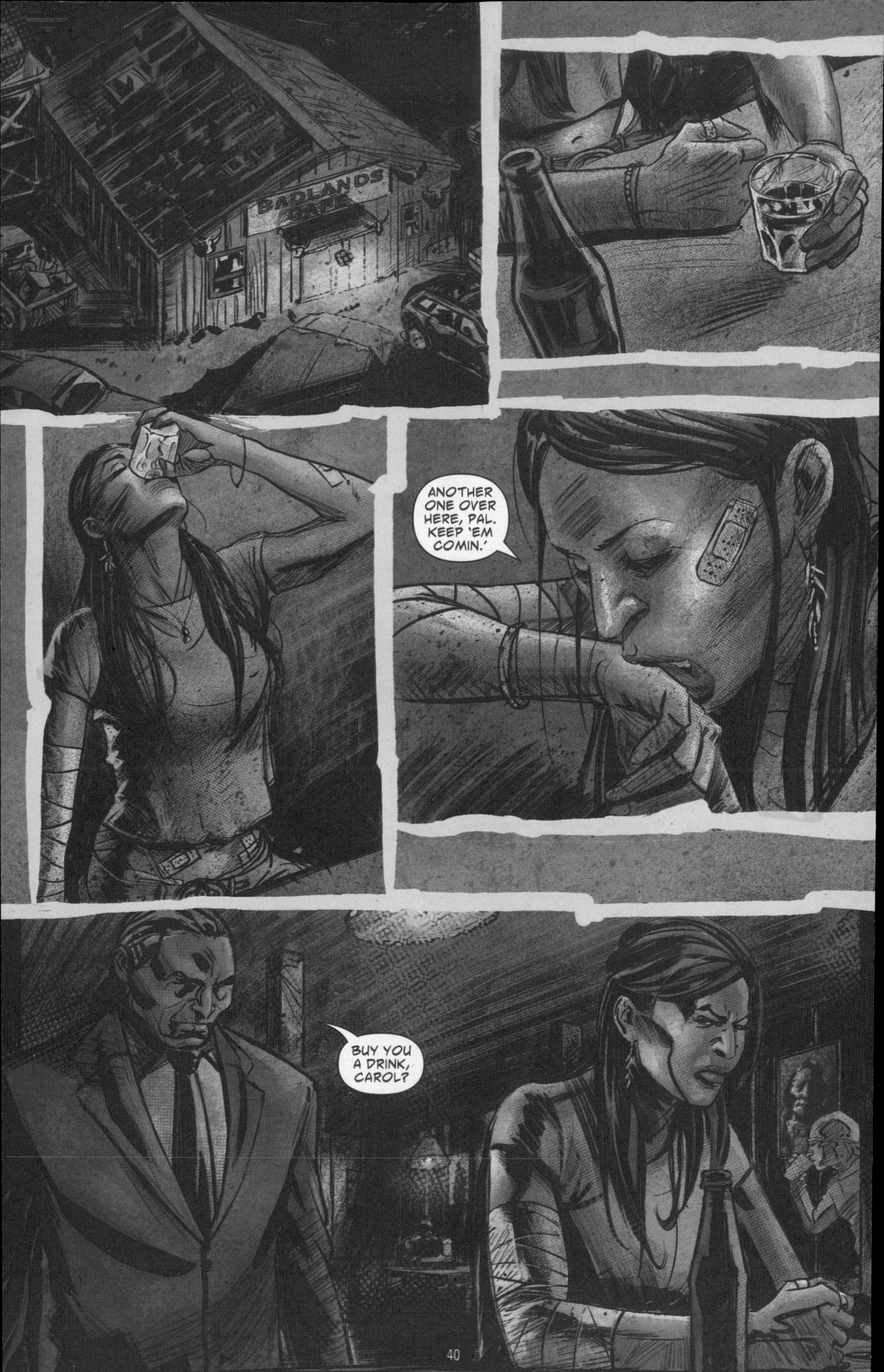
BADLANDS CAFE
ANOTHER ONE OVER HERE, PAL. KEEP 'EM COMIN.'
BUY YOU A DRINK, CAROL?

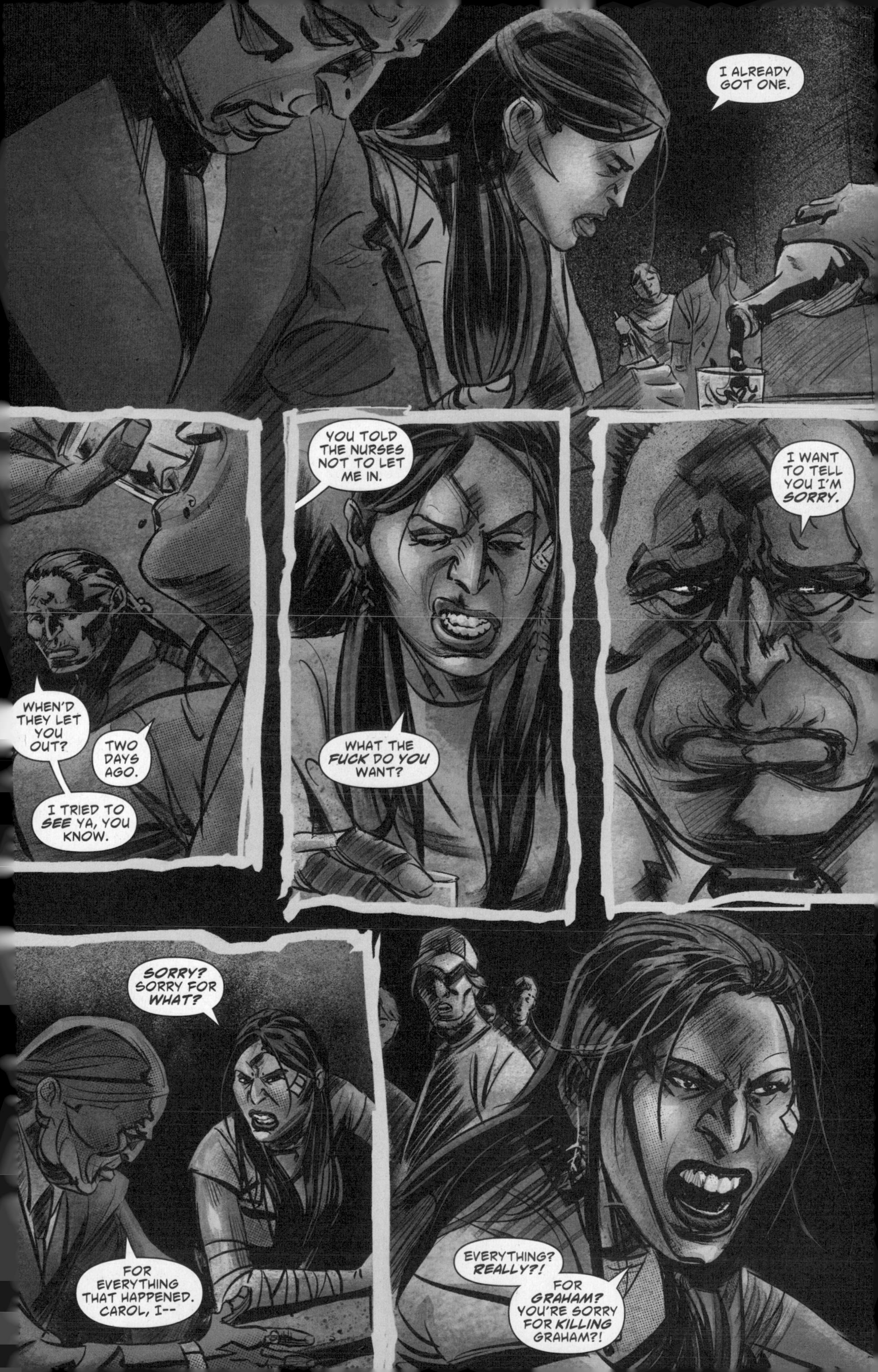
I ALREADY GOT ONE.
WHEN'D THEY LET YOU OUT?
TWO DAYS AGO.
I TRIED TO SEE YA, YOU KNOW.
YOU TOLD THE NURSES NOT TO LET ME IN.
WHAT THE FUCK DO YOU WANT?
I WANT TO TELL YOU I'M SORRY.
SORRY? SORRY FOR WHAT?
FOR EVERYTHING THAT HAPPENED. CAROL, I--
EVERYTHING? REALLY?!
FOR GRAHAM? YOU'RE SORRY FOR KILLING GRAHAM?!

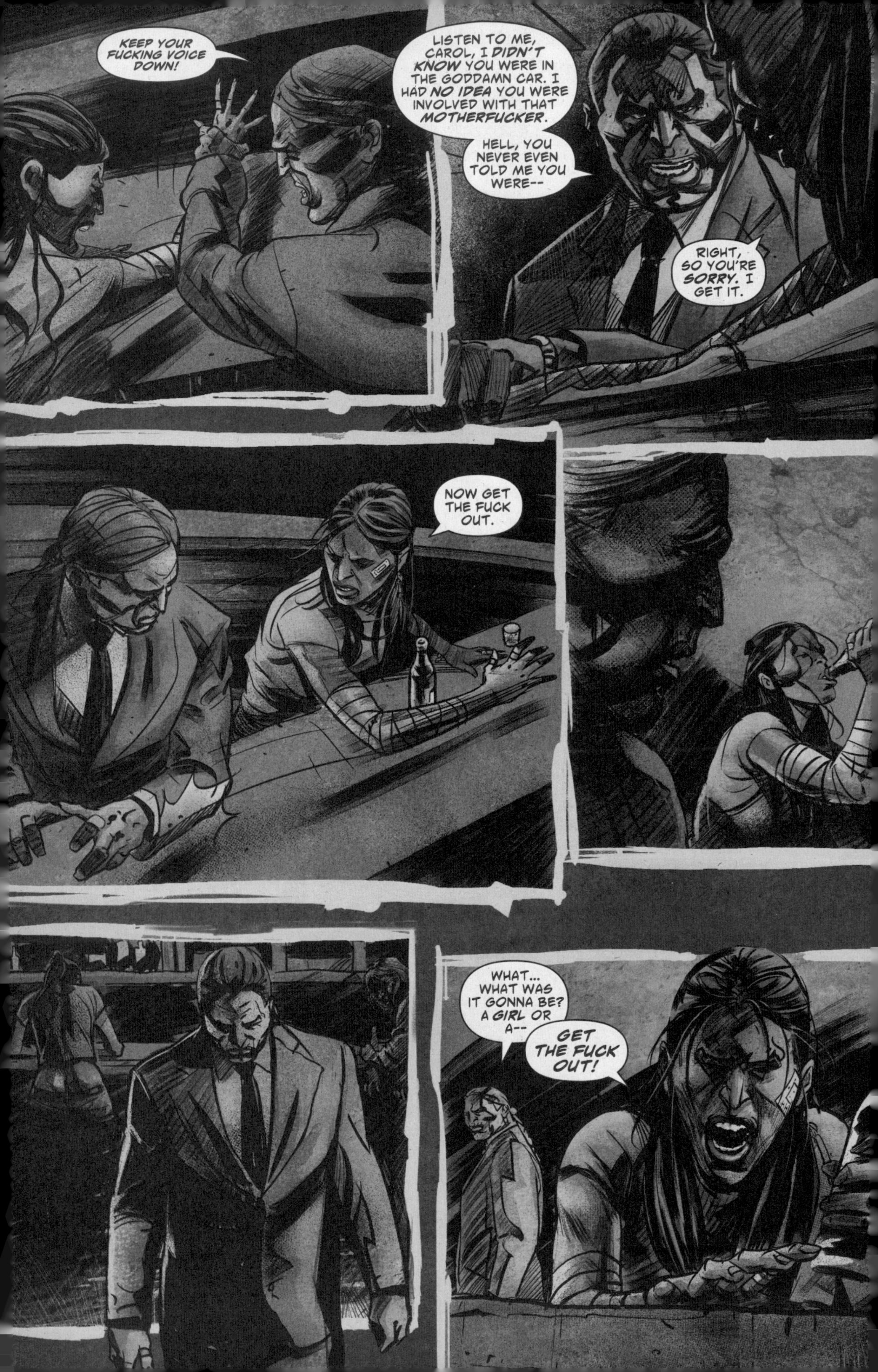
KEEP YOUR FUCKING VOICE DOWN!
LISTEN TO ME, CAROL, I *DIDN'T KNOW* YOU WERE IN THE GODDAMN CAR. I HAD *NO IDEA* YOU WERE INVOLVED WITH THAT *MOTHERFUCKER*.
HELL, YOU NEVER EVEN TOLD ME YOU WERE--
RIGHT, SO YOU'RE *SORRY*. I GET IT.
NOW GET THE FUCK OUT.
WHAT... WHAT WAS IT GONNA BE? A *GIRL* OR A--
GET THE FUCK OUT!

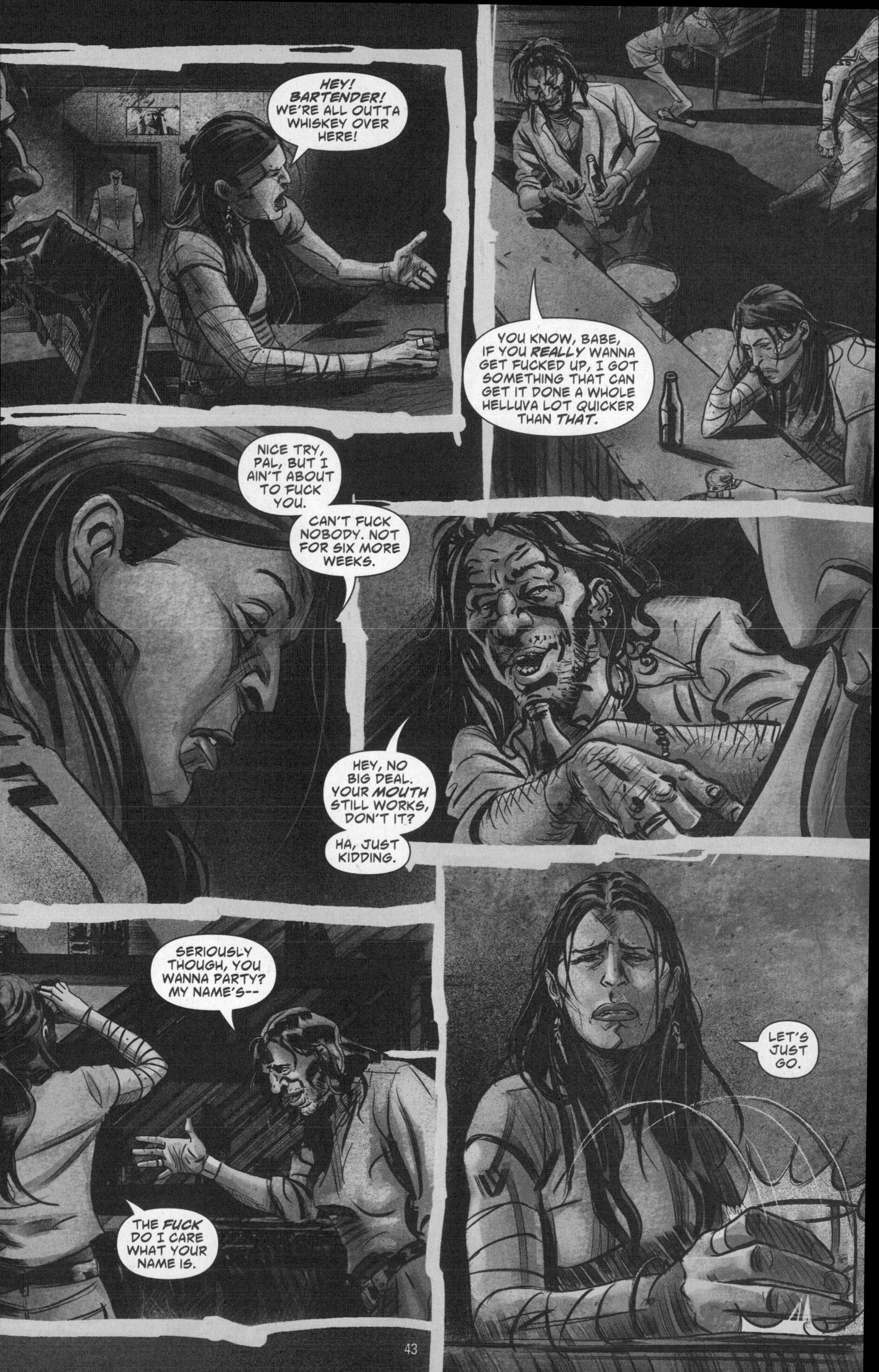
HEY! BARTENDER! WE'RE ALL OUTTA WHISKEY OVER HERE!
YOU KNOW, BABE, IF YOU REALLY WANNA GET FUCKED UP, I GOT SOMETHING THAT CAN GET IT DONE A WHOLE HELLUVA LOT QUICKER THAN THAT.
NICE TRY, PAL, BUT I AIN'T ABOUT TO FUCK YOU.
CAN'T FUCK NOBODY. NOT FOR SIX MORE WEEKS.
HEY, NO BIG DEAL. YOUR MOUTH STILL WORKS, DON'T IT?
HA, JUST KIDDING.
SERIOUSLY THOUGH, YOU WANNA PARTY? MY NAME'S--
THE FUCK DO I CARE WHAT YOUR NAME IS.
LET'S JUST GO.

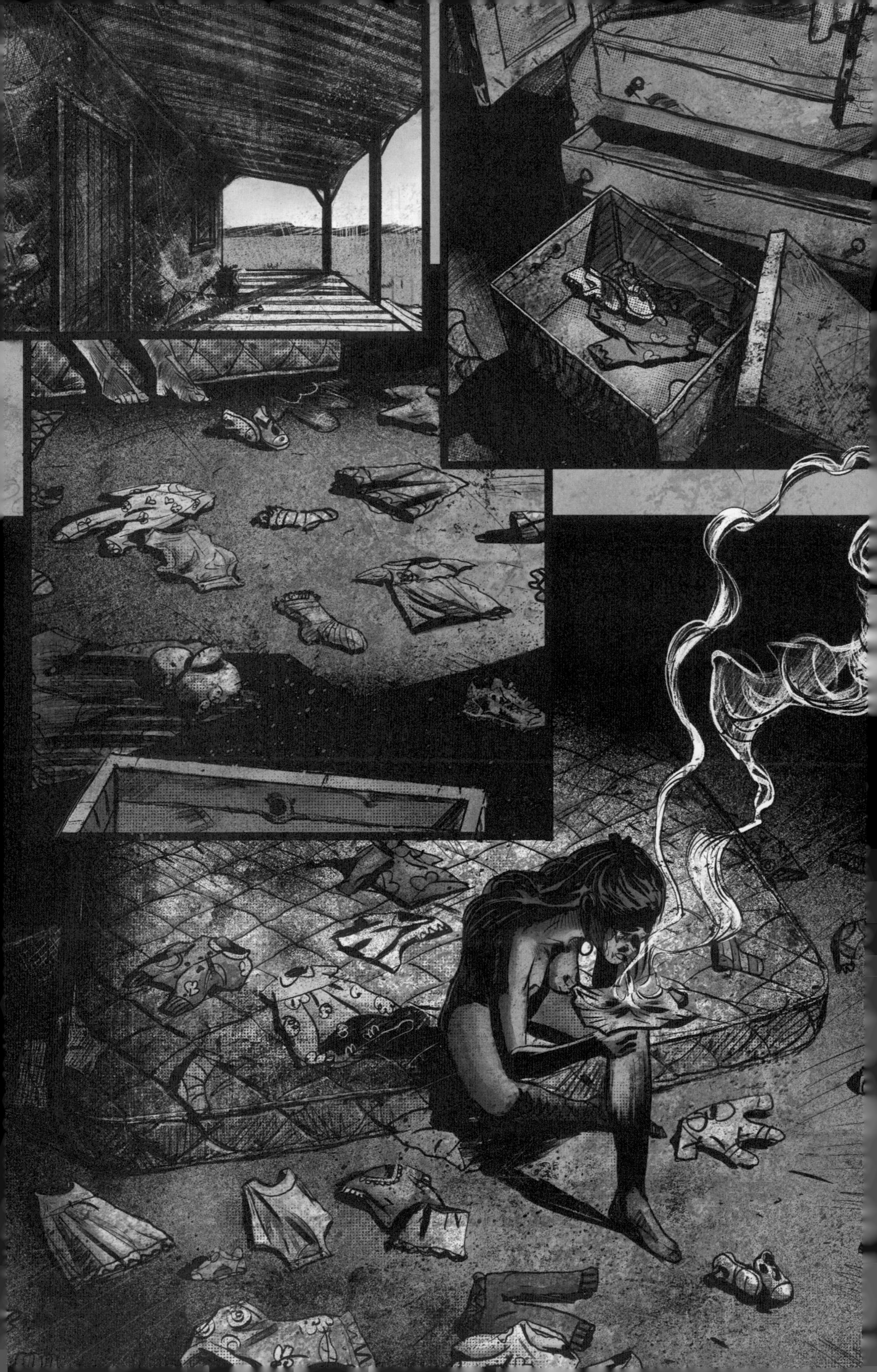

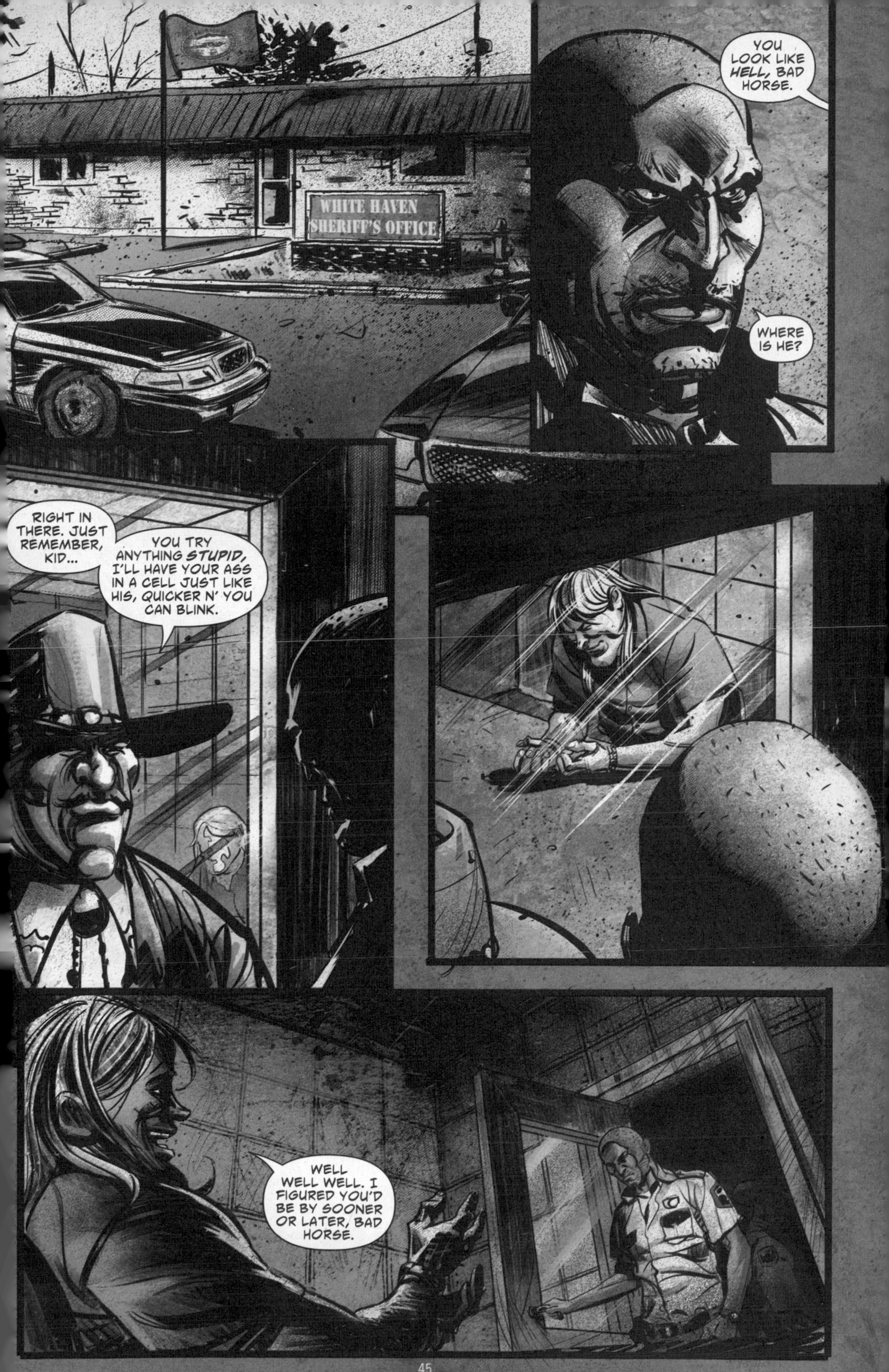
WHITE HAVEN SHERIFF'S OFFICE
YOU LOOK LIKE HELL, BAD HORSE.
WHERE IS HE?
RIGHT IN THERE. JUST REMEMBER, KID...
YOU TRY ANYTHING STUPID, I'LL HAVE YOUR ASS IN A CELL JUST LIKE HIS, QUICKER N' YOU CAN BLINK.
WELL WELL WELL. I FIGURED YOU'D BE BY SOONER OR LATER, BAD HORSE.

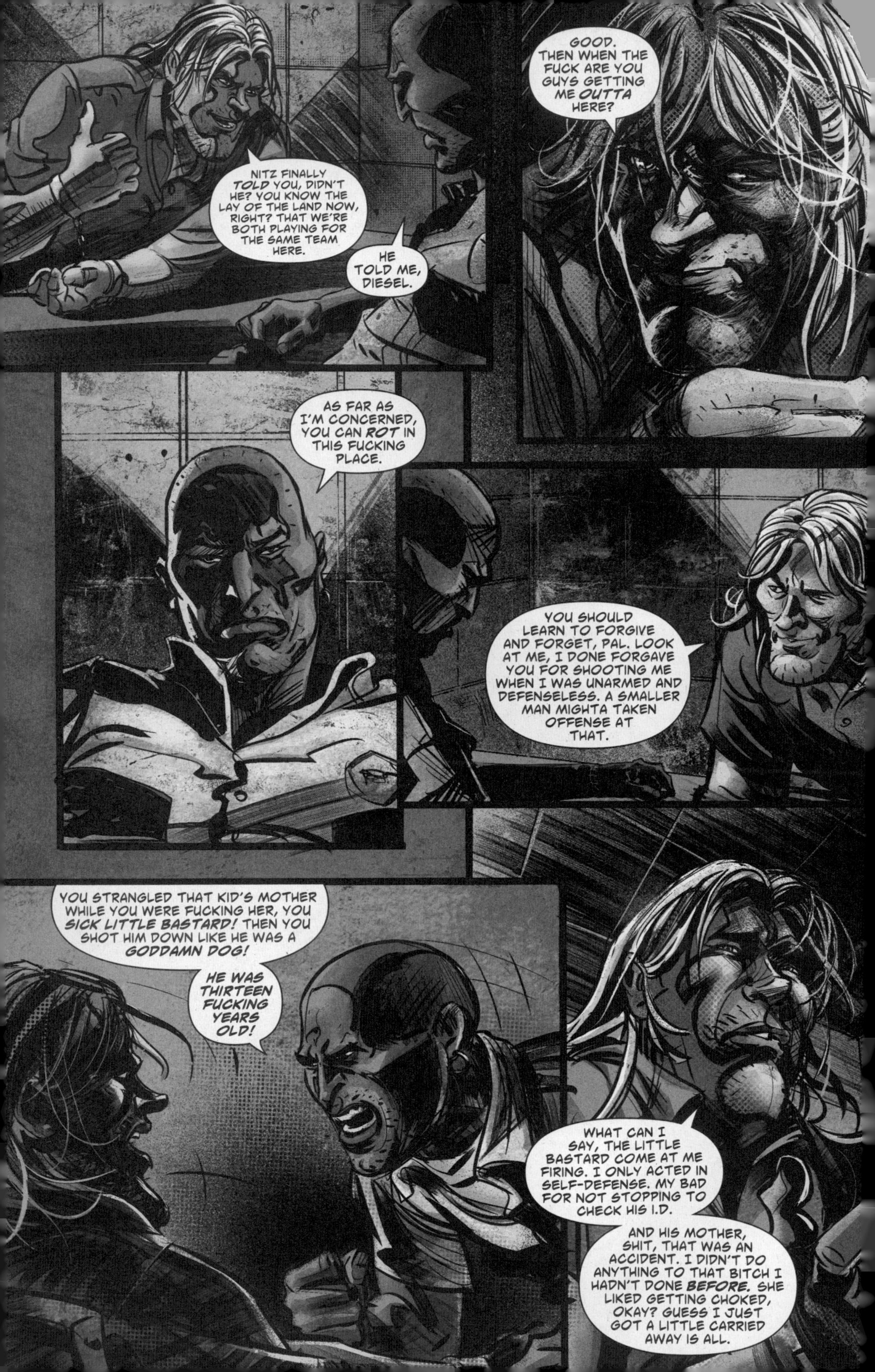
NITZ FINALLY *TOLD* YOU, DIDN'T HE? YOU KNOW THE LAY OF THE LAND NOW, RIGHT? THAT WE'RE BOTH PLAYING FOR THE SAME TEAM HERE.
HE TOLD ME, DIESEL.
GOOD. THEN WHEN THE FUCK ARE YOU GUYS GETTING ME *OUTTA* HERE?
AS FAR AS I'M CONCERNED, YOU CAN *ROT* IN THIS FUCKING PLACE.
YOU SHOULD LEARN TO FORGIVE AND FORGET, PAL. LOOK AT ME, I DONE FORGAVE YOU FOR SHOOTING ME WHEN I WAS UNARMED AND DEFENSELESS. A SMALLER MAN MIGHTA TAKEN OFFENSE AT THAT.
YOU STRANGLED THAT KID'S MOTHER WHILE YOU WERE FUCKING HER, YOU *SICK LITTLE BASTARD!* THEN YOU SHOT HIM DOWN LIKE HE WAS A *GODDAMN DOG!*
HE WAS THIRTEEN FUCKING YEARS OLD!
WHAT CAN I SAY, THE LITTLE BASTARD COME AT ME FIRING. I ONLY ACTED IN SELF-DEFENSE. MY BAD FOR NOT STOPPING TO CHECK HIS I.D.
AND HIS MOTHER, SHIT, THAT WAS AN ACCIDENT. I DIDN'T DO ANYTHING TO THAT BITCH I HADN'T DONE *BEFORE.* SHE LIKED GETTING CHOKED, OKAY? GUESS I JUST GOT A LITTLE CARRIED AWAY IS ALL.

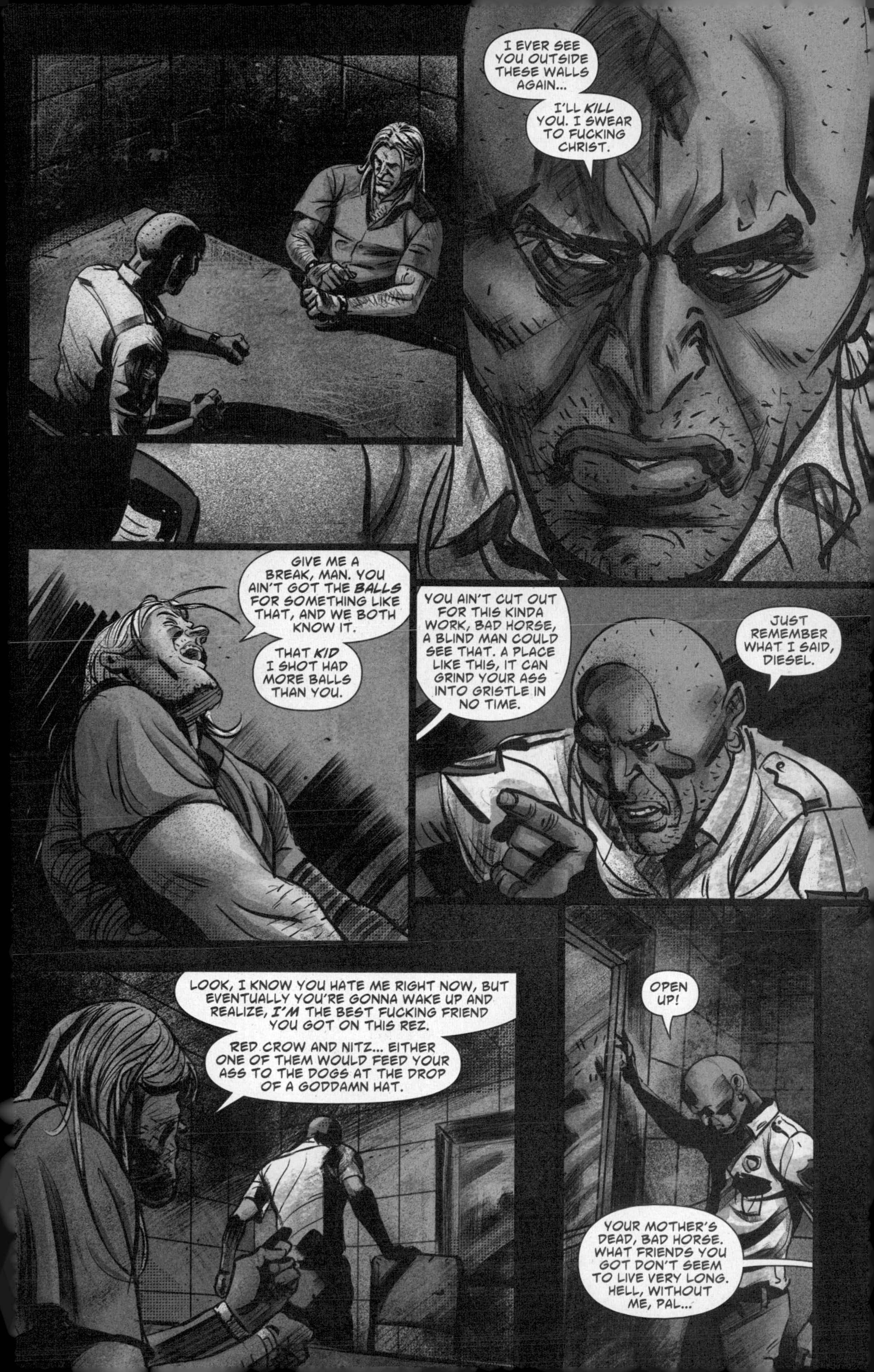
I EVER SEE YOU OUTSIDE THESE WALLS AGAIN...
I'LL *KILL* YOU. I SWEAR TO FUCKING CHRIST.
GIVE ME A BREAK, MAN. YOU AIN'T GOT THE *BALLS* FOR SOMETHING LIKE THAT, AND WE BOTH KNOW IT.
THAT *KID* I SHOT HAD MORE BALLS THAN YOU.
YOU AIN'T CUT OUT FOR THIS KINDA WORK, BAD HORSE, A BLIND MAN COULD SEE THAT. A PLACE LIKE THIS, IT CAN GRIND YOUR ASS INTO GRISTLE IN NO TIME.
JUST REMEMBER WHAT I SAID, DIESEL.
LOOK, I KNOW YOU HATE ME RIGHT NOW, BUT EVENTUALLY YOU'RE GONNA WAKE UP AND REALIZE, *I'M* THE BEST FUCKING FRIEND YOU GOT ON THIS REZ.
RED CROW AND NITZ... EITHER ONE OF THEM WOULD FEED YOUR ASS TO THE DOGS AT THE DROP OF A GODDAMN HAT.
OPEN UP!
YOUR MOTHER'S DEAD, BAD HORSE. WHAT FRIENDS YOU GOT DON'T SEEM TO LIVE VERY LONG. HELL, WITHOUT ME, PAL...

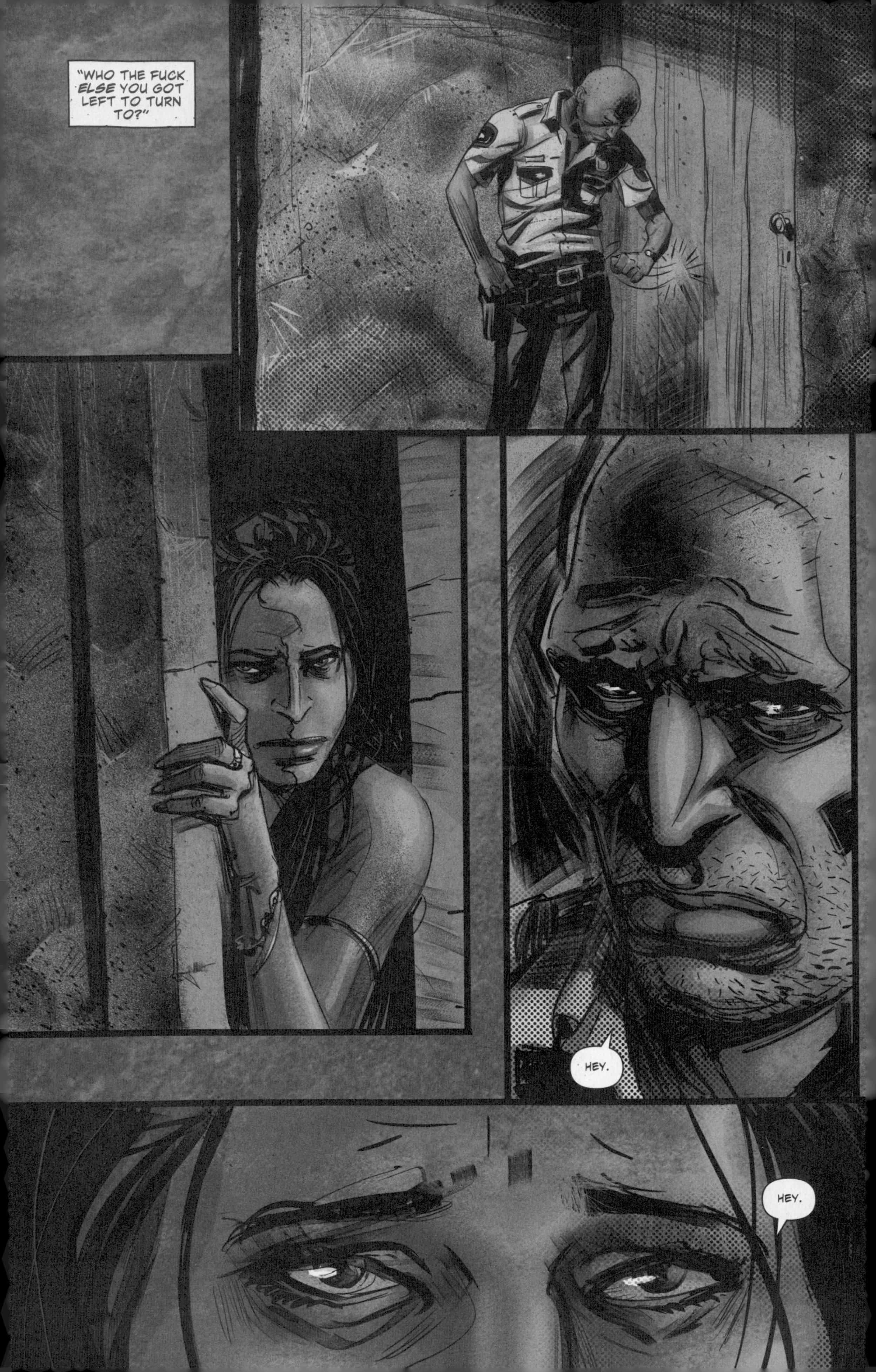
"WHO THE FUCK ELSE YOU GOT LEFT TO TURN TO?"
HEY.
HEY.

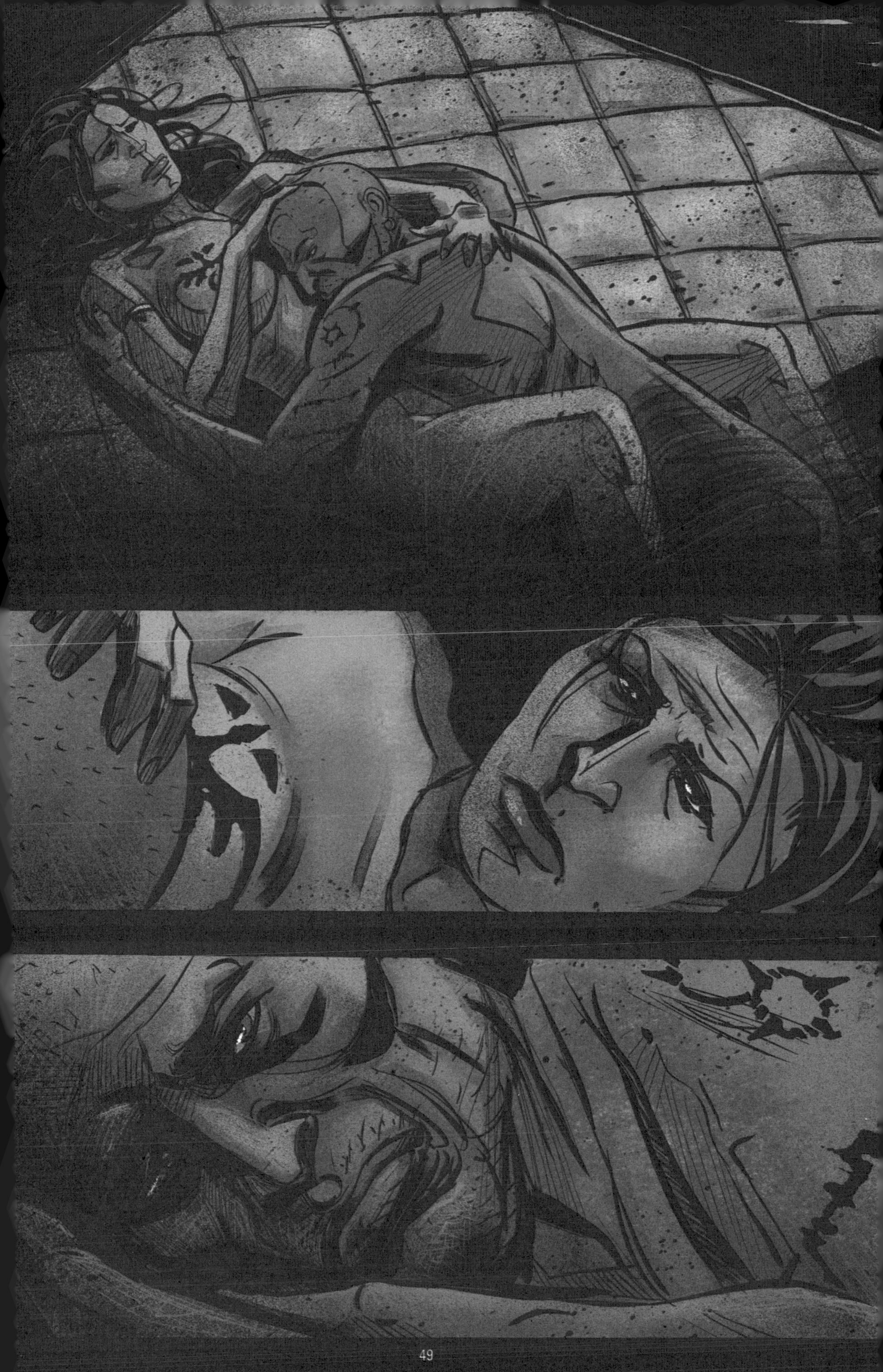

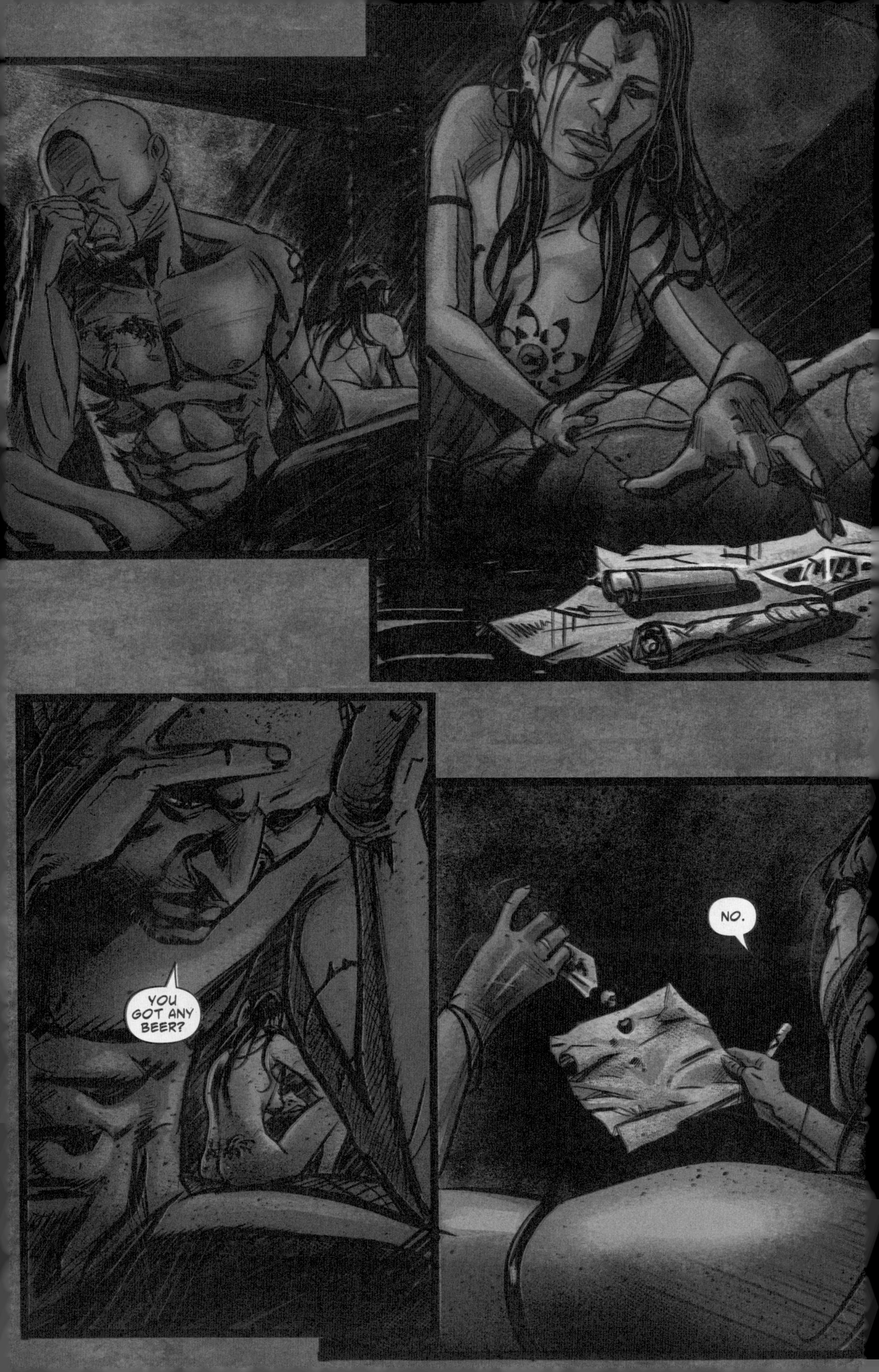
YOU GOT ANY BEER?
NO.

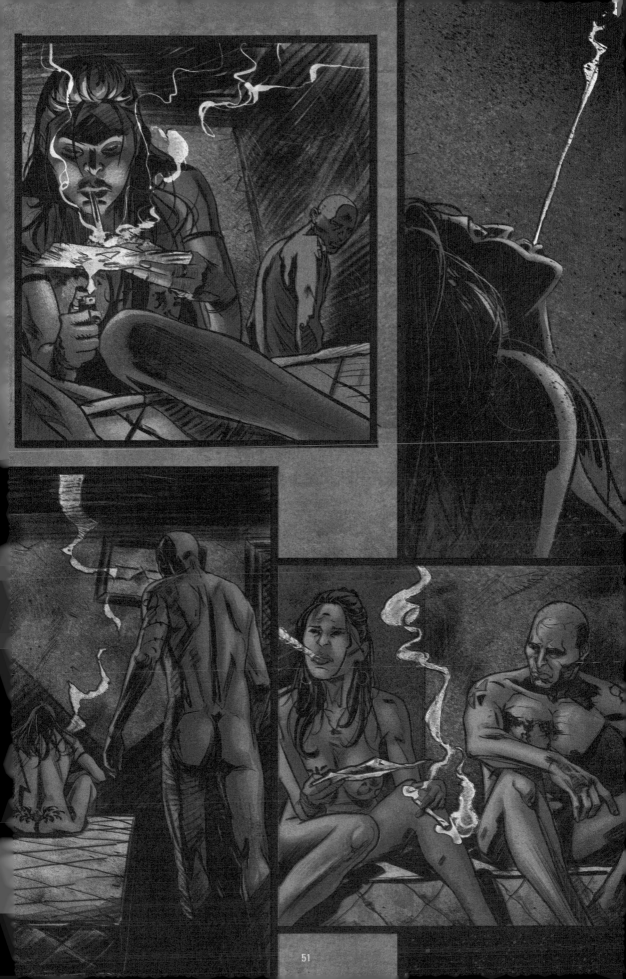

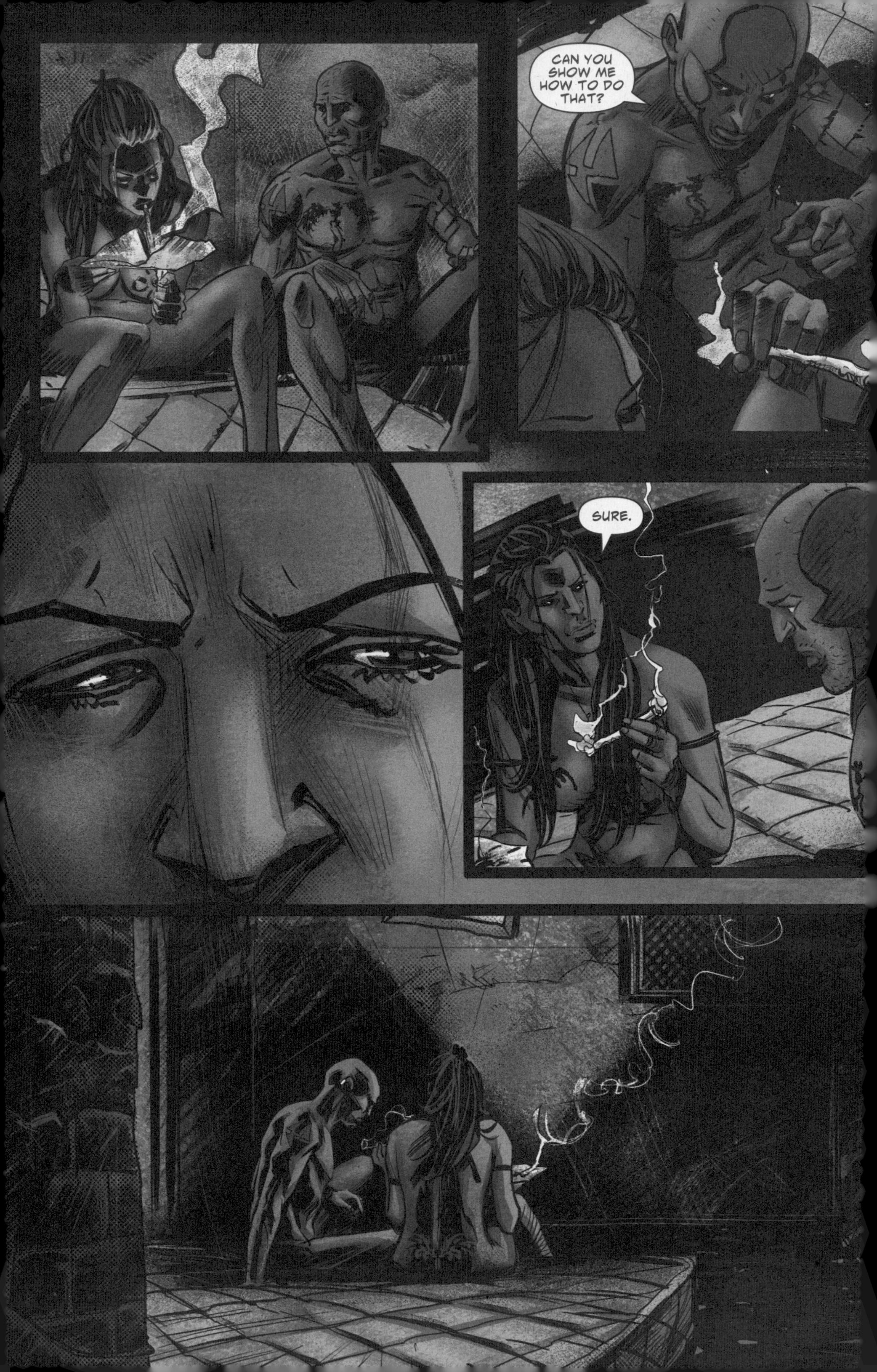
CAN YOU SHOW ME HOW TO DO THAT?
SURE.

THE GRAVEL IN YOUR GUTS PART 1

COVER ART BY JOCK

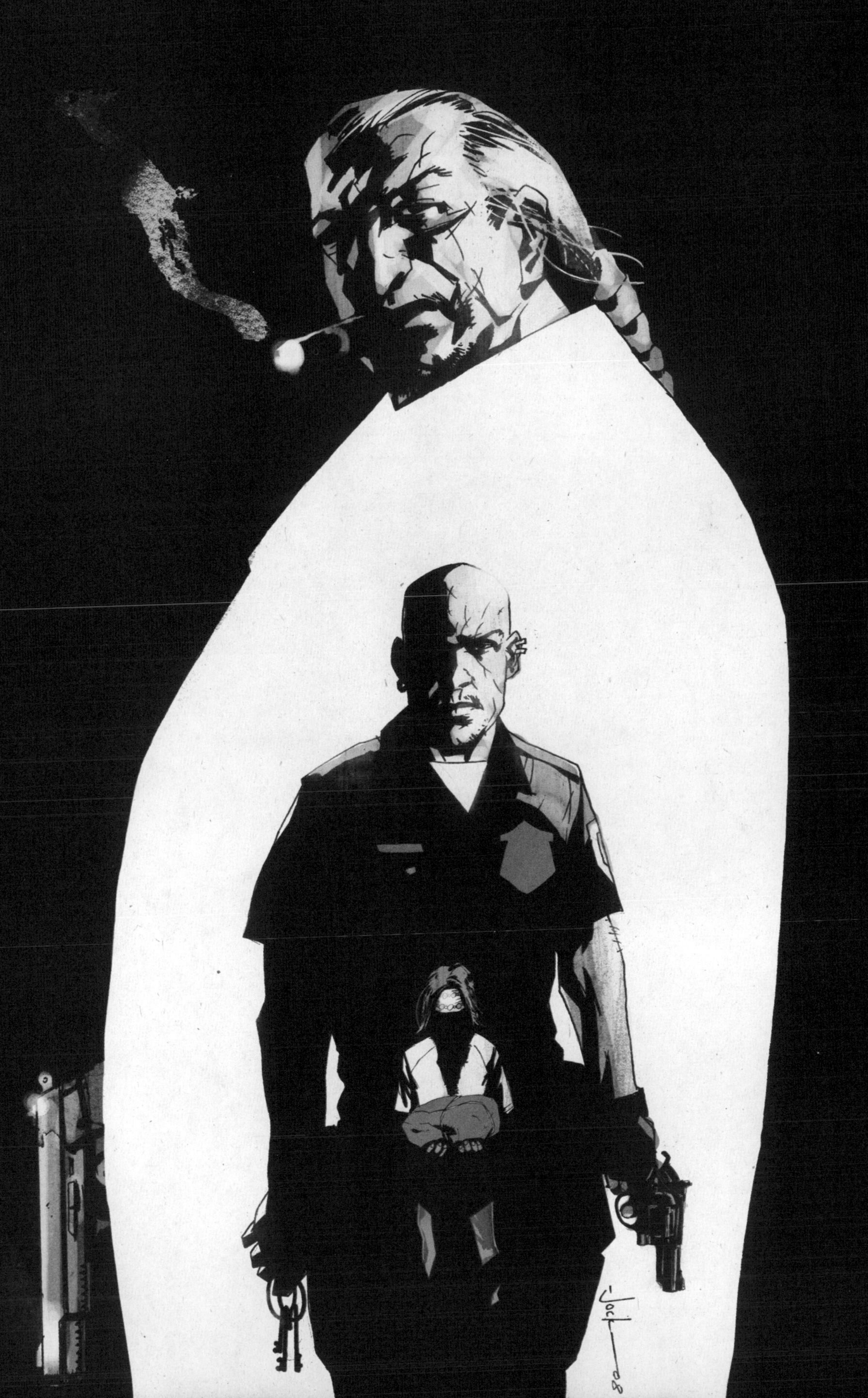
Jock '08

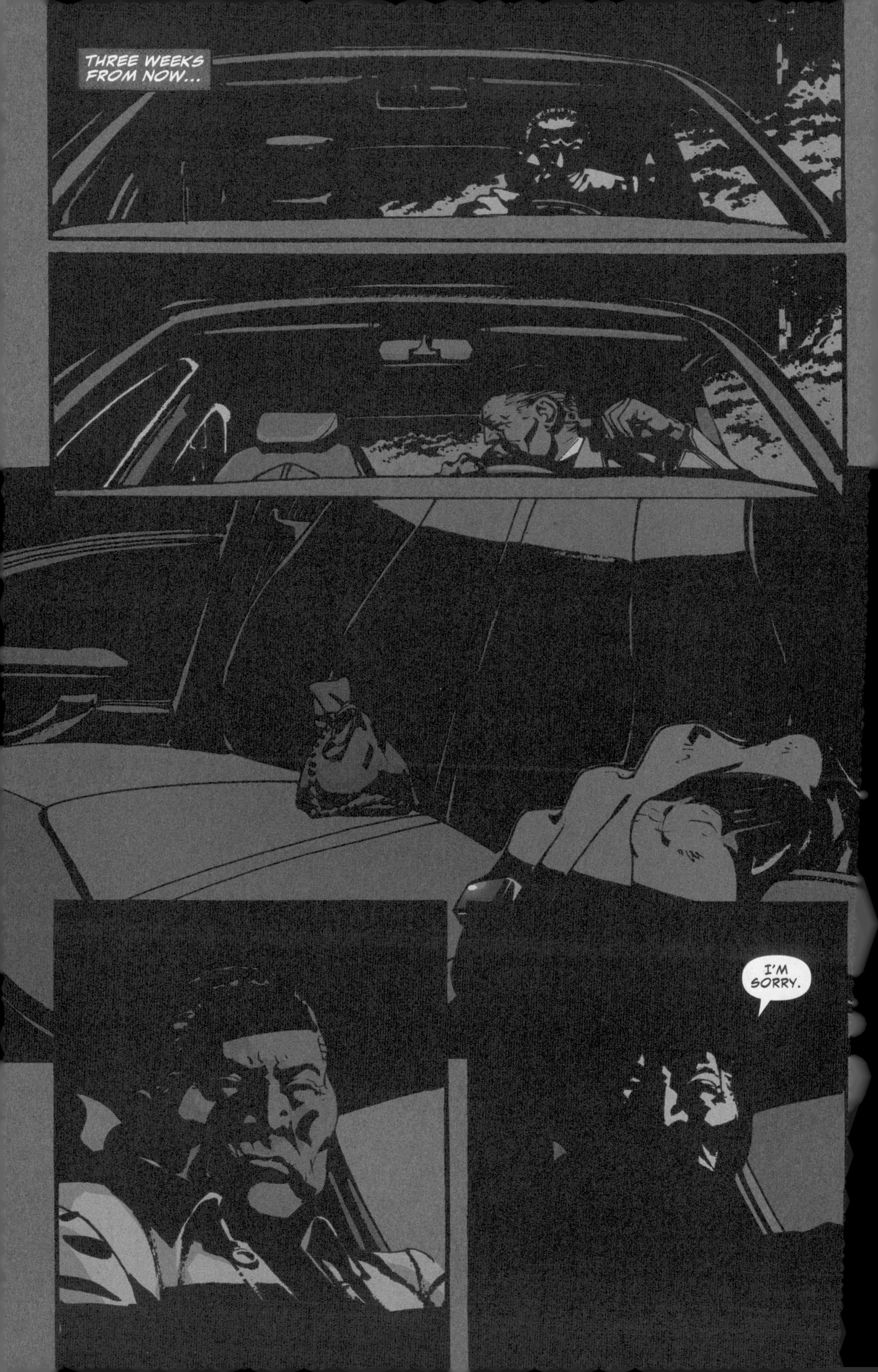
THREE WEEKS FROM NOW...
I'M SORRY.

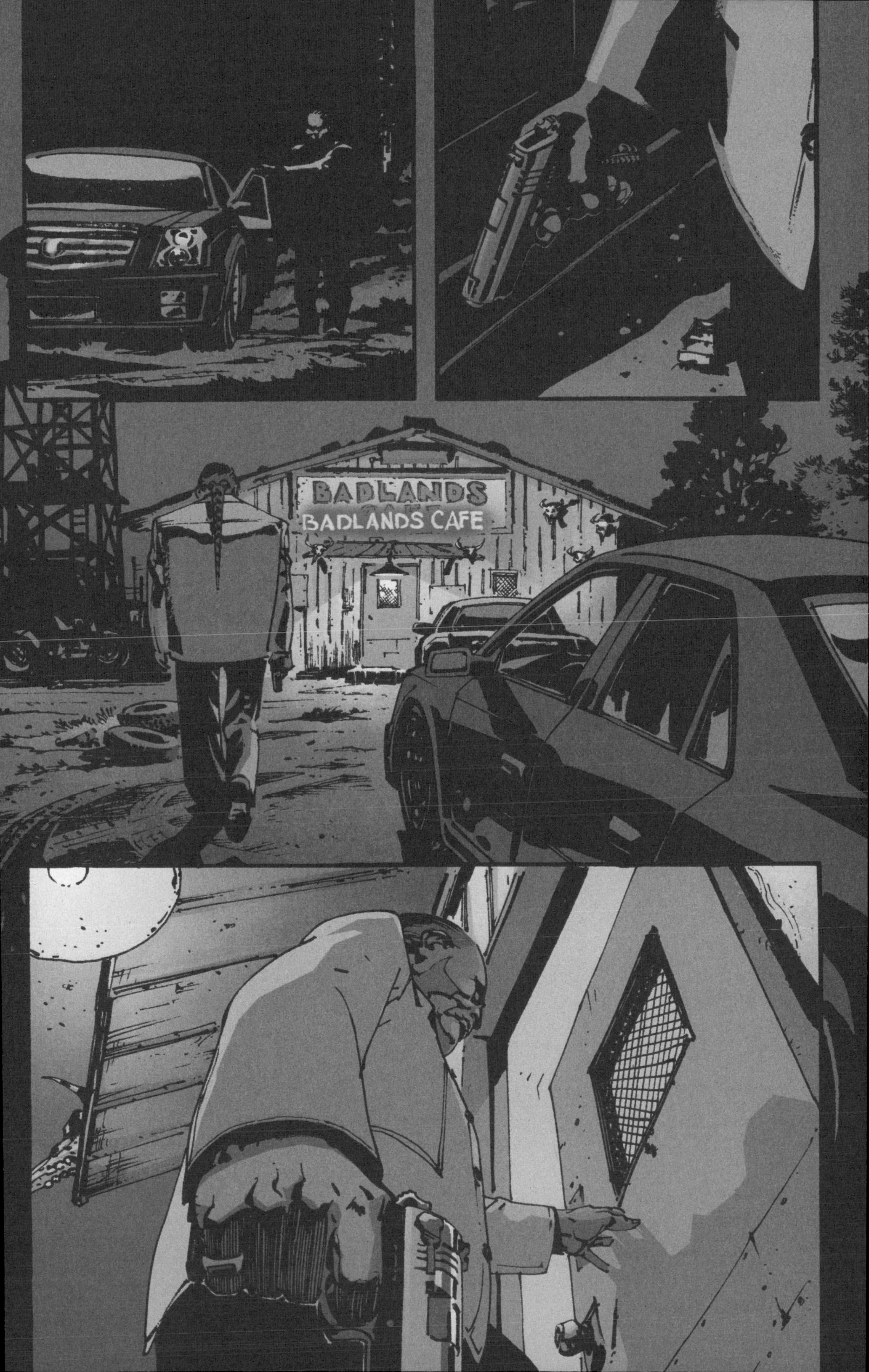
BADLANDS
BADLANDS CAFE

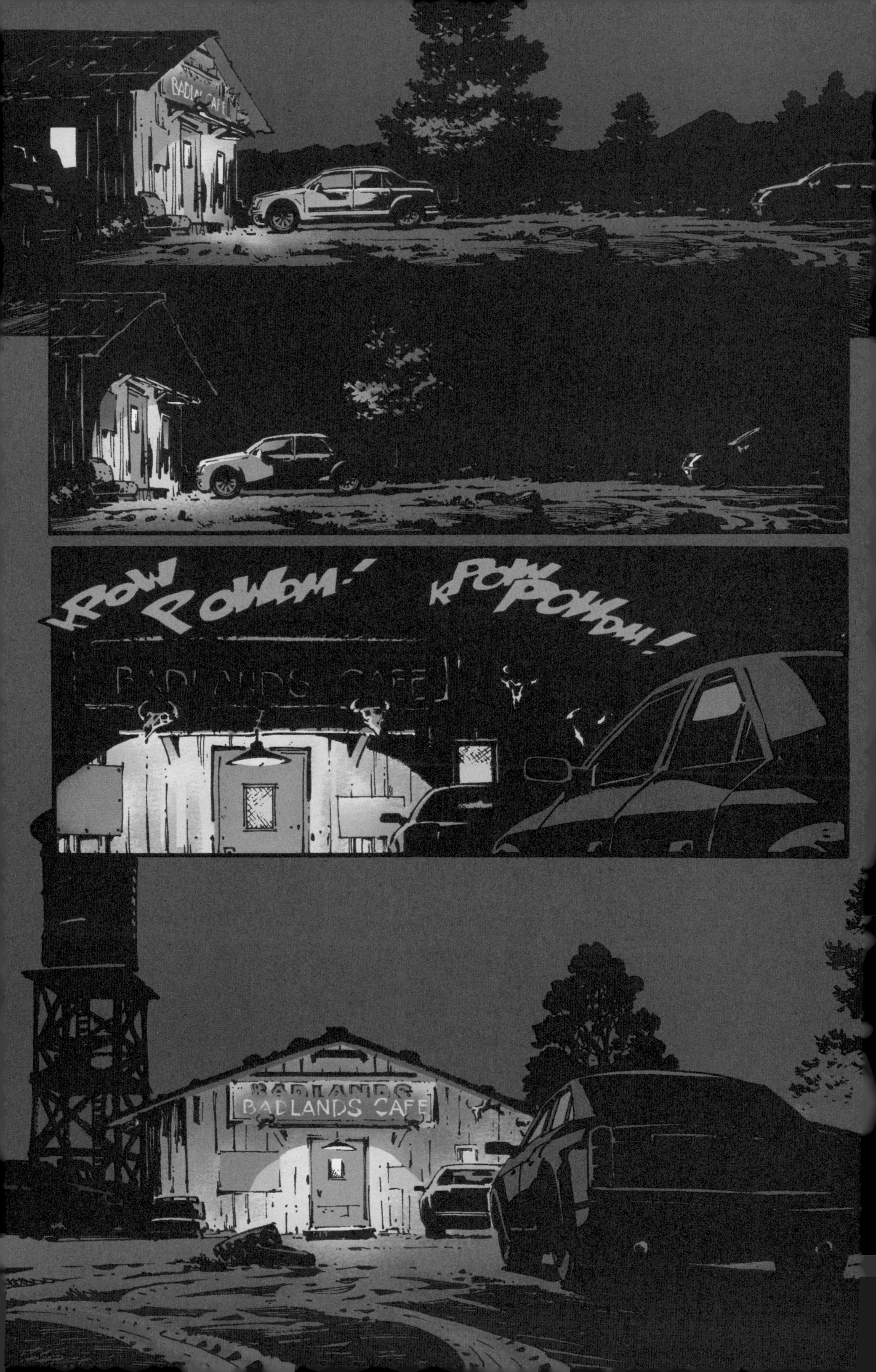
KPOW POWOW!
KPOW POWOW!
BADLANDS CAFE

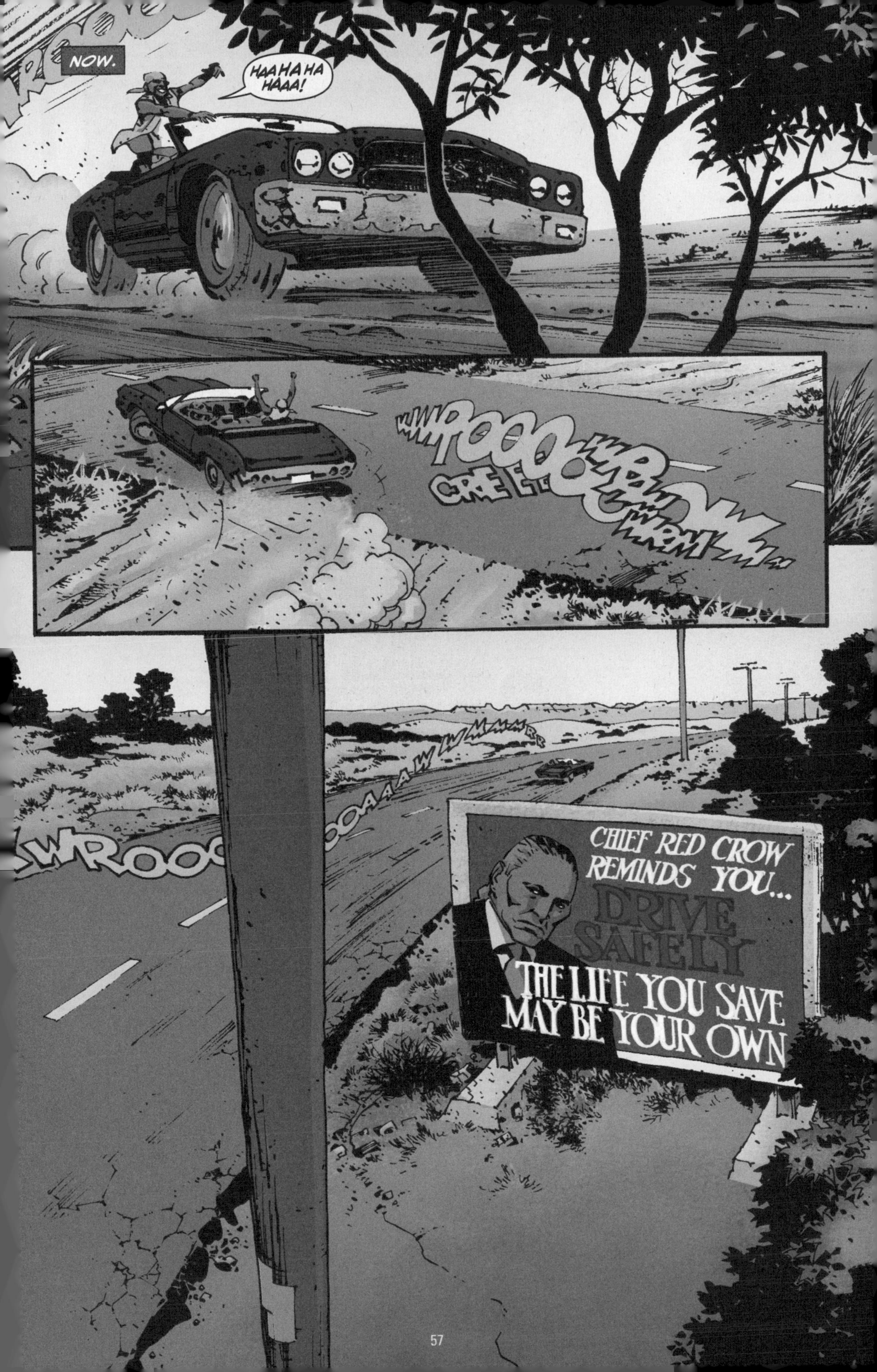
NOW.
HAAHAHA HAAA!
WWROOOOWRAWWWW
CREEEEE
WROOOOAAAAWWWMMMRR
CHIEF RED CROW REMINDS YOU...
DRIVE SAFELY
THE LIFE YOU SAVE MAY BE YOUR OWN

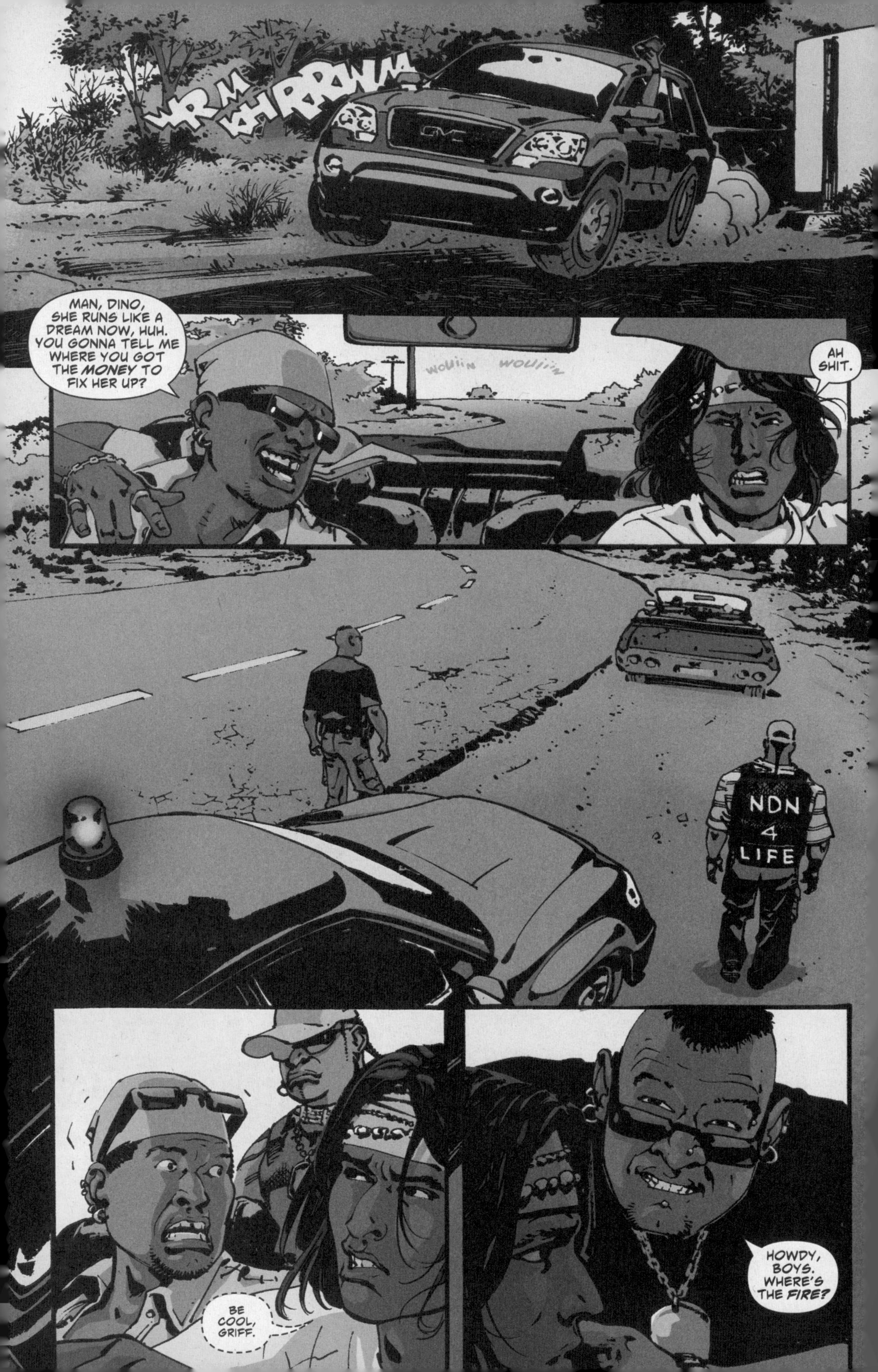
VRRM
KHRRRAAM
MAN, DINO, SHE RUNS LIKE A DREAM NOW, HUH. YOU GONNA TELL ME WHERE YOU GOT THE *MONEY* TO FIX HER UP?
WOUIIIN WOUIIIN
AH SHIT.
NDN 4 LIFE
BE COOL, GRIFF.
HOWDY, BOYS. WHERE'S THE *FIRE*?

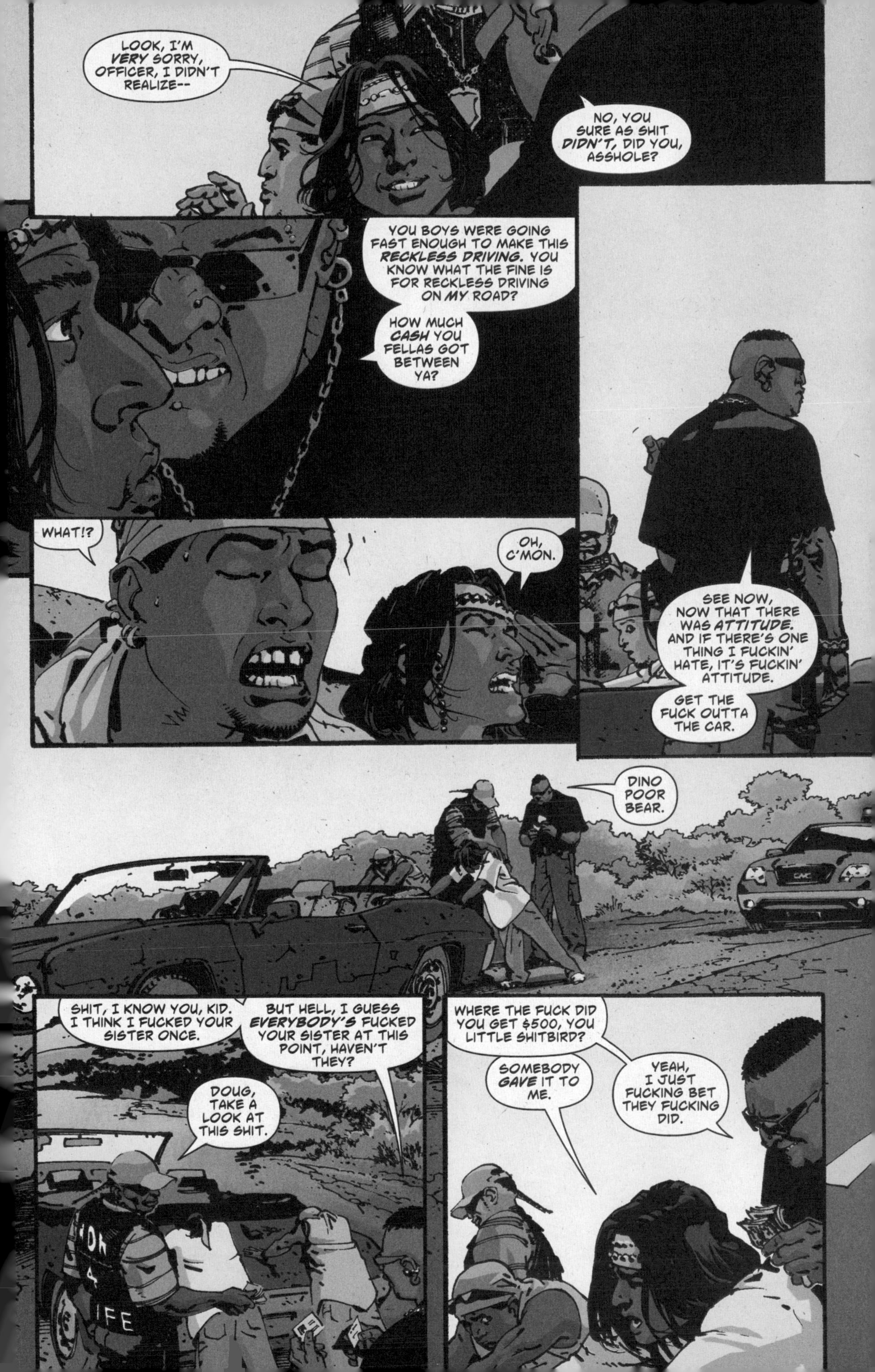

LOOK, I'M *VERY* SORRY, OFFICER, I DIDN'T REALIZE--
NO, YOU SURE AS SHIT *DIDN'T*, DID YOU, ASSHOLE?
YOU BOYS WERE GOING FAST ENOUGH TO MAKE THIS *RECKLESS DRIVING.* YOU KNOW WHAT THE FINE IS FOR RECKLESS DRIVING ON *MY* ROAD?
HOW MUCH *CASH* YOU FELLAS GOT BETWEEN YA?
WHAT!?
OH, C'MON.
SEE NOW, NOW THAT THERE WAS *ATTITUDE.* AND IF THERE'S ONE THING I FUCKIN' HATE, IT'S FUCKIN' ATTITUDE.
GET THE FUCK OUTTA THE CAR.
DINO POOR BEAR.
SHIT, I KNOW YOU, KID. I THINK I FUCKED YOUR SISTER ONCE.
BUT HELL, I GUESS *EVERYBODY'S* FUCKED YOUR SISTER AT THIS POINT, HAVEN'T THEY?
DOUG, TAKE A LOOK AT THIS SHIT.
WHERE THE FUCK DID YOU GET $500, YOU LITTLE SHITBIRD?
SOMEBODY *GAVE* IT TO ME.
YEAH, I JUST FUCKING BET THEY FUCKING DID.

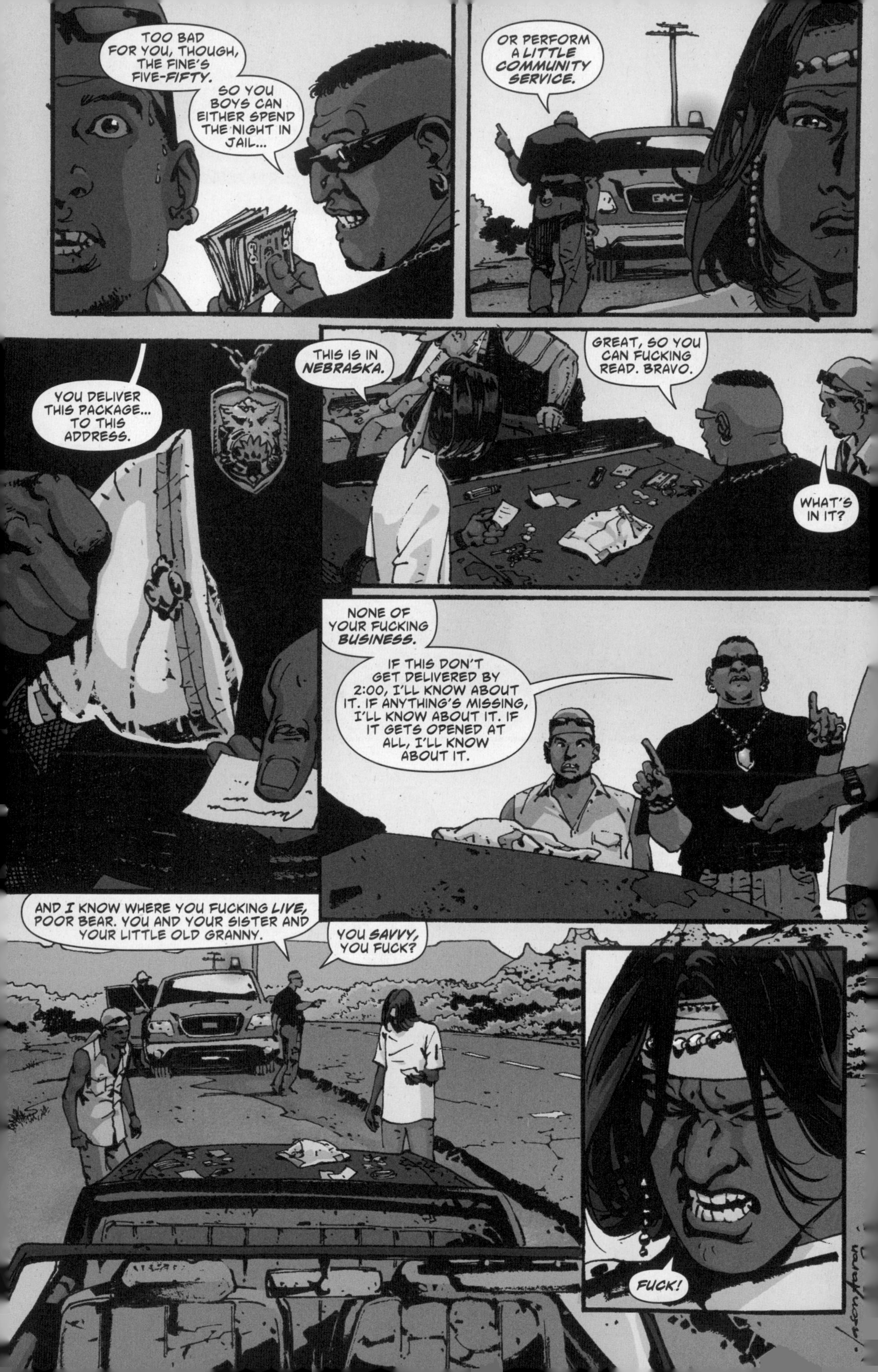
TOO BAD FOR YOU, THOUGH, THE FINE'S FIVE-FIFTY.
SO YOU BOYS CAN EITHER SPEND THE NIGHT IN JAIL...
OR PERFORM A LITTLE COMMUNITY SERVICE.
YOU DELIVER THIS PACKAGE... TO THIS ADDRESS.
THIS IS IN NEBRASKA.
GREAT, SO YOU CAN FUCKING READ. BRAVO.
WHAT'S IN IT?
NONE OF YOUR FUCKING BUSINESS.
IF THIS DON'T GET DELIVERED BY 2:00, I'LL KNOW ABOUT IT. IF ANYTHING'S MISSING, I'LL KNOW ABOUT IT. IF IT GETS OPENED AT ALL, I'LL KNOW ABOUT IT.
AND I KNOW WHERE YOU FUCKING LIVE, POOR BEAR. YOU AND YOUR SISTER AND YOUR LITTLE OLD GRANNY.
YOU SAVVY, YOU FUCK?
FUCK!

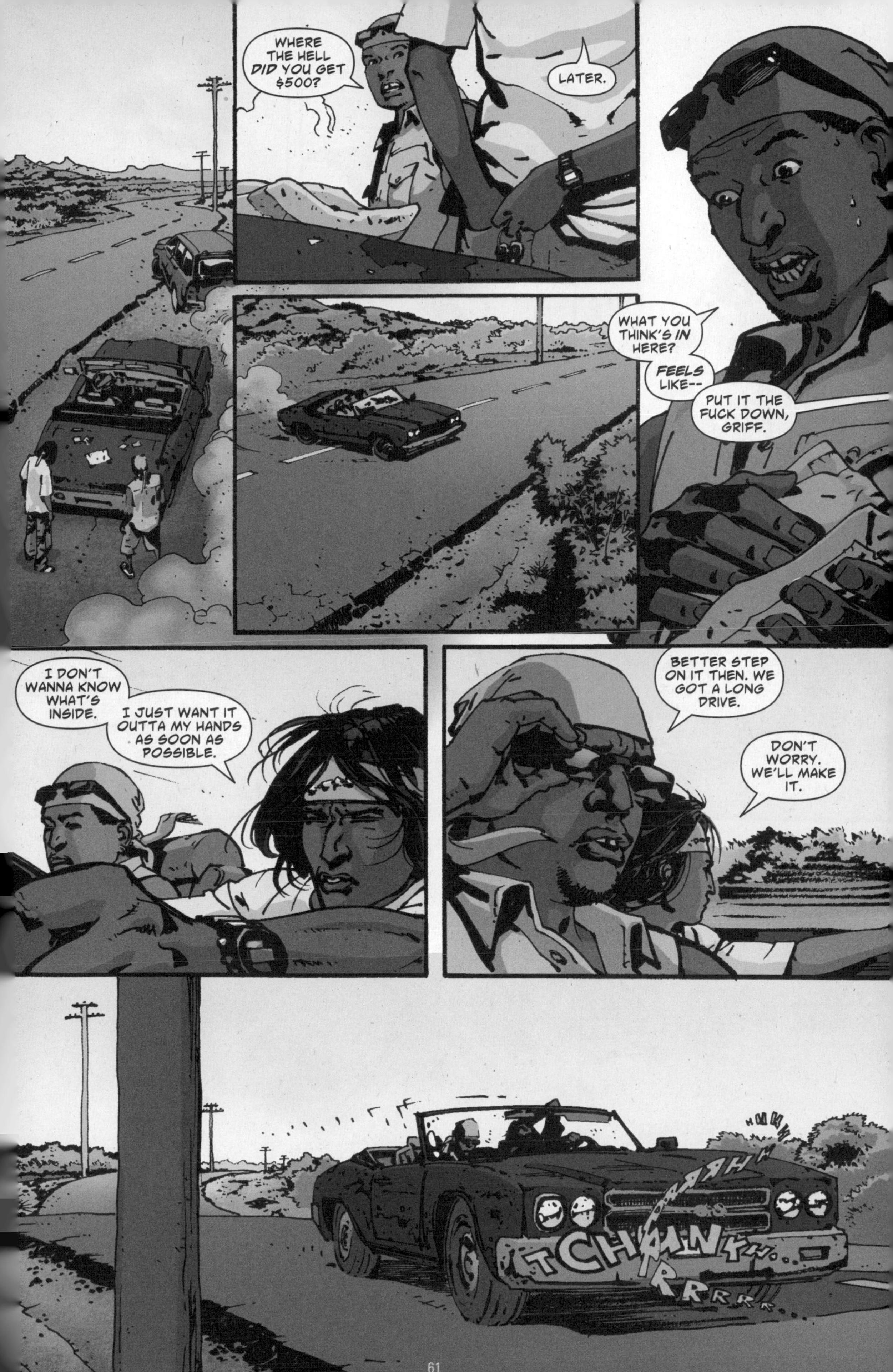
WHERE THE HELL DID YOU GET $500?
LATER.
WHAT YOU THINK'S IN HERE?
FEELS LIKE--
PUT IT THE FUCK DOWN, GRIFF.
I DON'T WANNA KNOW WHAT'S INSIDE.
I JUST WANT IT OUTTA MY HANDS AS SOON AS POSSIBLE.
BETTER STEP ON IT THEN. WE GOT A LONG DRIVE.
DON'T WORRY. WE'LL MAKE IT.
TCHANK
RRRRR

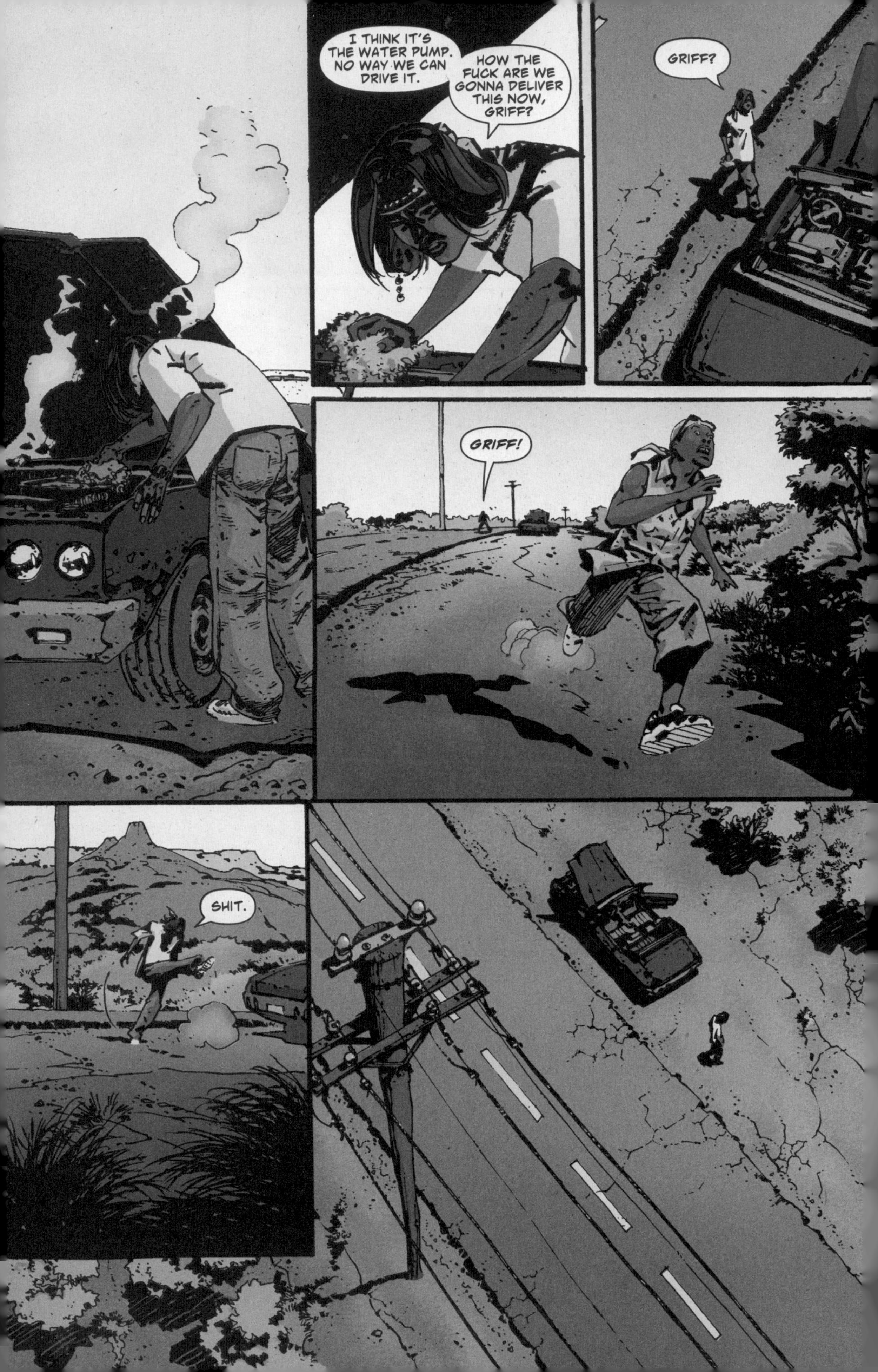
I THINK IT'S THE WATER PUMP. NO WAY WE CAN DRIVE IT.
HOW THE FUCK ARE WE GONNA DELIVER THIS NOW, GRIFF?
GRIFF?
GRIFF!
SHIT.

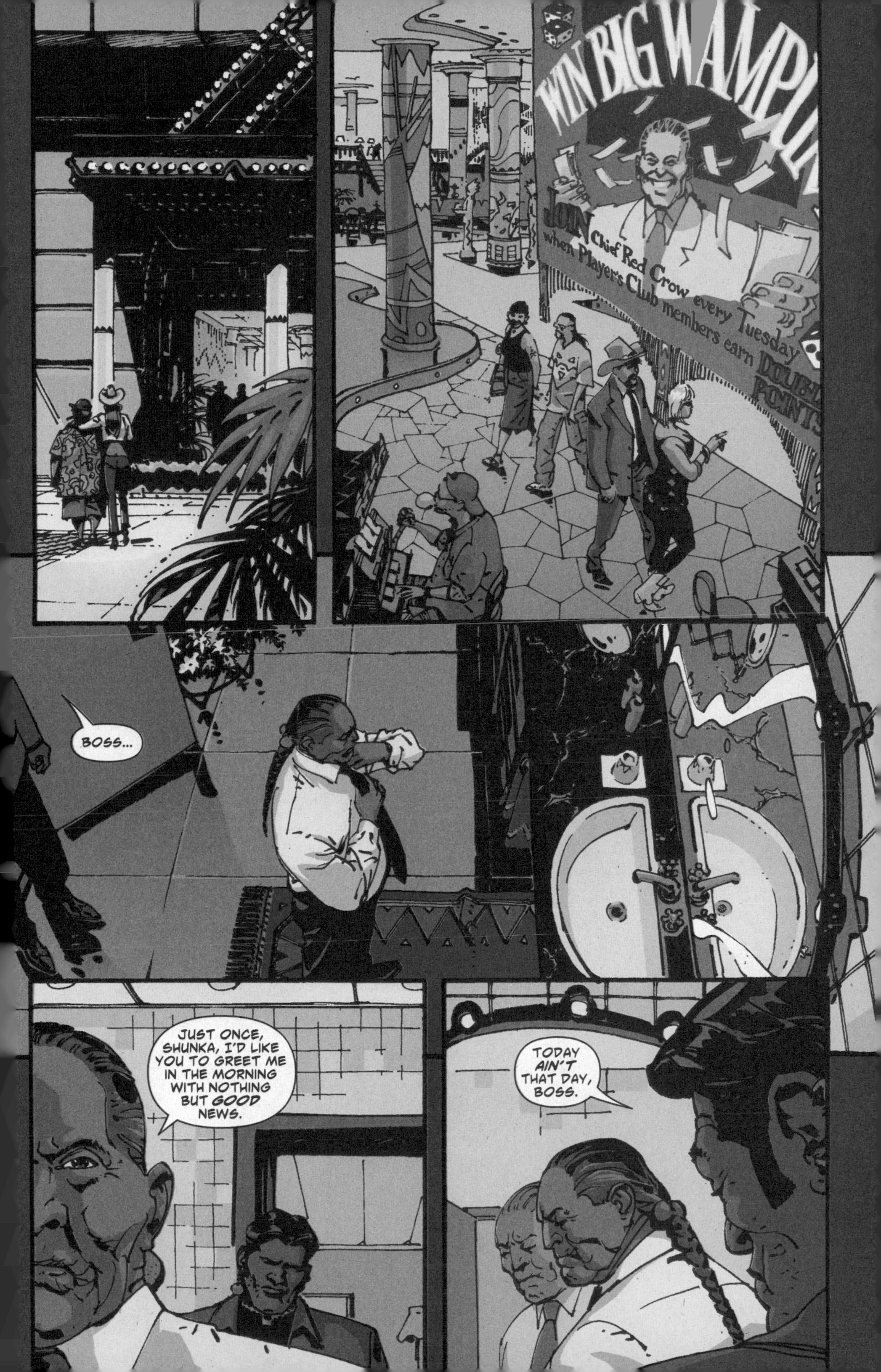
WIN BIG WAMPUM
JOIN Chief Red Crow every Tuesday
when Player's Club members earn DOUBLE POINTS
BOSS...
JUST ONCE, SHUNKA, I'D LIKE YOU TO GREET ME IN THE MORNING WITH NOTHING BUT GOOD NEWS.
TODAY AIN'T THAT DAY, BOSS.

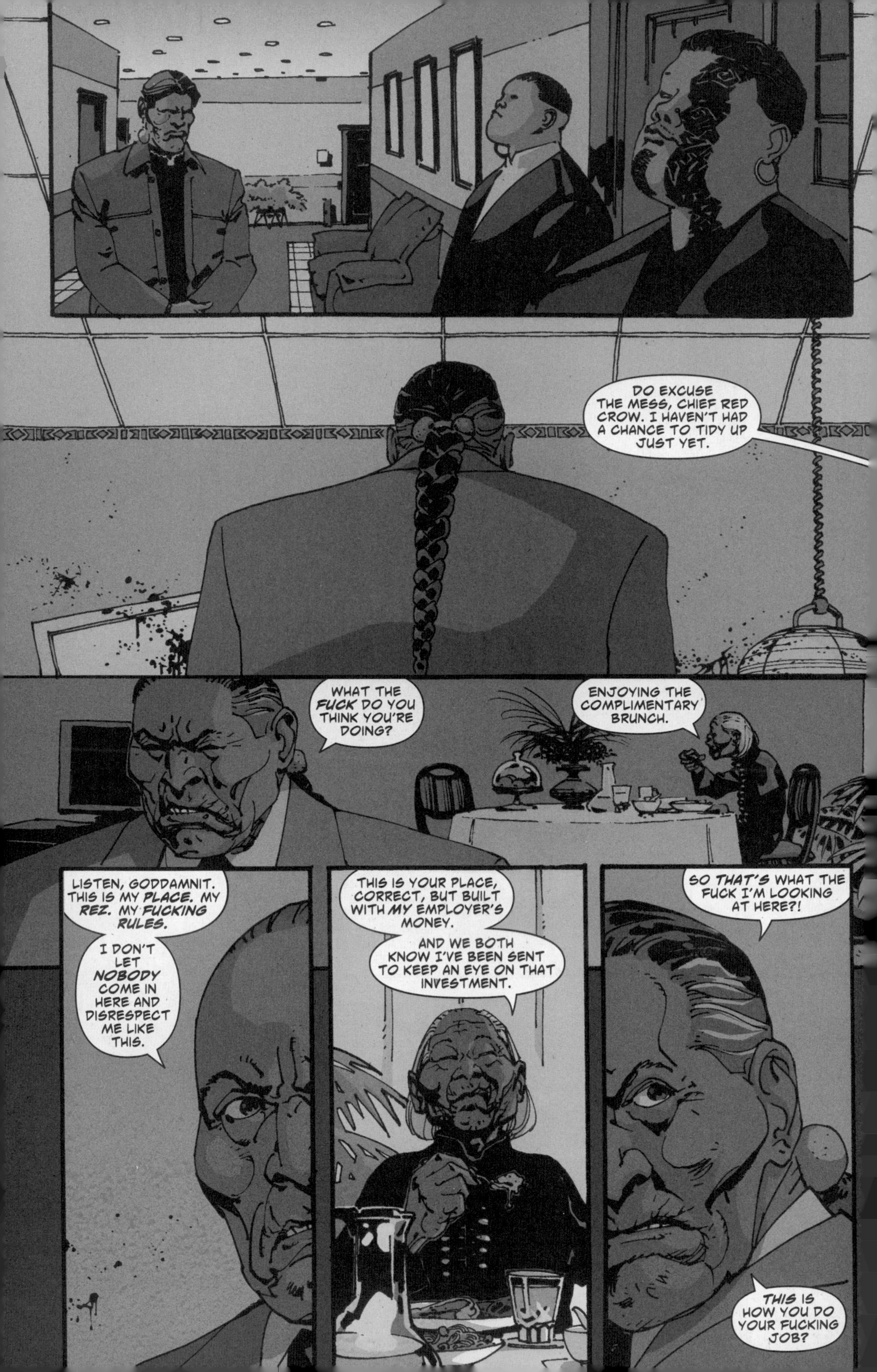
DO EXCUSE THE MESS, CHIEF RED CROW. I HAVEN'T HAD A CHANCE TO TIDY UP JUST YET.
WHAT THE *FUCK* DO YOU THINK YOU'RE DOING?
ENJOYING THE COMPLIMENTARY BRUNCH.
LISTEN, GODDAMNIT. THIS IS MY *PLACE*. MY *REZ*. MY *FUCKING RULES*.
I DON'T LET *NOBODY* COME IN HERE AND DISRESPECT ME LIKE THIS.
THIS IS YOUR PLACE, CORRECT, BUT BUILT WITH *MY* EMPLOYER'S MONEY.
AND WE BOTH KNOW I'VE BEEN SENT TO KEEP AN EYE ON THAT INVESTMENT.
SO *THAT'S* WHAT THE FUCK I'M LOOKING AT HERE?!
THIS IS HOW YOU DO YOUR FUCKING JOB?

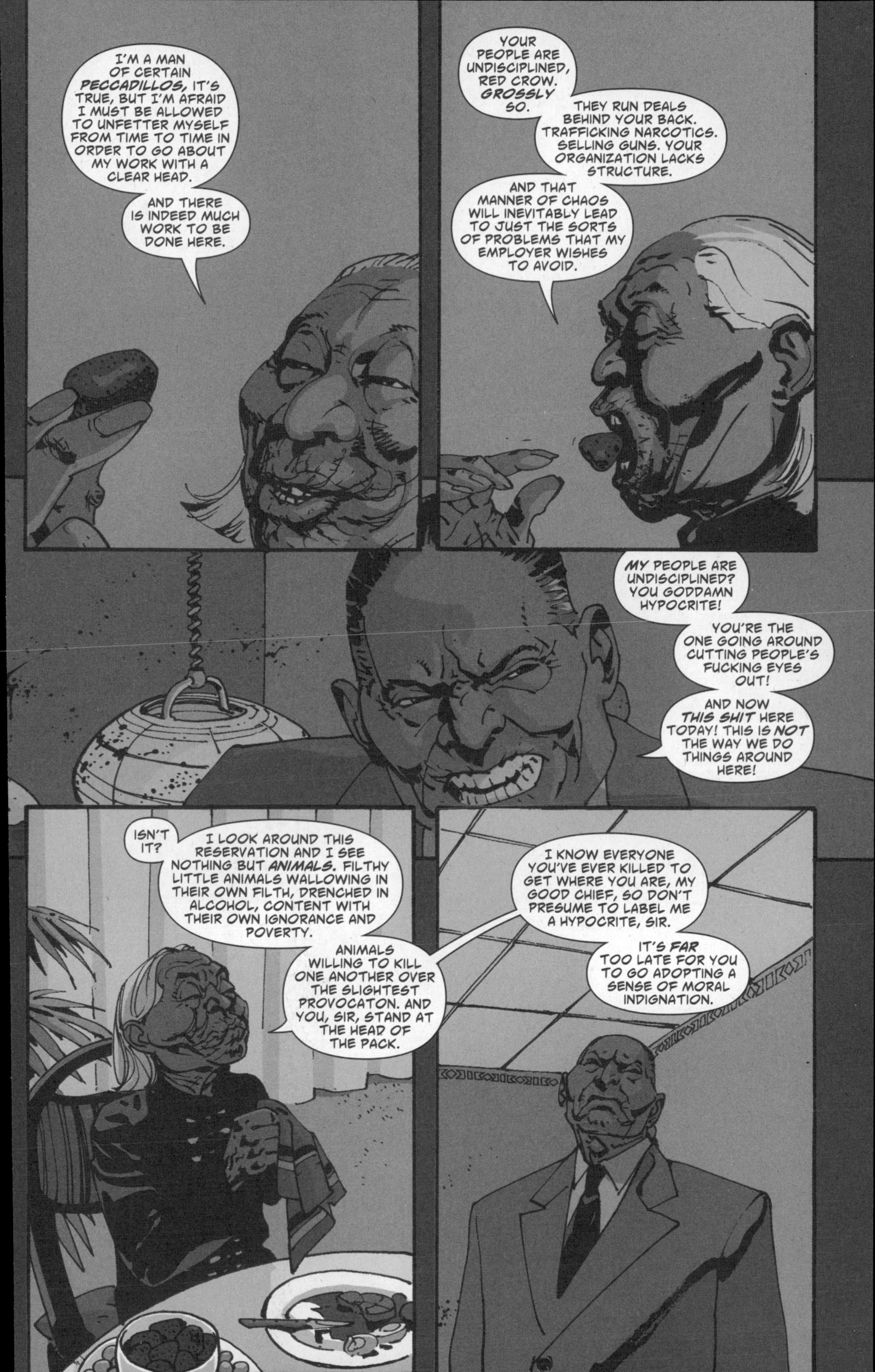

I'M A MAN OF CERTAIN PECCADILLOS, IT'S TRUE, BUT I'M AFRAID I MUST BE ALLOWED TO UNFETTER MYSELF FROM TIME TO TIME IN ORDER TO GO ABOUT MY WORK WITH A CLEAR HEAD.
AND THERE IS INDEED MUCH WORK TO BE DONE HERE.
YOUR PEOPLE ARE UNDISCIPLINED, RED CROW. GROSSLY SO.
THEY RUN DEALS BEHIND YOUR BACK. TRAFFICKING NARCOTICS. SELLING GUNS. YOUR ORGANIZATION LACKS STRUCTURE.
AND THAT MANNER OF CHAOS WILL INEVITABLY LEAD TO JUST THE SORTS OF PROBLEMS THAT MY EMPLOYER WISHES TO AVOID.
MY PEOPLE ARE UNDISCIPLINED? YOU GODDAMN HYPOCRITE!
YOU'RE THE ONE GOING AROUND CUTTING PEOPLE'S FUCKING EYES OUT!
AND NOW THIS SHIT HERE TODAY! THIS IS NOT THE WAY WE DO THINGS AROUND HERE!
ISN'T IT?
I LOOK AROUND THIS RESERVATION AND I SEE NOTHING BUT ANIMALS. FILTHY LITTLE ANIMALS WALLOWING IN THEIR OWN FILTH, DRENCHED IN ALCOHOL, CONTENT WITH THEIR OWN IGNORANCE AND POVERTY.
ANIMALS WILLING TO KILL ONE ANOTHER OVER THE SLIGHTEST PROVOCATON. AND YOU, SIR, STAND AT THE HEAD OF THE PACK.
I KNOW EVERYONE YOU'VE EVER KILLED TO GET WHERE YOU ARE, MY GOOD CHIEF, SO DON'T PRESUME TO LABEL ME A HYPOCRITE, SIR.
IT'S FAR TOO LATE FOR YOU TO GO ADOPTING A SENSE OF MORAL INDIGNATION.

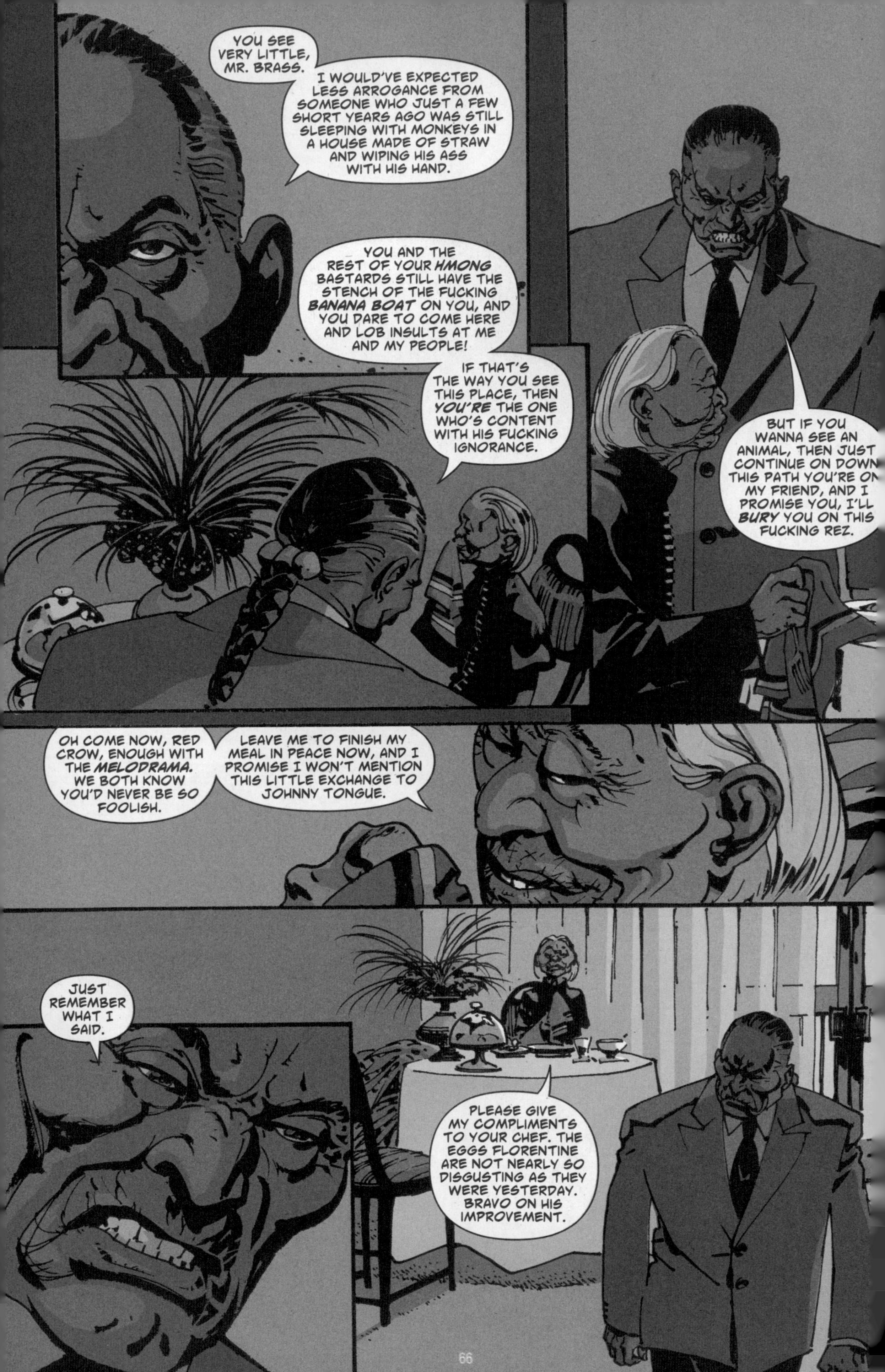
YOU SEE VERY LITTLE, MR. BRASS.
I WOULD'VE EXPECTED LESS ARROGANCE FROM SOMEONE WHO JUST A FEW SHORT YEARS AGO WAS STILL SLEEPING WITH MONKEYS IN A HOUSE MADE OF STRAW AND WIPING HIS ASS WITH HIS HAND.
YOU AND THE REST OF YOUR HMONG BASTARDS STILL HAVE THE STENCH OF THE FUCKING BANANA BOAT ON YOU, AND YOU DARE TO COME HERE AND LOB INSULTS AT ME AND MY PEOPLE!
IF THAT'S THE WAY YOU SEE THIS PLACE, THEN YOU'RE THE ONE WHO'S CONTENT WITH HIS FUCKING IGNORANCE.
BUT IF YOU WANNA SEE AN ANIMAL, THEN JUST CONTINUE ON DOWN THIS PATH YOU'RE ON MY FRIEND, AND I PROMISE YOU, I'LL BURY YOU ON THIS FUCKING REZ.
OH COME NOW, RED CROW, ENOUGH WITH THE MELODRAMA. WE BOTH KNOW YOU'D NEVER BE SO FOOLISH.
LEAVE ME TO FINISH MY MEAL IN PEACE NOW, AND I PROMISE I WON'T MENTION THIS LITTLE EXCHANGE TO JOHNNY TONGUE.
JUST REMEMBER WHAT I SAID.
PLEASE GIVE MY COMPLIMENTS TO YOUR CHEF. THE EGGS FLORENTINE ARE NOT NEARLY SO DISGUSTING AS THEY WERE YESTERDAY. BRAVO ON HIS IMPROVEMENT.

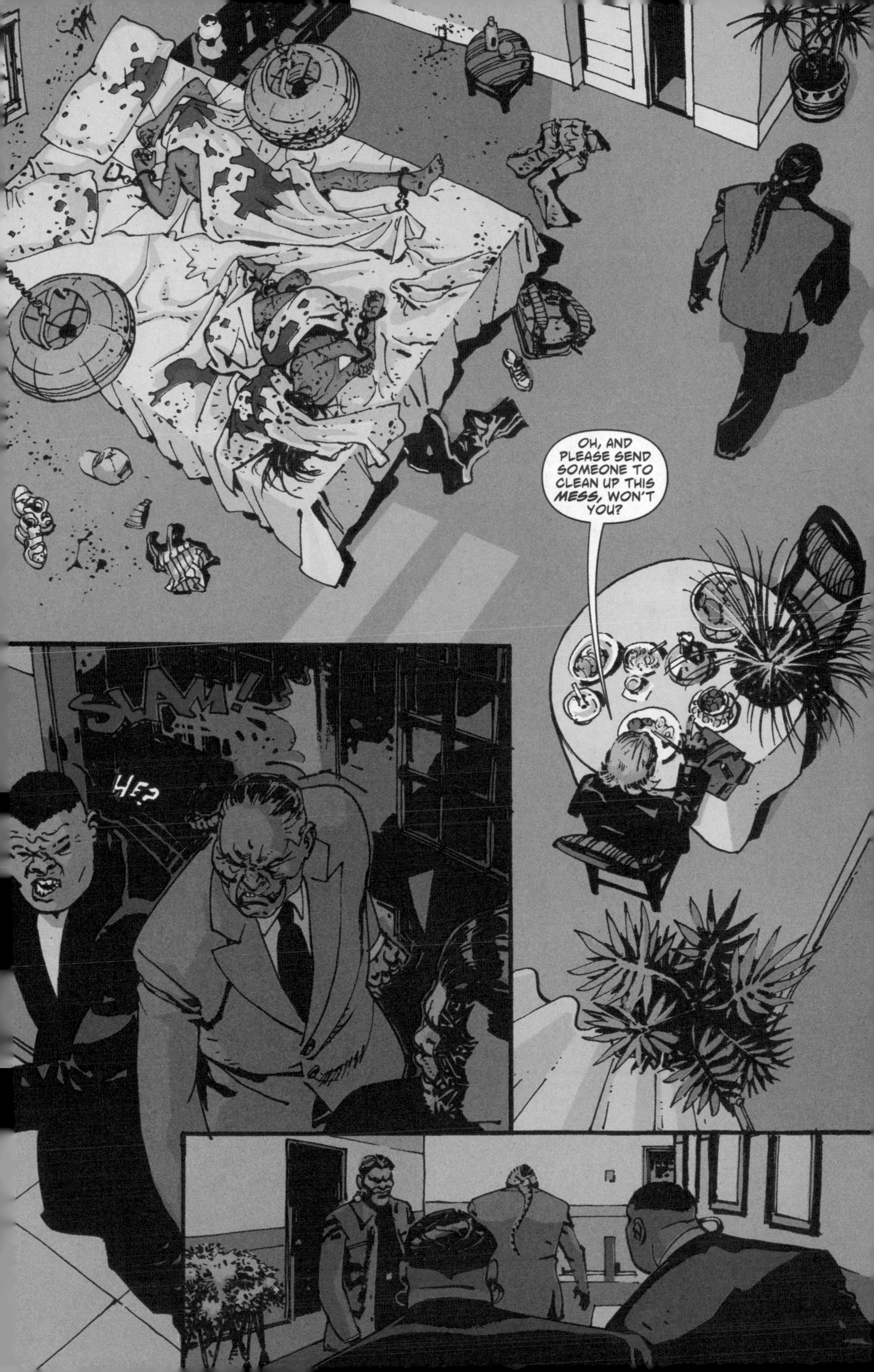
OH, AND PLEASE SEND SOMEONE TO CLEAN UP THIS MESS, WON'T YOU?
SLAM!
HE?

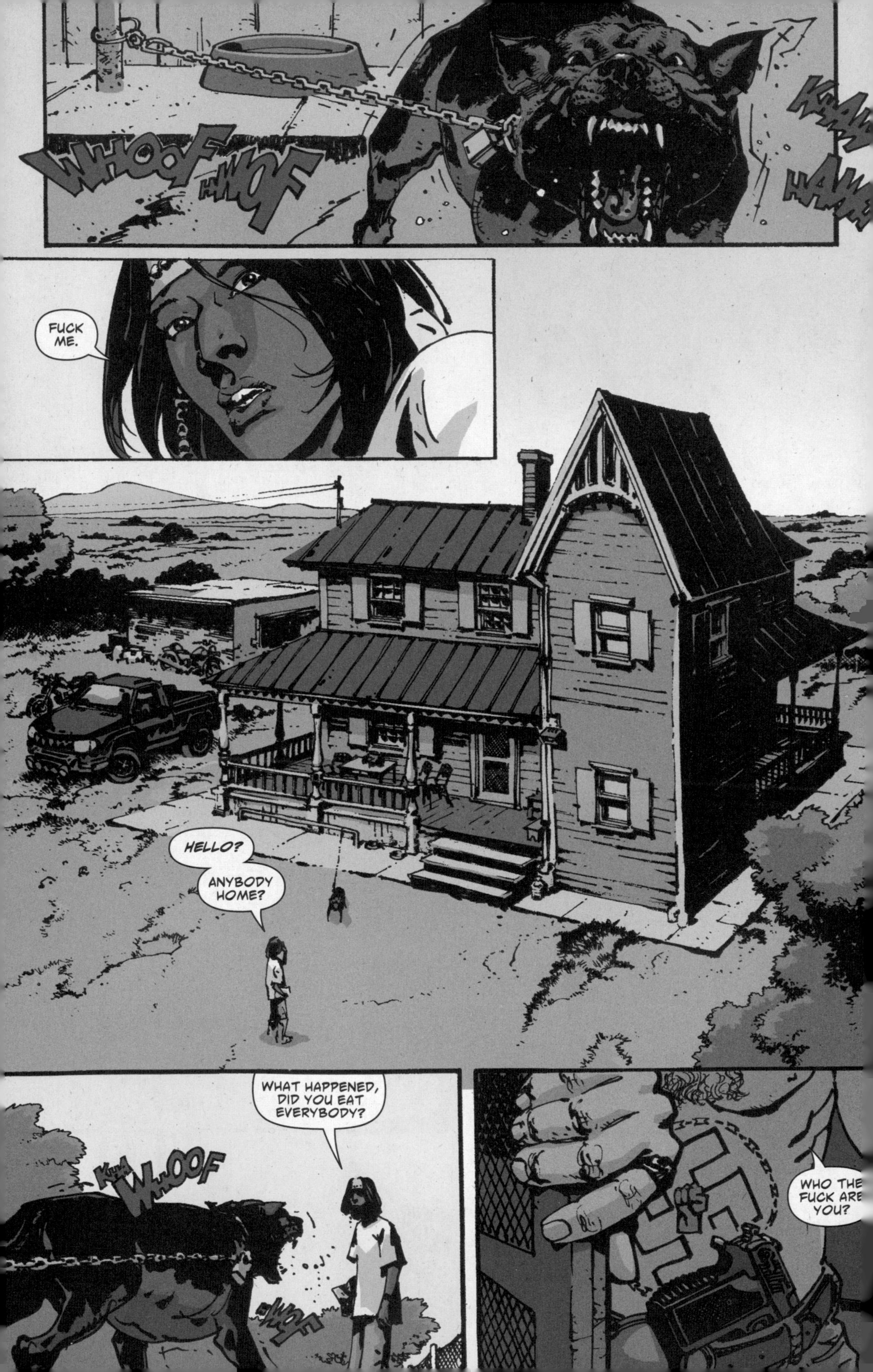

WHOOF
HWOF
KWAW
HAWW
FUCK ME.
HELLO?
ANYBODY HOME?
KWA
WHOOF
WHAT HAPPENED, DID YOU EAT EVERYBODY?
HWOF
WHO THE FUCK ARE YOU?

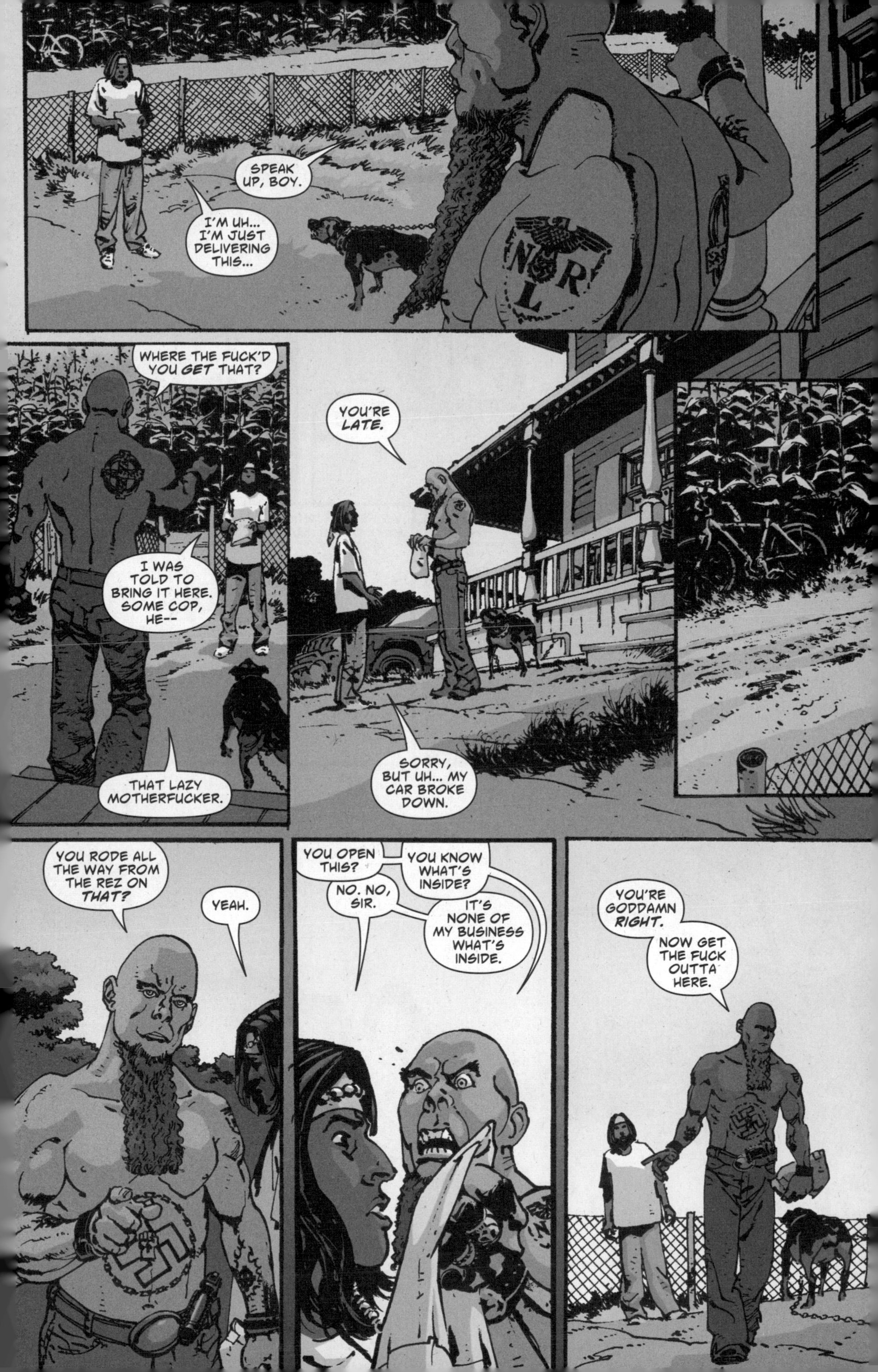
SPEAK UP, BOY.
I'M UH... I'M JUST DELIVERING THIS...
WHERE THE FUCK'D YOU GET THAT?
I WAS TOLD TO BRING IT HERE. SOME COP, HE--
THAT LAZY MOTHERFUCKER.
YOU'RE LATE.
SORRY, BUT UH... MY CAR BROKE DOWN.
YOU RODE ALL THE WAY FROM THE REZ ON THAT?
YEAH.
YOU OPEN THIS?
YOU KNOW WHAT'S INSIDE?
NO. NO, SIR.
IT'S NONE OF MY BUSINESS WHAT'S INSIDE.
YOU'RE GODDAMN RIGHT.
NOW GET THE FUCK OUTTA HERE.

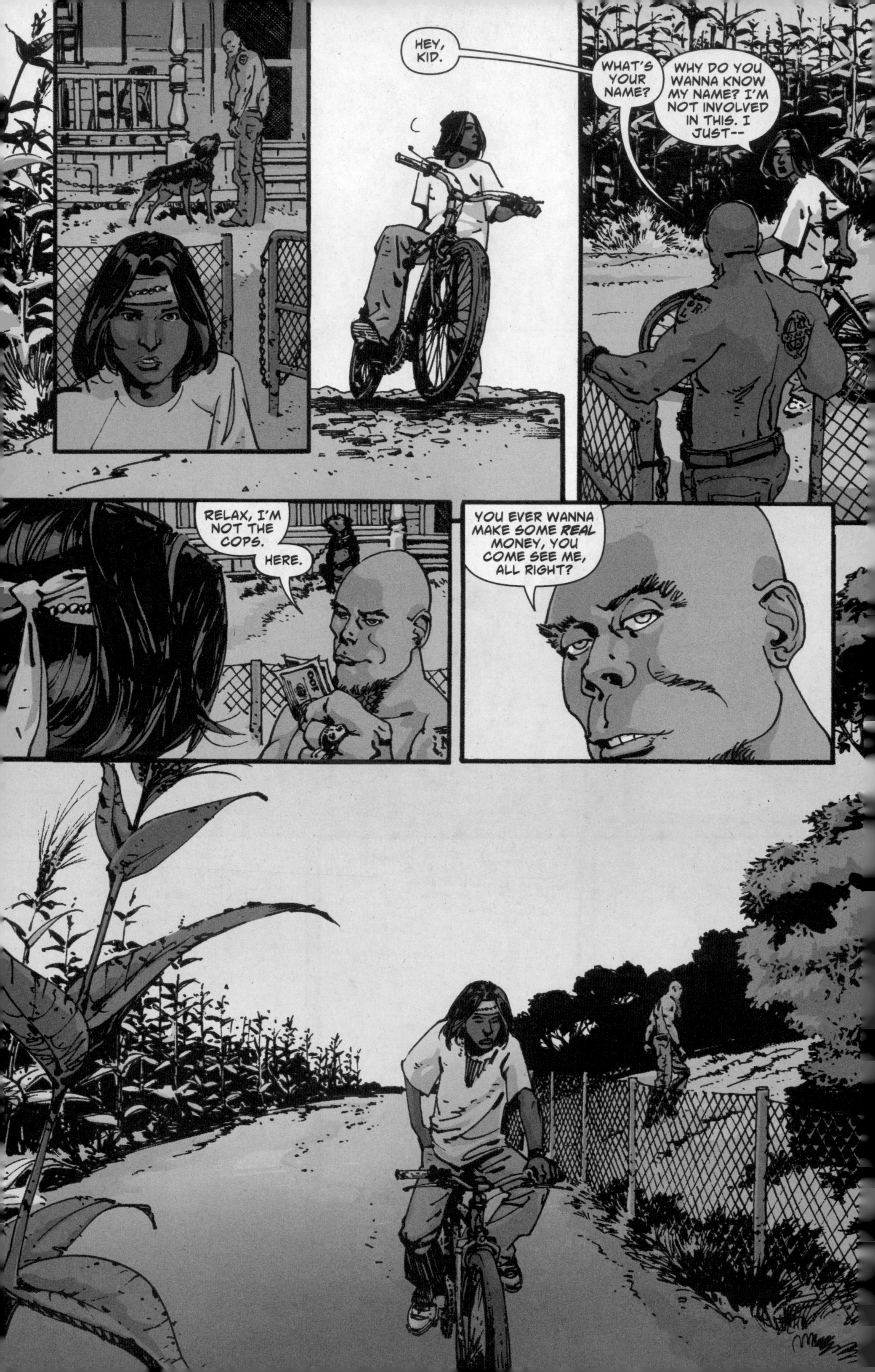
HEY, KID.
WHAT'S YOUR NAME?
WHY DO YOU WANNA KNOW MY NAME? I'M NOT INVOLVED IN THIS. I JUST--
RELAX, I'M NOT THE COPS.
HERE.
YOU EVER WANNA MAKE SOME *REAL* MONEY, YOU COME SEE ME, ALL RIGHT?

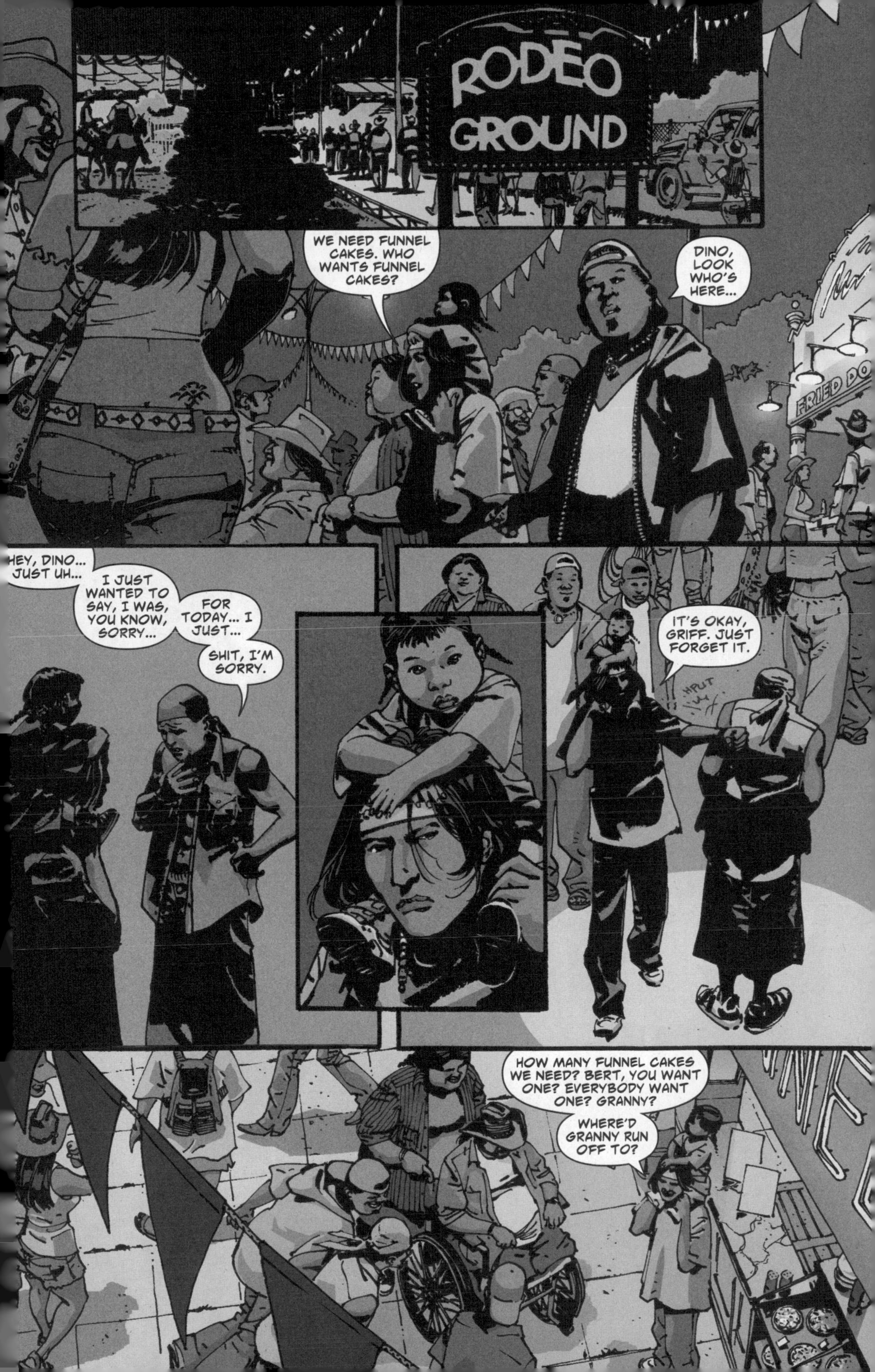
RODEO GROUND
WE NEED FUNNEL CAKES. WHO WANTS FUNNEL CAKES?
DINO, LOOK WHO'S HERE...
FRIED DO
HEY, DINO... JUST UH...
I JUST WANTED TO SAY, I WAS, YOU KNOW, SORRY...
FOR TODAY... I JUST...
SHIT, I'M SORRY.
IT'S OKAY, GRIFF. JUST FORGET IT.
HOW MANY FUNNEL CAKES WE NEED? BERT, YOU WANT ONE? EVERYBODY WANT ONE? GRANNY?
WHERE'D GRANNY RUN OFF TO?

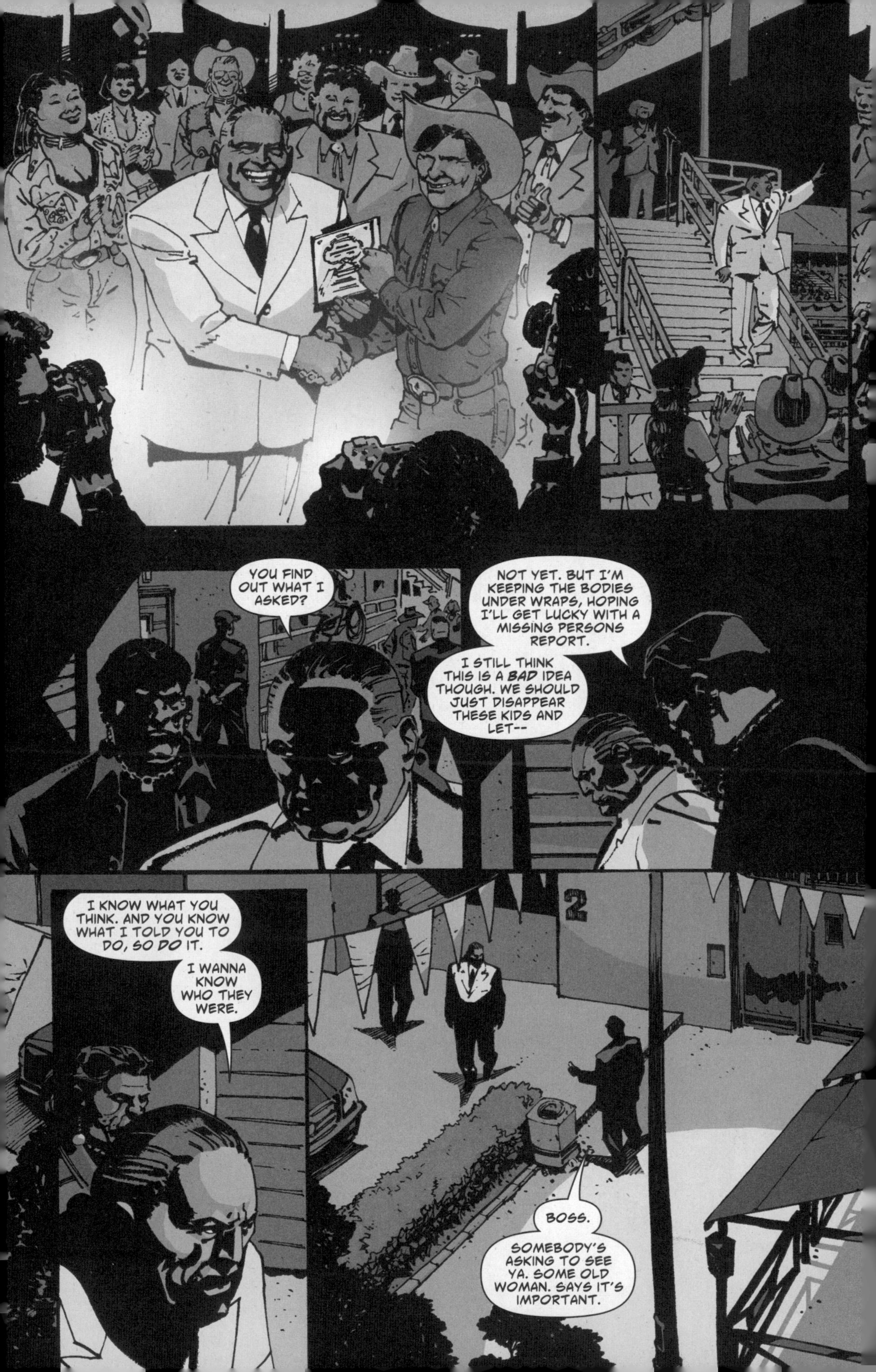
YOU FIND OUT WHAT I ASKED?
NOT YET. BUT I'M KEEPING THE BODIES UNDER WRAPS, HOPING I'LL GET LUCKY WITH A MISSING PERSONS REPORT.
I STILL THINK THIS IS A BAD IDEA THOUGH. WE SHOULD JUST DISAPPEAR THESE KIDS AND LET--
I KNOW WHAT YOU THINK. AND YOU KNOW WHAT I TOLD YOU TO DO, SO DO IT.
I WANNA KNOW WHO THEY WERE.
2
BOSS.
SOMEBODY'S ASKING TO SEE YA. SOME OLD WOMAN. SAYS IT'S IMPORTANT.

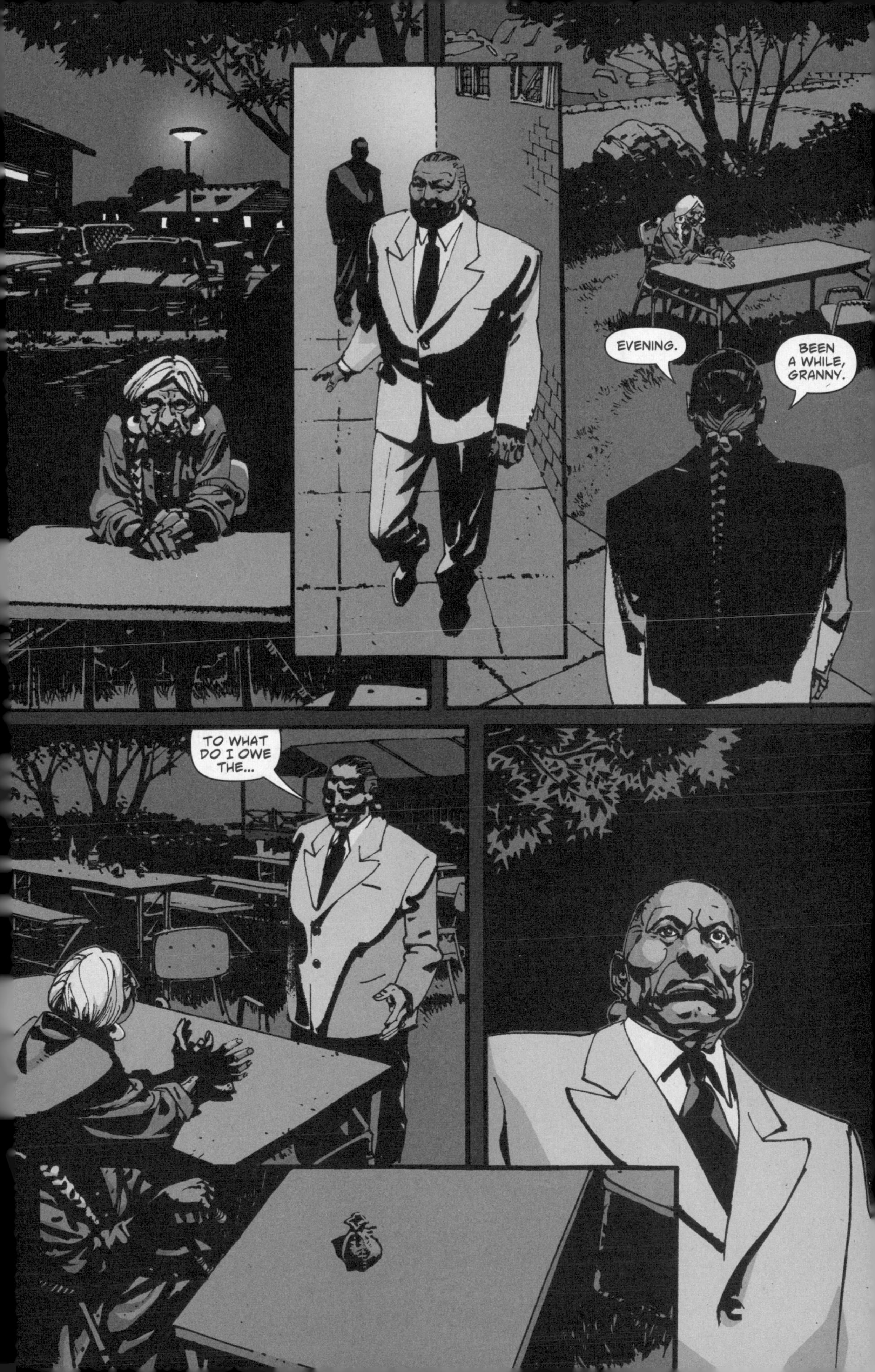
EVENING.
BEEN A WHILE, GRANNY.
TO WHAT DO I OWE THE...

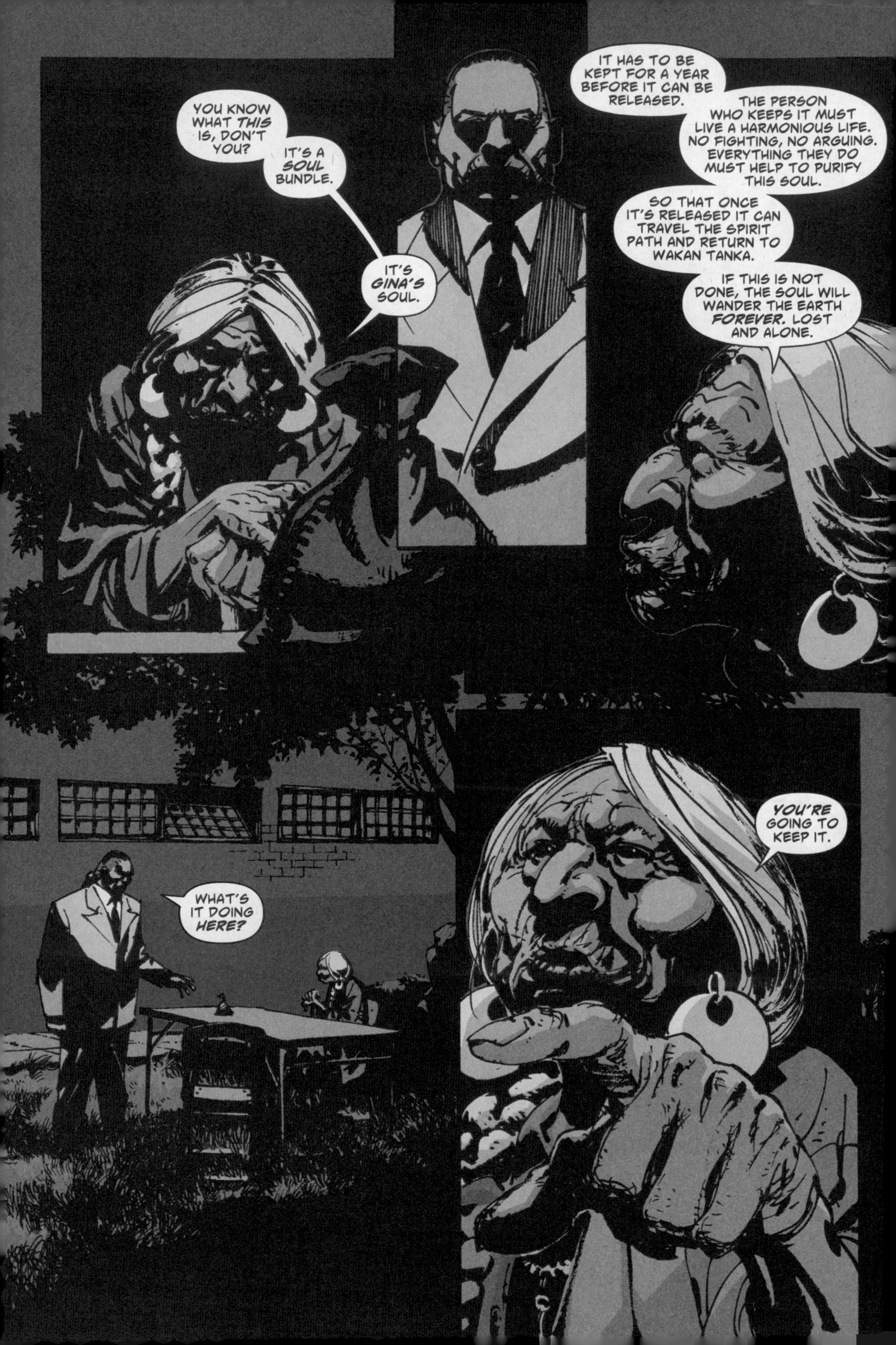

YOU KNOW WHAT THIS IS, DON'T YOU?
IT'S A SOUL BUNDLE.
IT'S GINA'S SOUL.
IT HAS TO BE KEPT FOR A YEAR BEFORE IT CAN BE RELEASED.
THE PERSON WHO KEEPS IT MUST LIVE A HARMONIOUS LIFE. NO FIGHTING, NO ARGUING. EVERYTHING THEY DO MUST HELP TO PURIFY THIS SOUL.
SO THAT ONCE IT'S RELEASED IT CAN TRAVEL THE SPIRIT PATH AND RETURN TO WAKAN TANKA.
IF THIS IS NOT DONE, THE SOUL WILL WANDER THE EARTH FOREVER. LOST AND ALONE.
WHAT'S IT DOING HERE?
YOU'RE GOING TO KEEP IT.

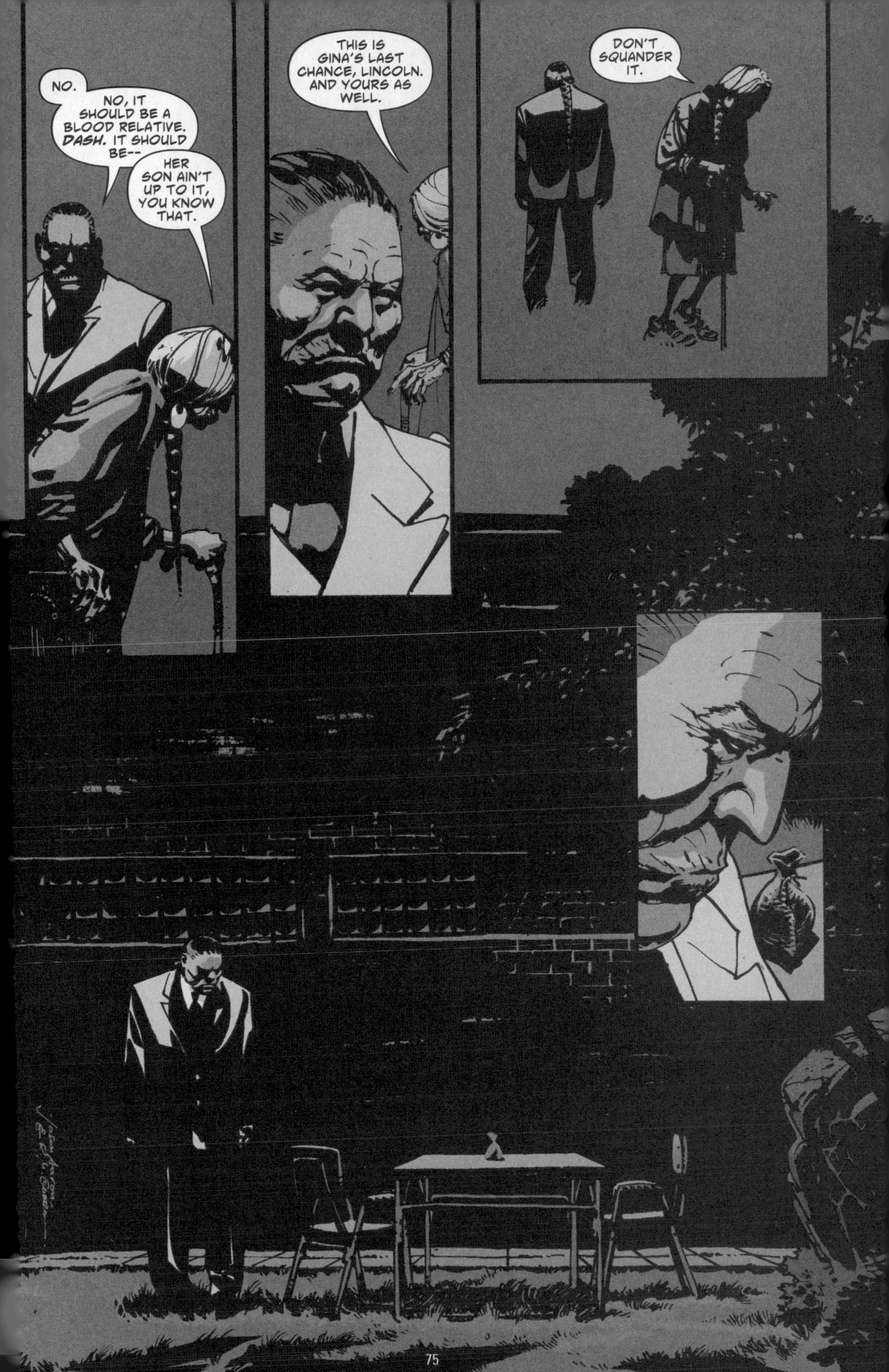
NO.
NO, IT SHOULD BE A BLOOD RELATIVE. DASH. IT SHOULD BE--
HER SON AIN'T UP TO IT, YOU KNOW THAT.
THIS IS GINA'S LAST CHANCE, LINCOLN. AND YOURS AS WELL.
DON'T SQUANDER IT.

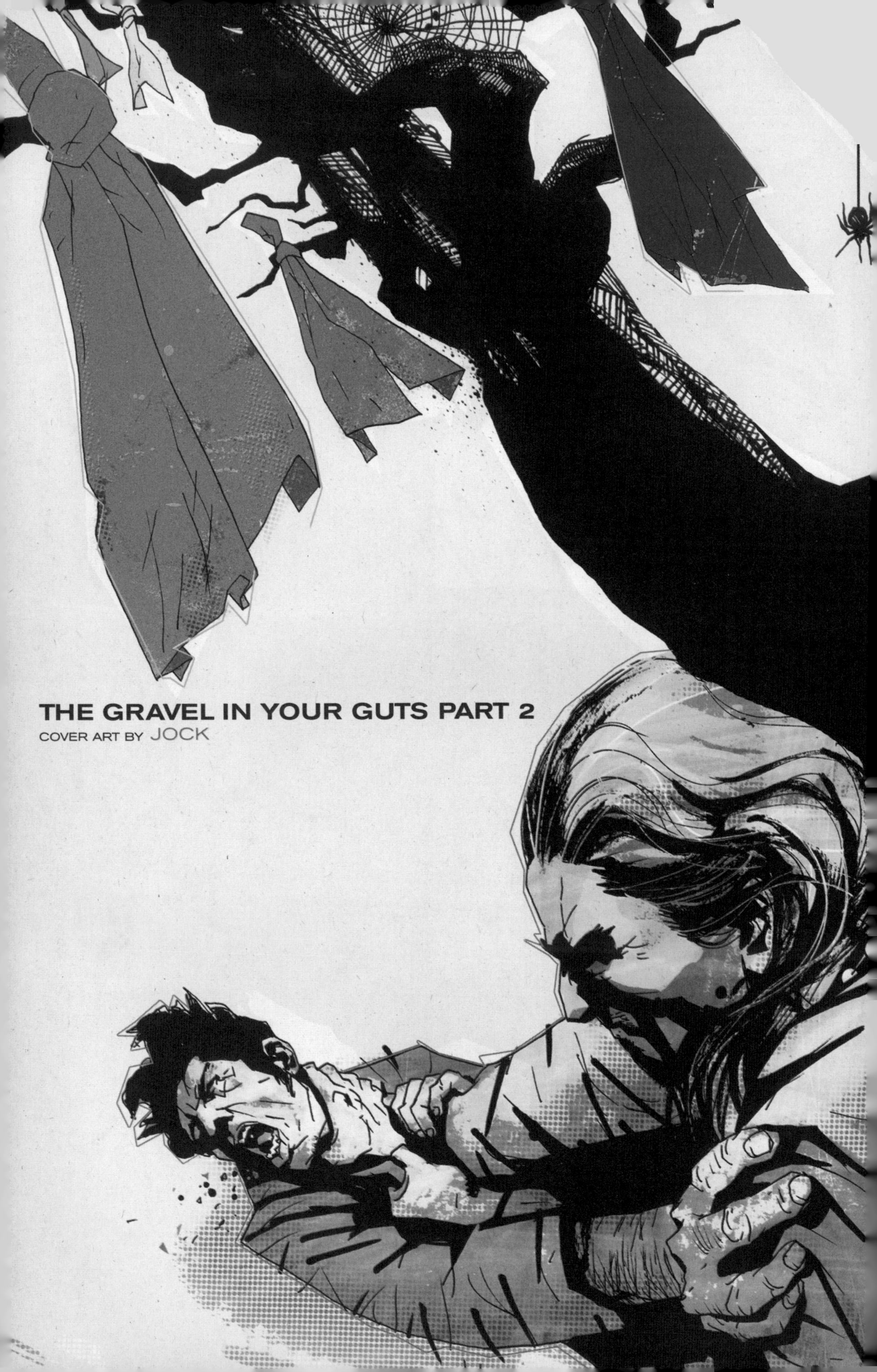

THE GRAVEL IN YOUR GUTS PART 2

COVER ART BY JOCK

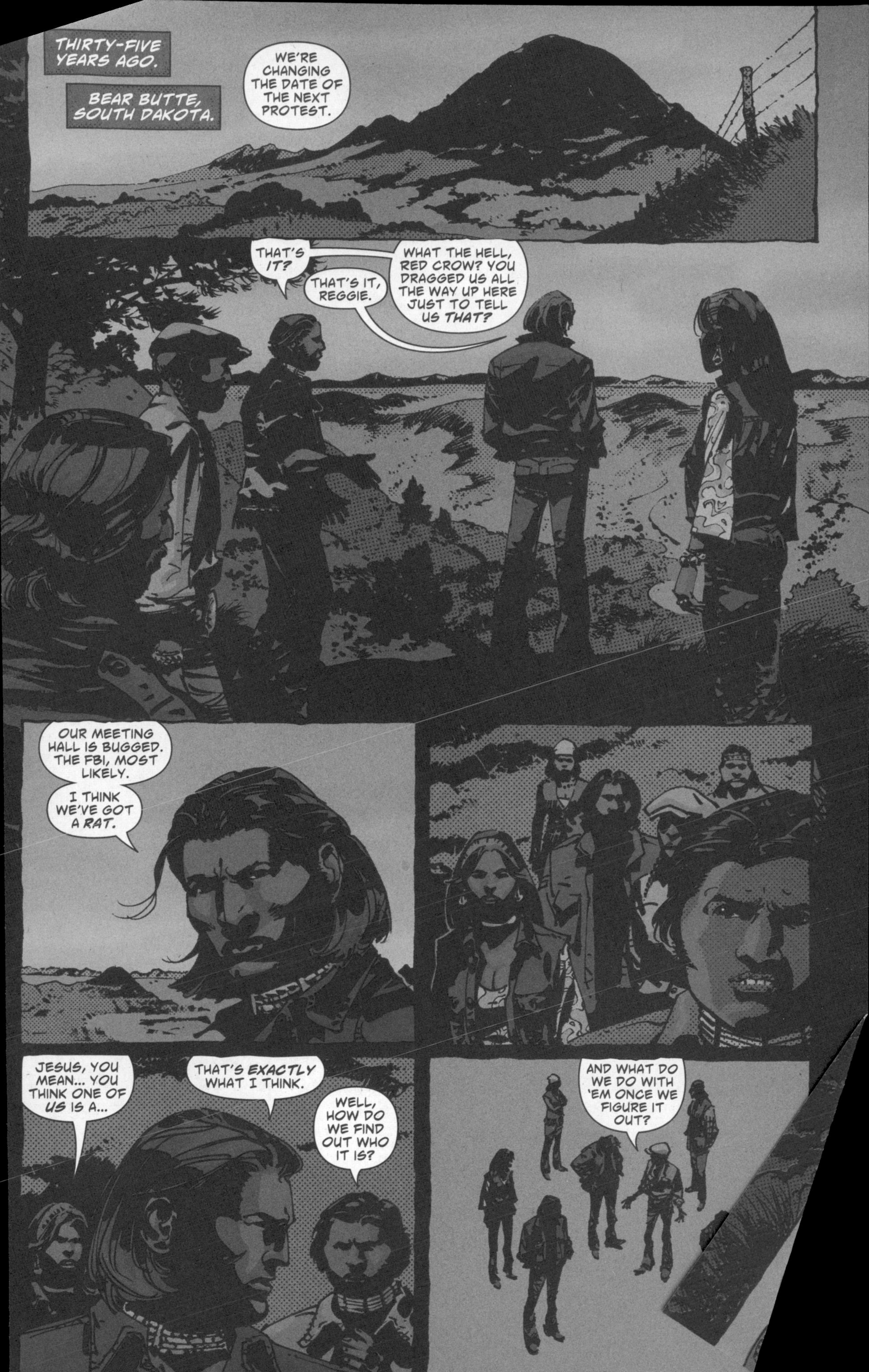
THIRTY-FIVE YEARS AGO.
BEAR BUTTE, SOUTH DAKOTA.
WE'RE CHANGING THE DATE OF THE NEXT PROTEST.
THAT'S *IT?*
WHAT THE HELL, RED CROW? YOU DRAGGED US ALL THE WAY UP HERE JUST TO TELL US *THAT?*
THAT'S IT, REGGIE.
OUR MEETING HALL IS BUGGED. THE FBI, MOST LIKELY.
I THINK WE'VE GOT A *RAT.*
JESUS, YOU MEAN... YOU THINK ONE OF *US* IS A...
THAT'S *EXACTLY* WHAT I THINK.
WELL, HOW DO WE FIND OUT WHO IT IS?
AND WHAT DO WE DO WITH 'EM ONCE WE FIGURE IT OUT?

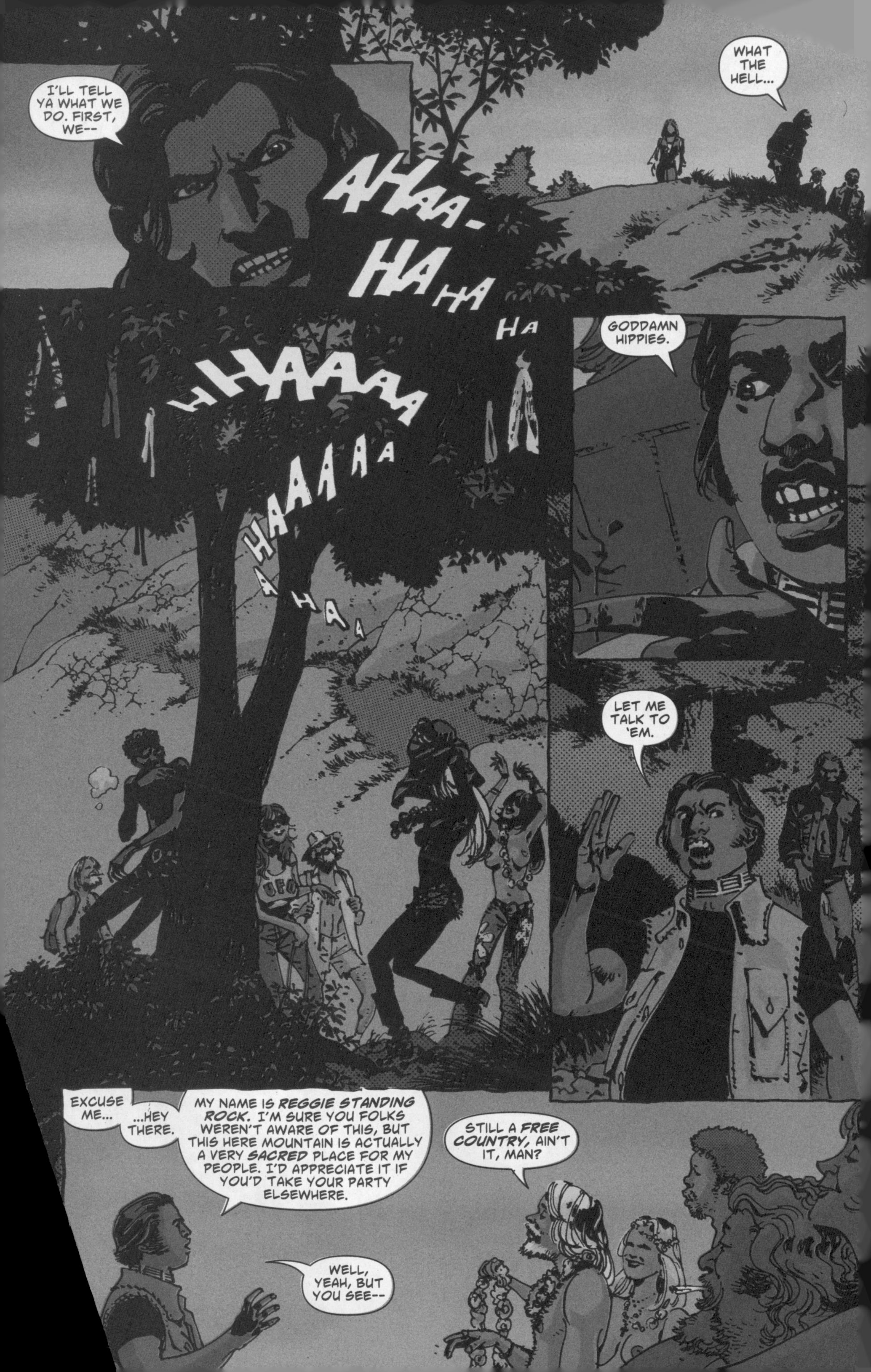
I'LL TELL YA WHAT WE DO. FIRST, WE--
WHAT THE HELL...
AHAA-HA HA HA HA
HHAAAA AAAAAA HAHA HA A
GODDAMN HIPPIES.
LET ME TALK TO 'EM.
EXCUSE ME...
...HEY THERE.
MY NAME IS REGGIE STANDING ROCK. I'M SURE YOU FOLKS WEREN'T AWARE OF THIS, BUT THIS HERE MOUNTAIN IS ACTUALLY A VERY SACRED PLACE FOR MY PEOPLE. I'D APPRECIATE IT IF YOU'D TAKE YOUR PARTY ELSEWHERE.
STILL A FREE COUNTRY, AIN'T IT, MAN?
WELL, YEAH, BUT YOU SEE--

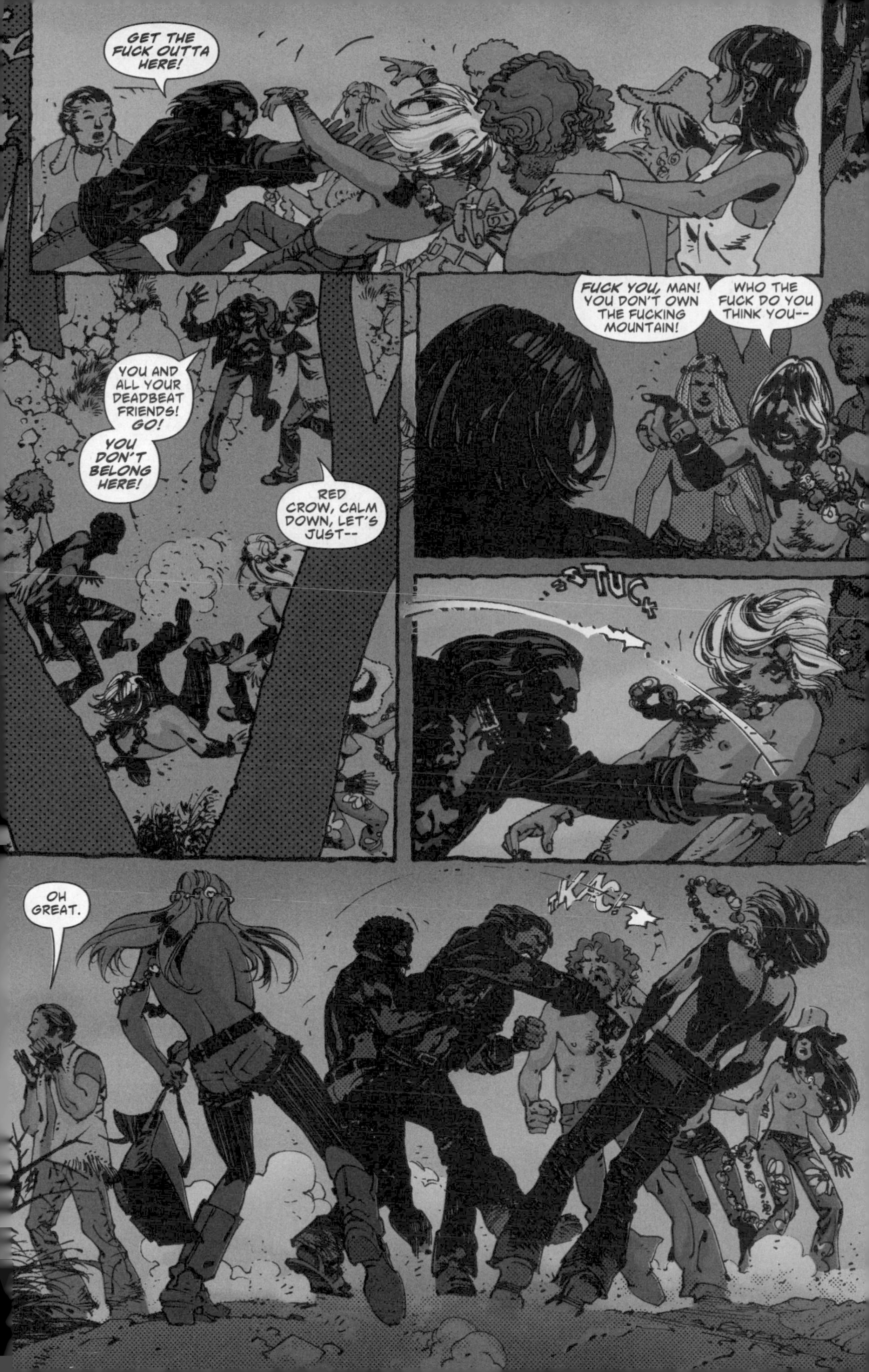
GET THE FUCK OUTTA HERE!
YOU AND ALL YOUR DEADBEAT FRIENDS! GO!
YOU DON'T BELONG HERE!
RED CROW, CALM DOWN, LET'S JUST--
FUCK YOU, MAN! YOU DON'T OWN THE FUCKING MOUNTAIN!
WHO THE FUCK DO YOU THINK YOU--
STUCK
OH GREAT.
KAC!

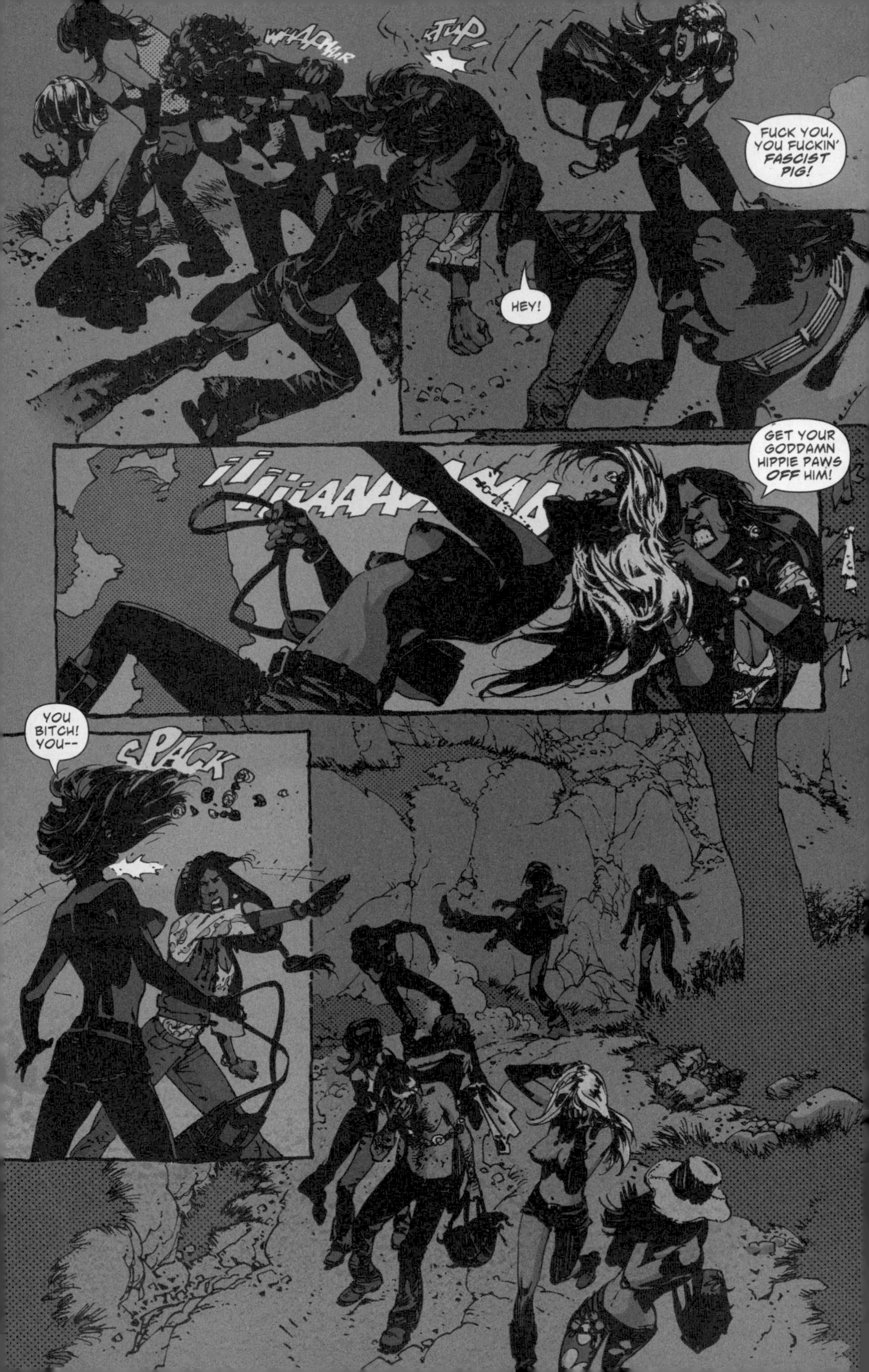
WHAPWHR
KTUP!
FUCK YOU, YOU FUCKIN' FASCIST PIG!
HEY!
GET YOUR GODDAMN HIPPIE PAWS OFF HIM!
YOU BITCH! YOU--
SPACK

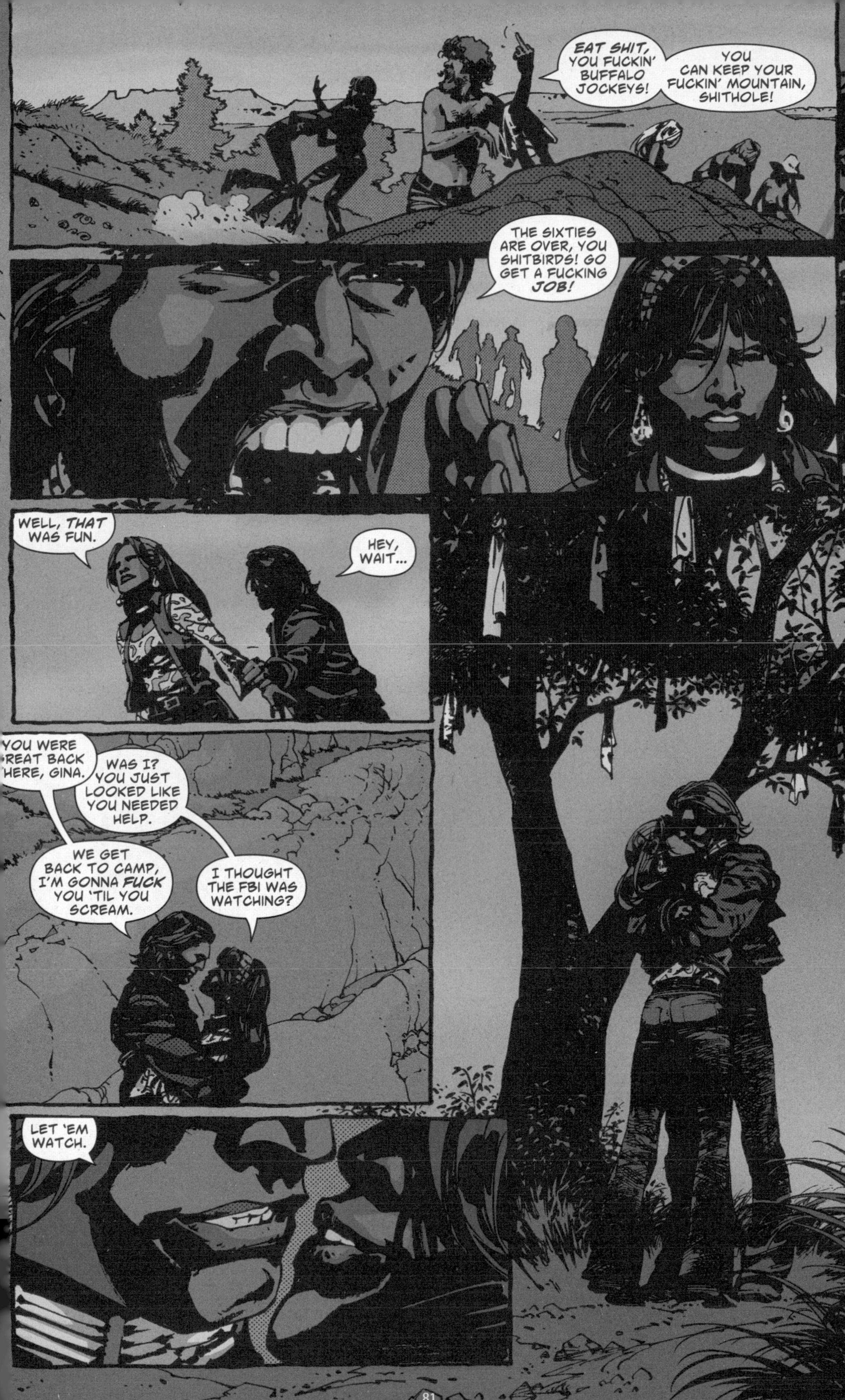
EAT SHIT, YOU FUCKIN' BUFFALO JOCKEYS!
YOU CAN KEEP YOUR FUCKIN' MOUNTAIN, SHITHOLE!
THE SIXTIES ARE OVER, YOU SHITBIRDS! GO GET A FUCKING JOB!
WELL, THAT WAS FUN.
HEY, WAIT...
YOU WERE GREAT BACK THERE, GINA.
WAS I? YOU JUST LOOKED LIKE YOU NEEDED HELP.
WE GET BACK TO CAMP, I'M GONNA FUCK YOU 'TIL YOU SCREAM.
I THOUGHT THE FBI WAS WATCHING?
LET 'EM WATCH.

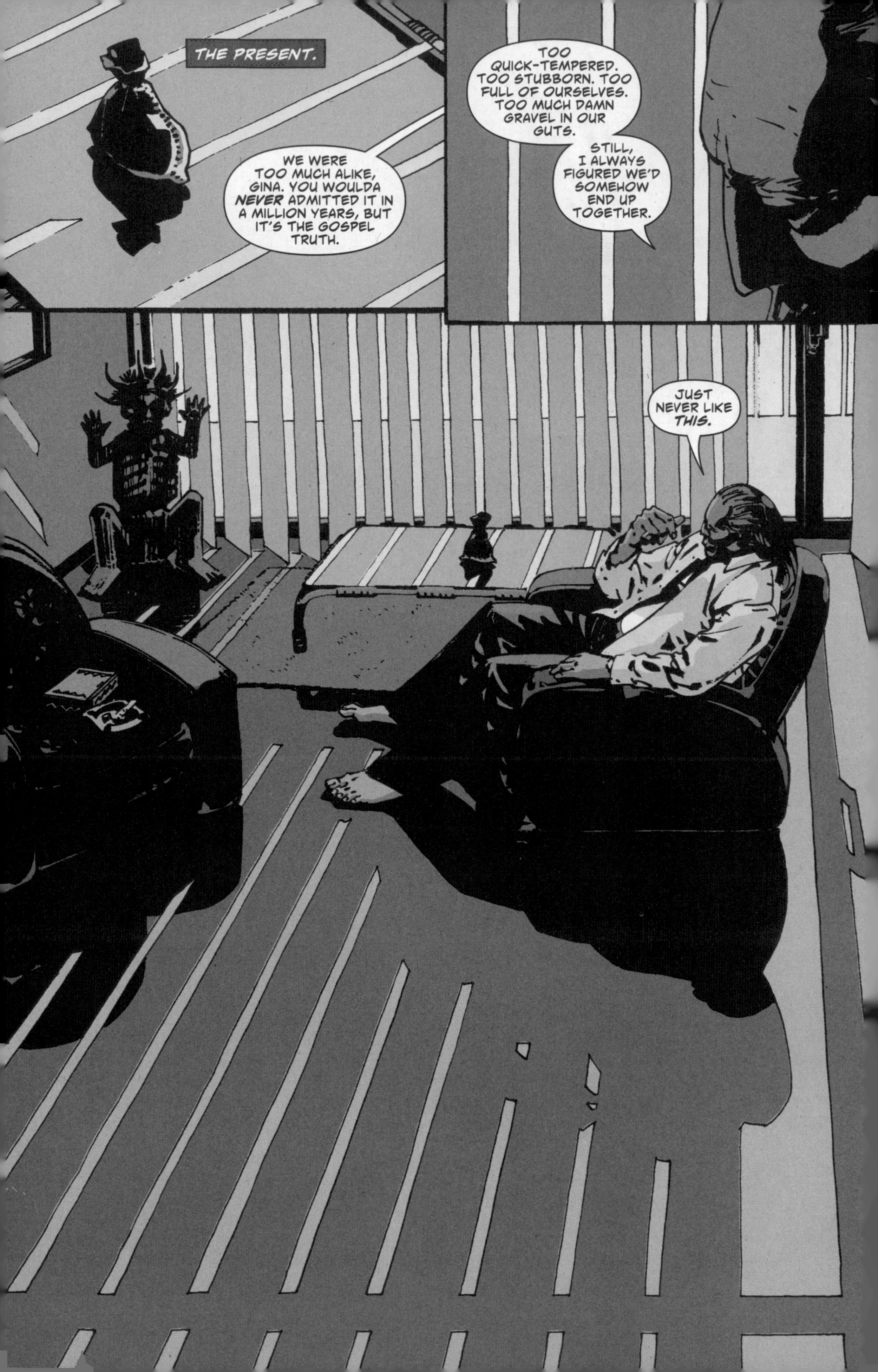
THE PRESENT.
WE WERE TOO MUCH ALIKE, GINA. YOU WOULDA NEVER ADMITTED IT IN A MILLION YEARS, BUT IT'S THE GOSPEL TRUTH.
TOO QUICK-TEMPERED. TOO STUBBORN. TOO FULL OF OURSELVES. TOO MUCH DAMN GRAVEL IN OUR GUTS.
STILL, I ALWAYS FIGURED WE'D SOMEHOW END UP TOGETHER.
JUST NEVER LIKE THIS.

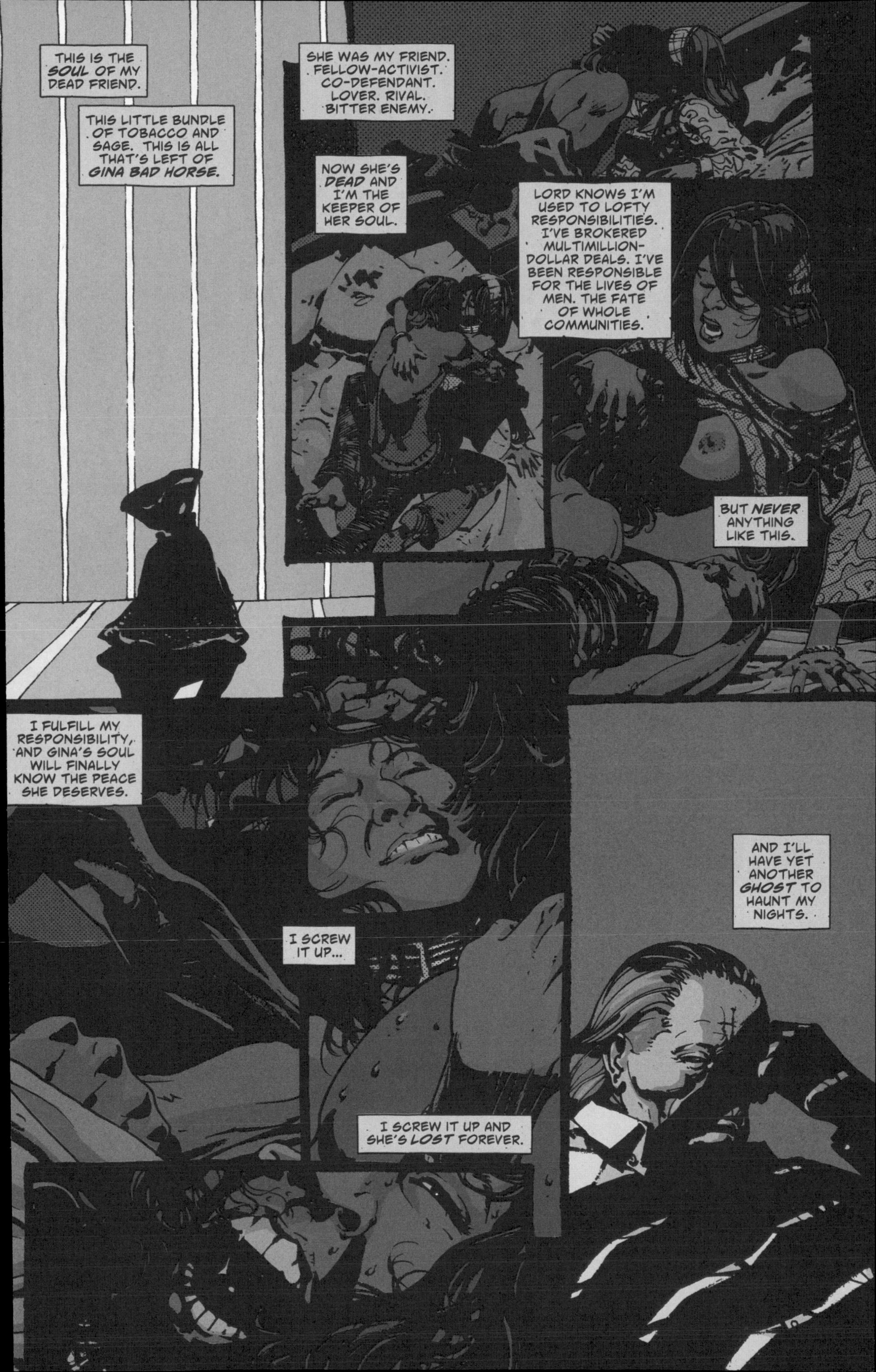
THIS IS THE SOUL OF MY DEAD FRIEND.
THIS LITTLE BUNDLE OF TOBACCO AND SAGE. THIS IS ALL THAT'S LEFT OF GINA BAD HORSE.
SHE WAS MY FRIEND. FELLOW-ACTIVIST. CO-DEFENDANT. LOVER. RIVAL. BITTER ENEMY.
NOW SHE'S DEAD AND I'M THE KEEPER OF HER SOUL.
LORD KNOWS I'M USED TO LOFTY RESPONSIBILITIES. I'VE BROKERED MULTIMILLION-DOLLAR DEALS. I'VE BEEN RESPONSIBLE FOR THE LIVES OF MEN. THE FATE OF WHOLE COMMUNITIES.
BUT NEVER ANYTHING LIKE THIS.
I FULFILL MY RESPONSIBILITY, AND GINA'S SOUL WILL FINALLY KNOW THE PEACE SHE DESERVES.
I SCREW IT UP...
I SCREW IT UP AND SHE'S LOST FOREVER.
AND I'LL HAVE YET ANOTHER GHOST TO HAUNT MY NIGHTS.

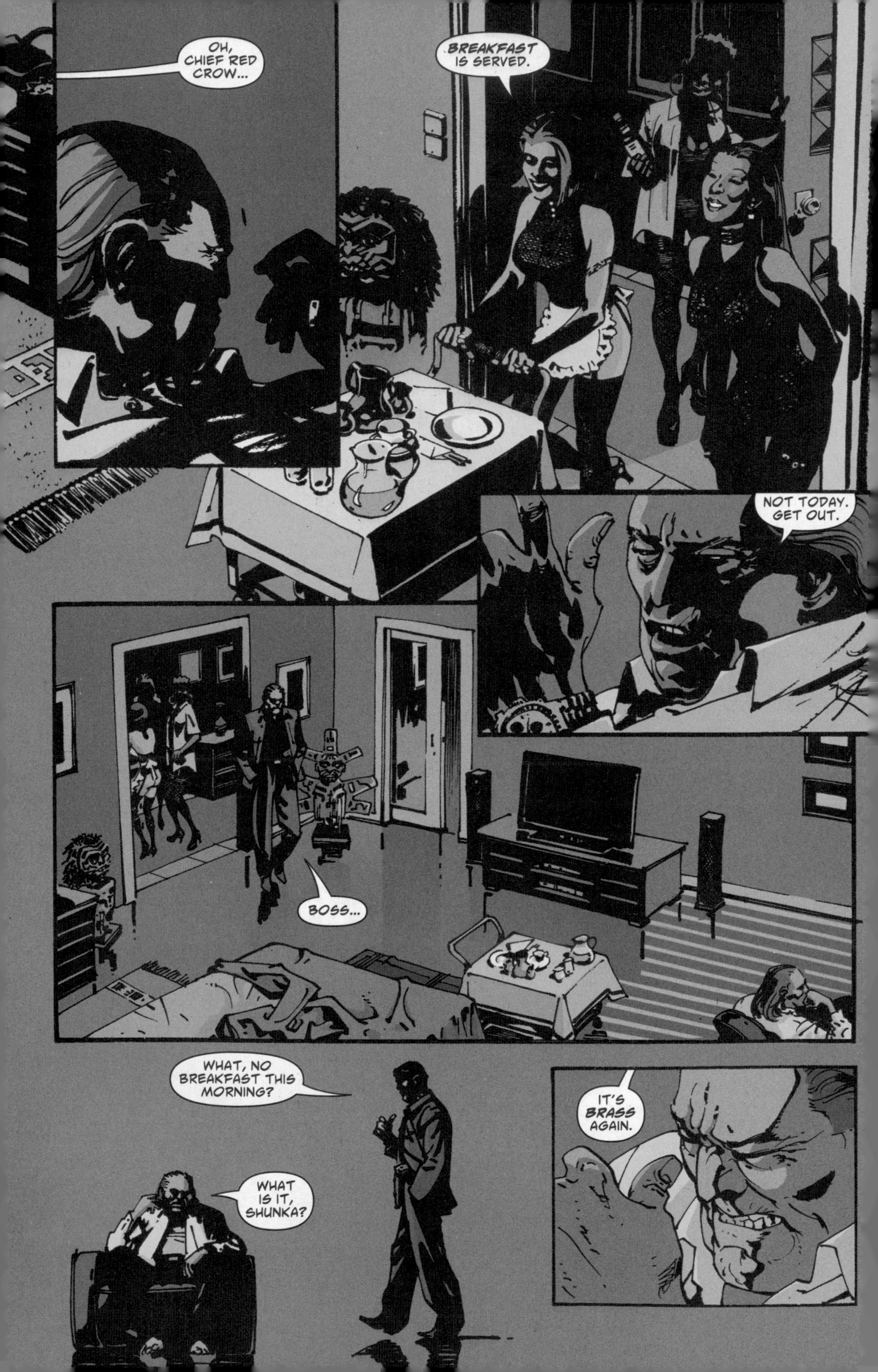
OH, CHIEF RED CROW...
BREAKFAST IS SERVED.
NOT TODAY. GET OUT.
BOSS...
WHAT, NO BREAKFAST THIS MORNING?
WHAT IS IT, SHUNKA?
IT'S BRASS AGAIN.

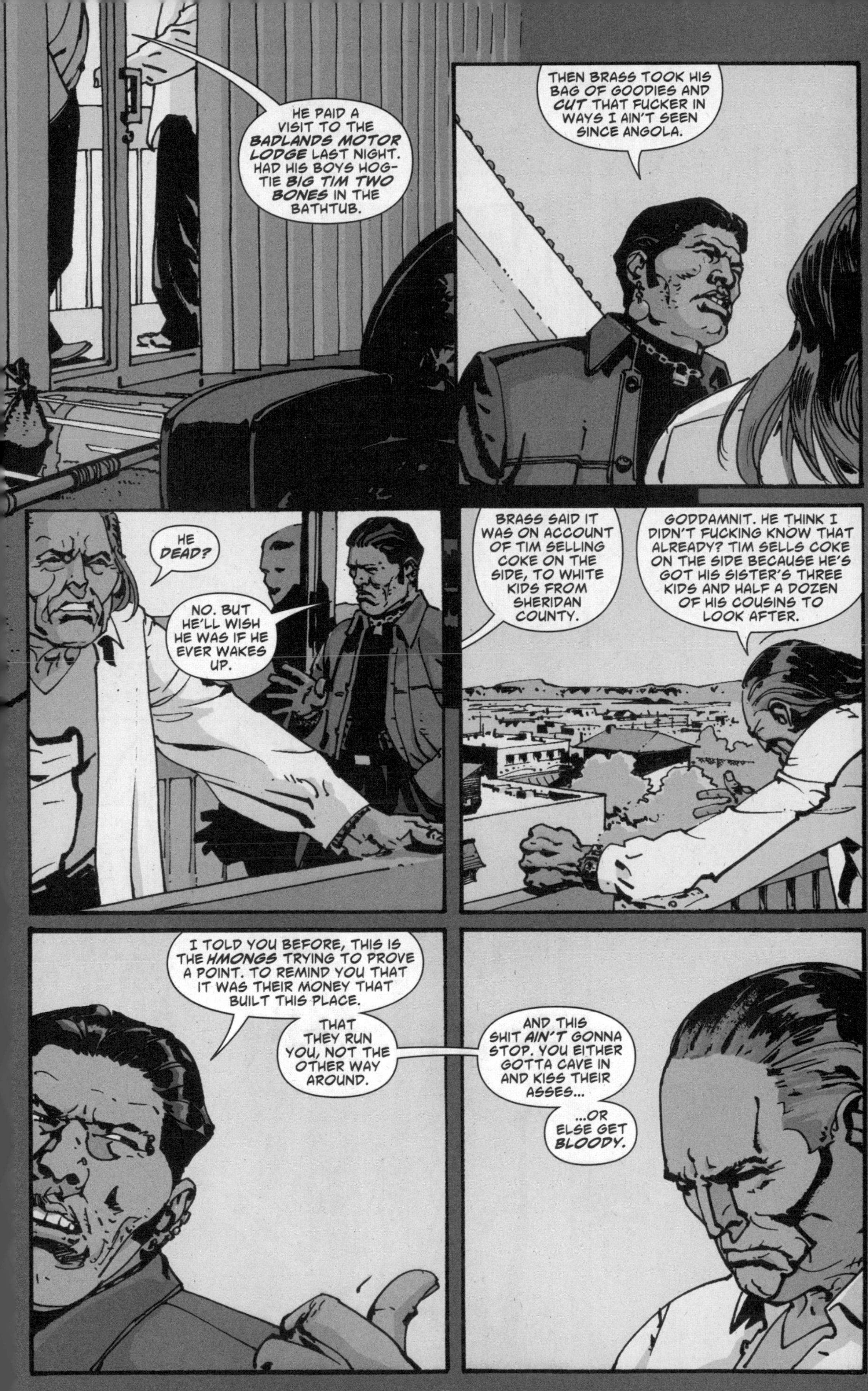
HE PAID A VISIT TO THE BADLANDS MOTOR LODGE LAST NIGHT. HAD HIS BOYS HOG-TIE BIG TIM TWO BONES IN THE BATHTUB.
THEN BRASS TOOK HIS BAG OF GOODIES AND CUT THAT FUCKER IN WAYS I AIN'T SEEN SINCE ANGOLA.
HE DEAD?
NO. BUT HE'LL WISH HE WAS IF HE EVER WAKES UP.
BRASS SAID IT WAS ON ACCOUNT OF TIM SELLING COKE ON THE SIDE, TO WHITE KIDS FROM SHERIDAN COUNTY.
GODDAMNIT. HE THINK I DIDN'T FUCKING KNOW THAT ALREADY? TIM SELLS COKE ON THE SIDE BECAUSE HE'S GOT HIS SISTER'S THREE KIDS AND HALF A DOZEN OF HIS COUSINS TO LOOK AFTER.
I TOLD YOU BEFORE, THIS IS THE HMONGS TRYING TO PROVE A POINT. TO REMIND YOU THAT IT WAS THEIR MONEY THAT BUILT THIS PLACE.
THAT THEY RUN YOU, NOT THE OTHER WAY AROUND.
AND THIS SHIT AIN'T GONNA STOP. YOU EITHER GOTTA CAVE IN AND KISS THEIR ASSES...
...OR ELSE GET BLOODY.

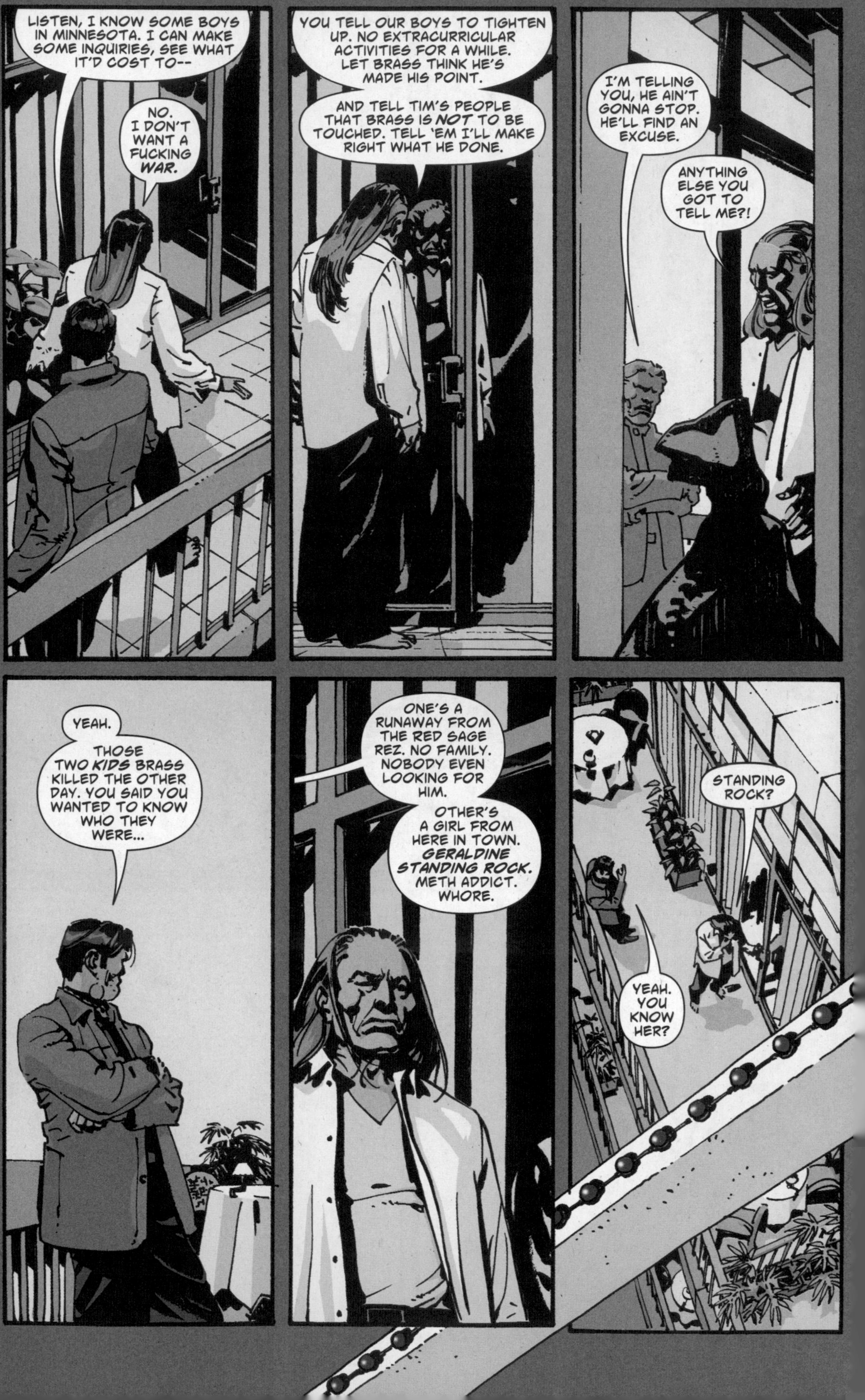
LISTEN, I KNOW SOME BOYS IN MINNESOTA. I CAN MAKE SOME INQUIRIES, SEE WHAT IT'D COST TO--
NO. I DON'T WANT A FUCKING WAR.
YOU TELL OUR BOYS TO TIGHTEN UP. NO EXTRACURRICULAR ACTIVITIES FOR A WHILE. LET BRASS THINK HE'S MADE HIS POINT.
AND TELL TIM'S PEOPLE THAT BRASS IS NOT TO BE TOUCHED. TELL 'EM I'LL MAKE RIGHT WHAT HE DONE.
I'M TELLING YOU, HE AIN'T GONNA STOP. HE'LL FIND AN EXCUSE.
ANYTHING ELSE YOU GOT TO TELL ME?!
YEAH.
THOSE TWO KIDS BRASS KILLED THE OTHER DAY. YOU SAID YOU WANTED TO KNOW WHO THEY WERE...
ONE'S A RUNAWAY FROM THE RED SAGE REZ. NO FAMILY. NOBODY EVEN LOOKING FOR HIM.
OTHER'S A GIRL FROM HERE IN TOWN. GERALDINE STANDING ROCK. METH ADDICT. WHORE.
STANDING ROCK?
YEAH. YOU KNOW HER?

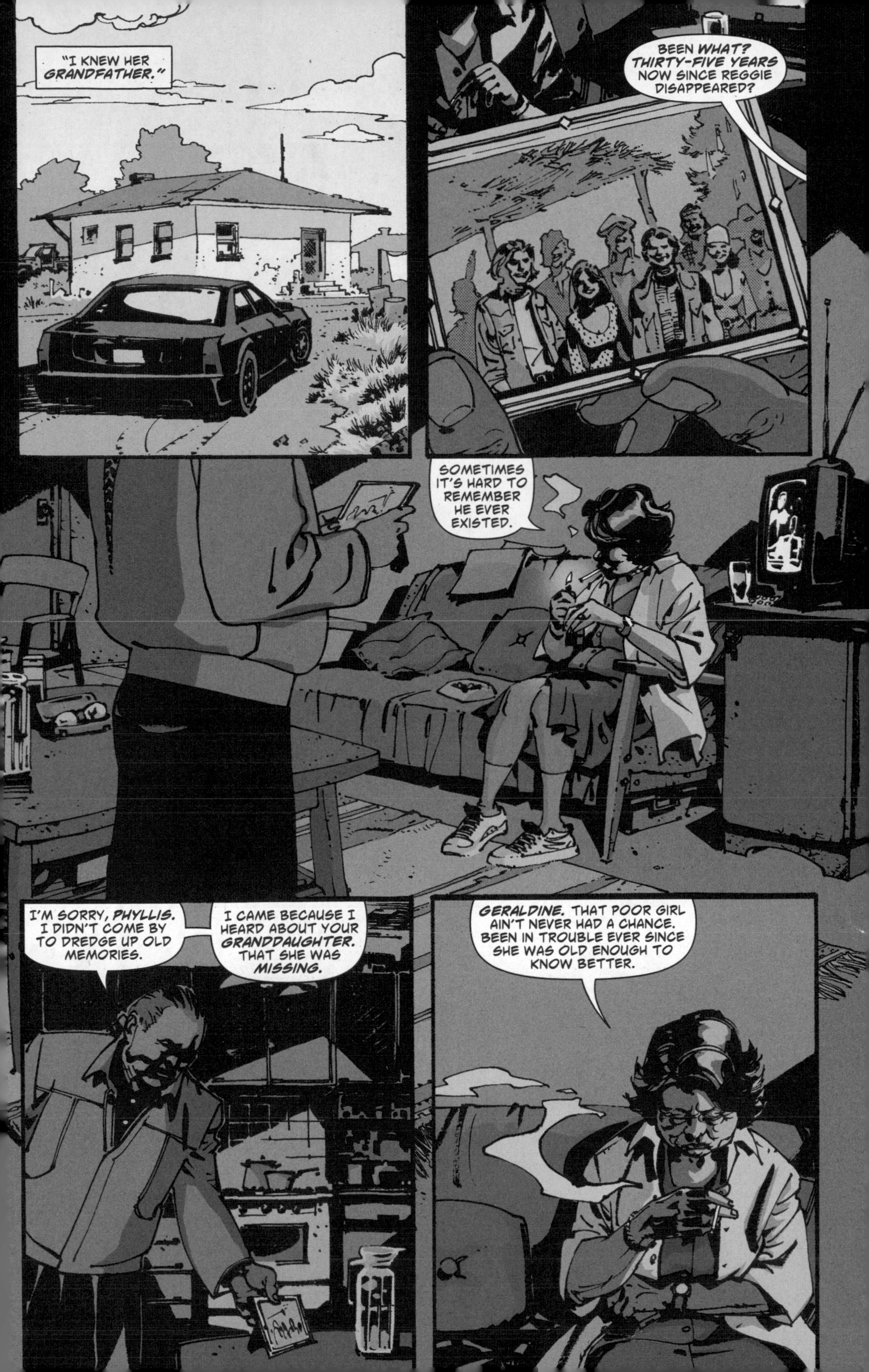
"I KNEW HER GRANDFATHER."
BEEN WHAT? THIRTY-FIVE YEARS NOW SINCE REGGIE DISAPPEARED?
SOMETIMES IT'S HARD TO REMEMBER HE EVER EXISTED.
I'M SORRY, PHYLLIS. I DIDN'T COME BY TO DREDGE UP OLD MEMORIES.
I CAME BECAUSE I HEARD ABOUT YOUR GRANDDAUGHTER. THAT SHE WAS MISSING.
GERALDINE. THAT POOR GIRL AIN'T NEVER HAD A CHANCE. BEEN IN TROUBLE EVER SINCE SHE WAS OLD ENOUGH TO KNOW BETTER.

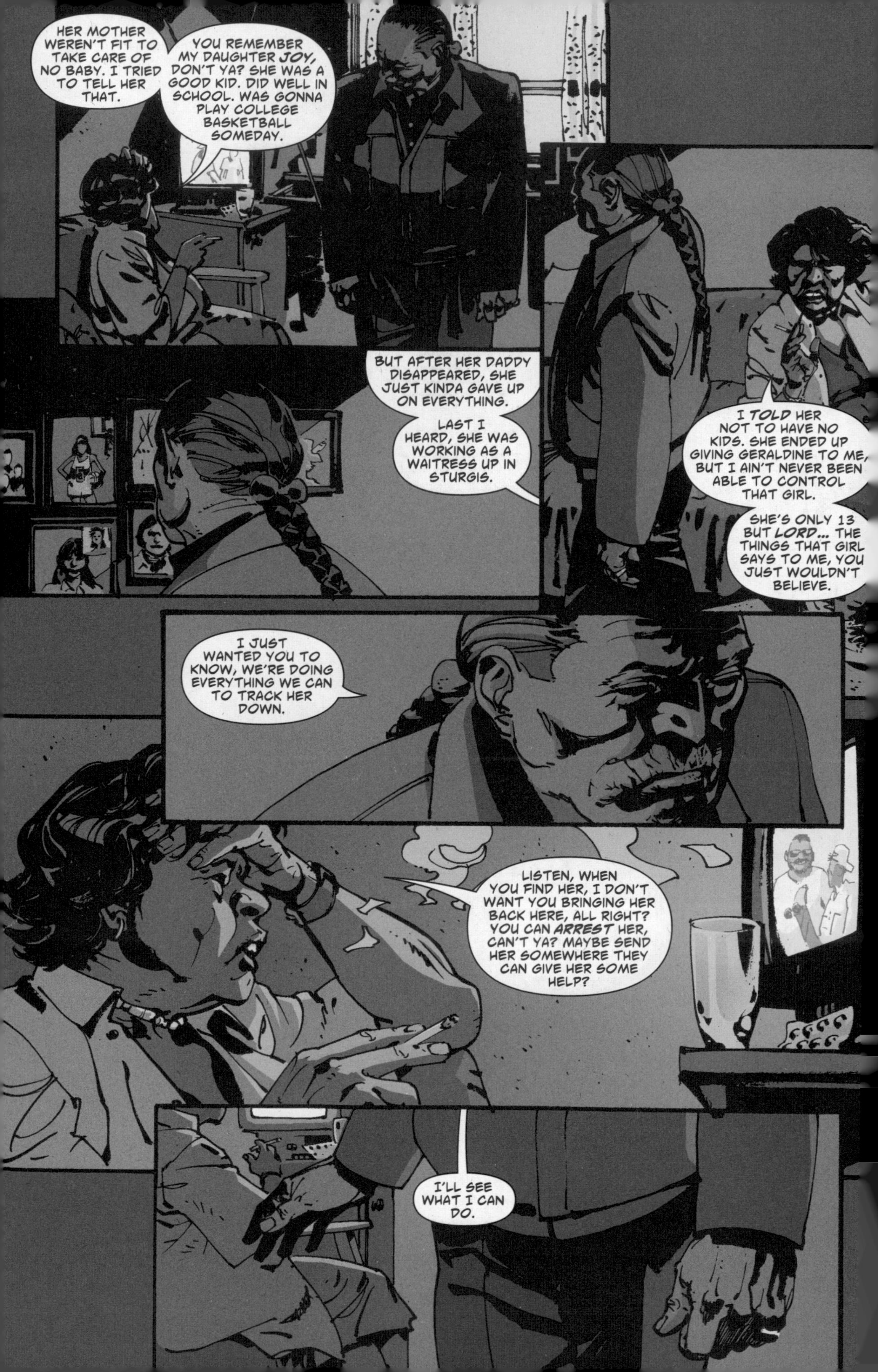

HER MOTHER WEREN'T FIT TO TAKE CARE OF NO BABY. I TRIED TO TELL HER THAT.
YOU REMEMBER MY DAUGHTER JOY, DON'T YA? SHE WAS A GOOD KID. DID WELL IN SCHOOL. WAS GONNA PLAY COLLEGE BASKETBALL SOMEDAY.
BUT AFTER HER DADDY DISAPPEARED, SHE JUST KINDA GAVE UP ON EVERYTHING.
LAST I HEARD, SHE WAS WORKING AS A WAITRESS UP IN STURGIS.
I TOLD HER NOT TO HAVE NO KIDS. SHE ENDED UP GIVING GERALDINE TO ME, BUT I AIN'T NEVER BEEN ABLE TO CONTROL THAT GIRL.
SHE'S ONLY 13 BUT LORD... THE THINGS THAT GIRL SAYS TO ME, YOU JUST WOULDN'T BELIEVE.
I JUST WANTED YOU TO KNOW, WE'RE DOING EVERYTHING WE CAN TO TRACK HER DOWN.
LISTEN, WHEN YOU FIND HER, I DON'T WANT YOU BRINGING HER BACK HERE, ALL RIGHT? YOU CAN ARREST HER, CAN'T YA? MAYBE SEND HER SOMEWHERE THEY CAN GIVE HER SOME HELP?
I'LL SEE WHAT I CAN DO.

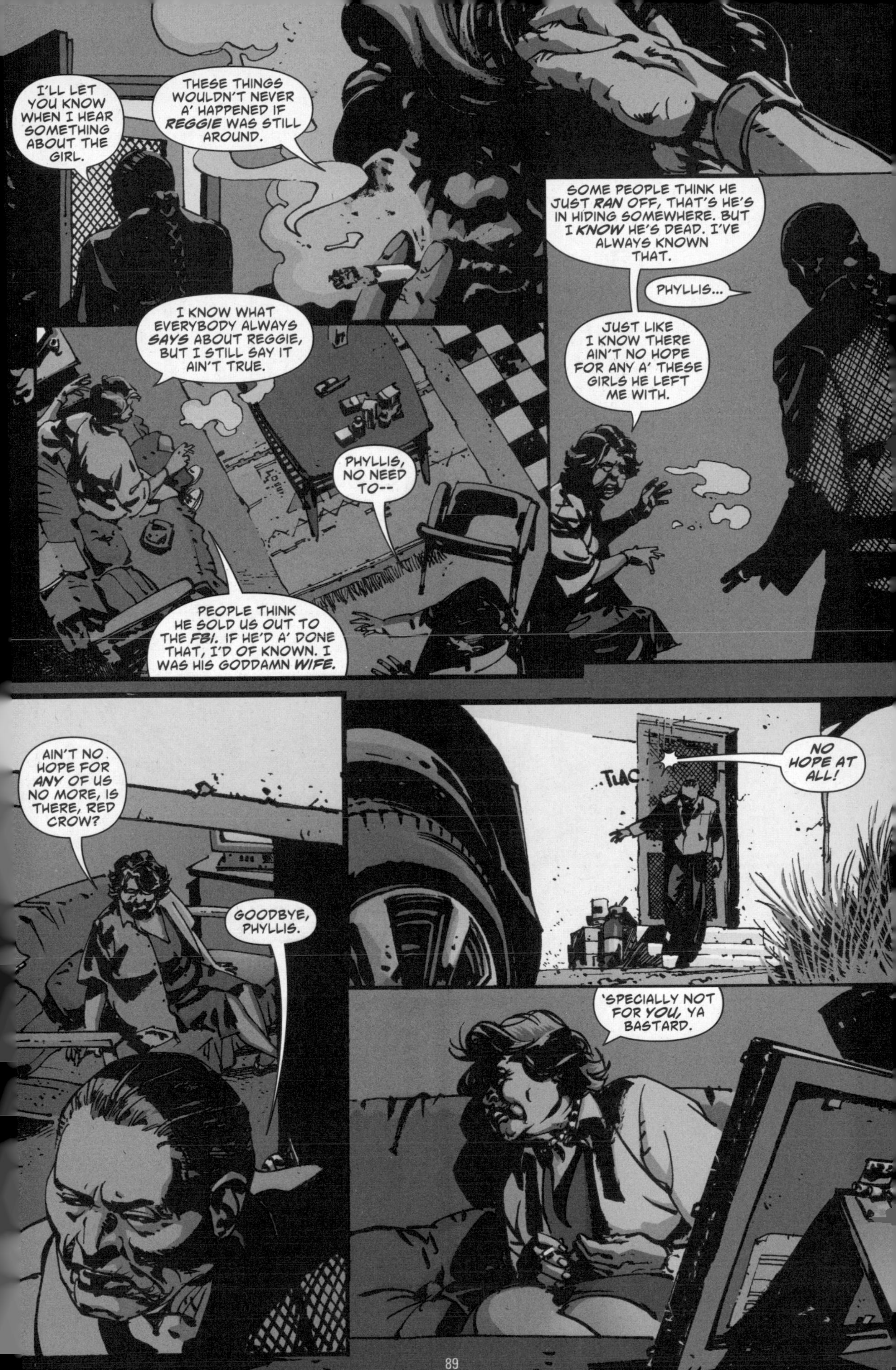
I'LL LET YOU KNOW WHEN I HEAR SOMETHING ABOUT THE GIRL.
THESE THINGS WOULDN'T NEVER A' HAPPENED IF REGGIE WAS STILL AROUND.
I KNOW WHAT EVERYBODY ALWAYS SAYS ABOUT REGGIE, BUT I STILL SAY IT AIN'T TRUE.
PHYLLIS, NO NEED TO--
PEOPLE THINK HE SOLD US OUT TO THE FBI. IF HE'D A' DONE THAT, I'D OF KNOWN. I WAS HIS GODDAMN WIFE.
SOME PEOPLE THINK HE JUST RAN OFF, THAT'S HE'S IN HIDING SOMEWHERE. BUT I KNOW HE'S DEAD. I'VE ALWAYS KNOWN THAT.
PHYLLIS...
JUST LIKE I KNOW THERE AIN'T NO HOPE FOR ANY A' THESE GIRLS HE LEFT ME WITH.
AIN'T NO HOPE FOR ANY OF US NO MORE, IS THERE, RED CROW?
GOODBYE, PHYLLIS.
TLAC
NO HOPE AT ALL!
'SPECIALLY NOT FOR YOU, YA BASTARD.

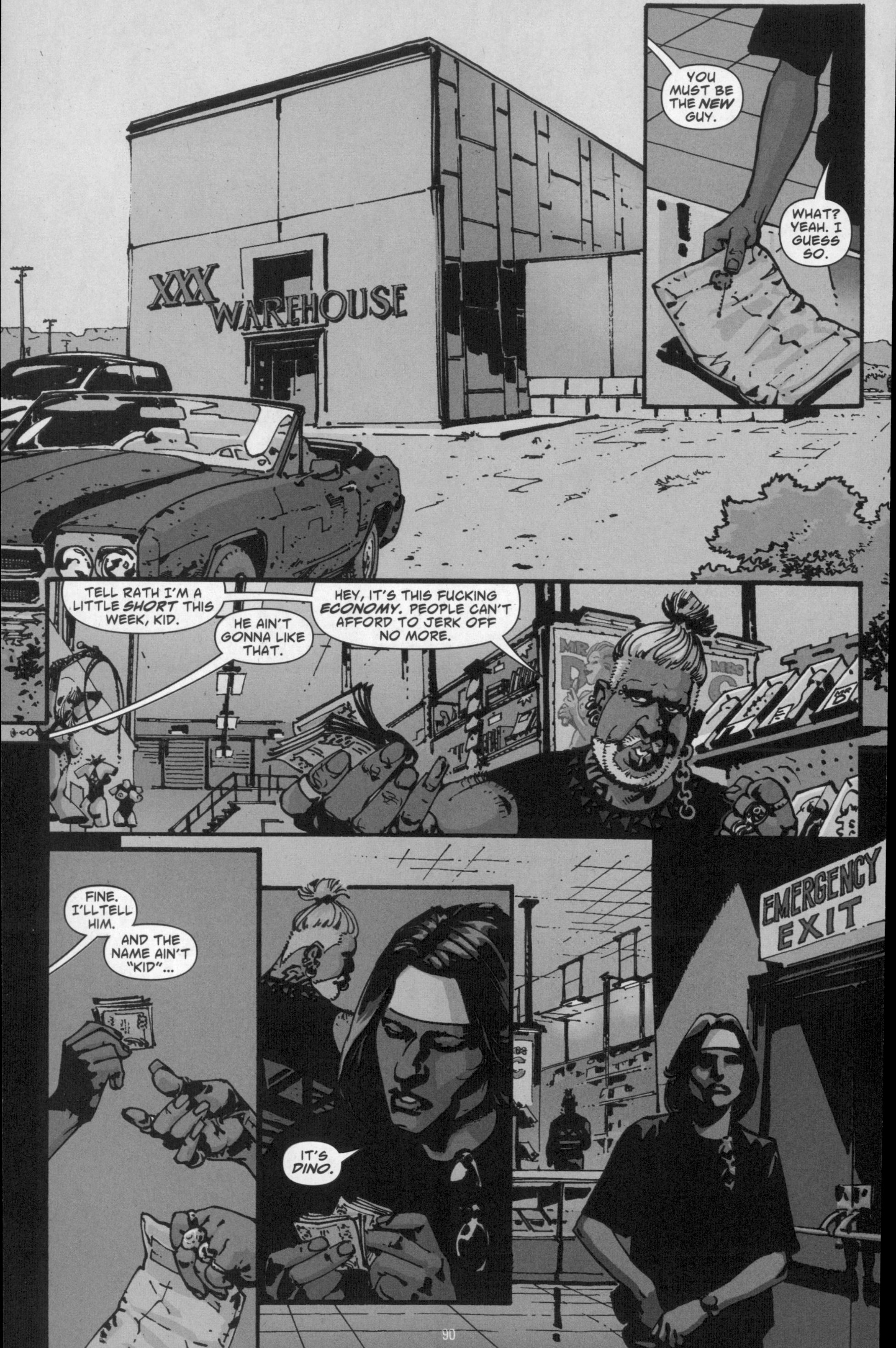
XXX WAREHOUSE
YOU MUST BE THE NEW GUY.
WHAT? YEAH. I GUESS SO.
TELL RATH I'M A LITTLE SHORT THIS WEEK, KID.
HE AIN'T GONNA LIKE THAT.
HEY, IT'S THIS FUCKING ECONOMY. PEOPLE CAN'T AFFORD TO JERK OFF NO MORE.
FINE. I'LLTELL HIM.
AND THE NAME AIN'T "KID"...
IT'S DINO.
EMERGENCY EXIT

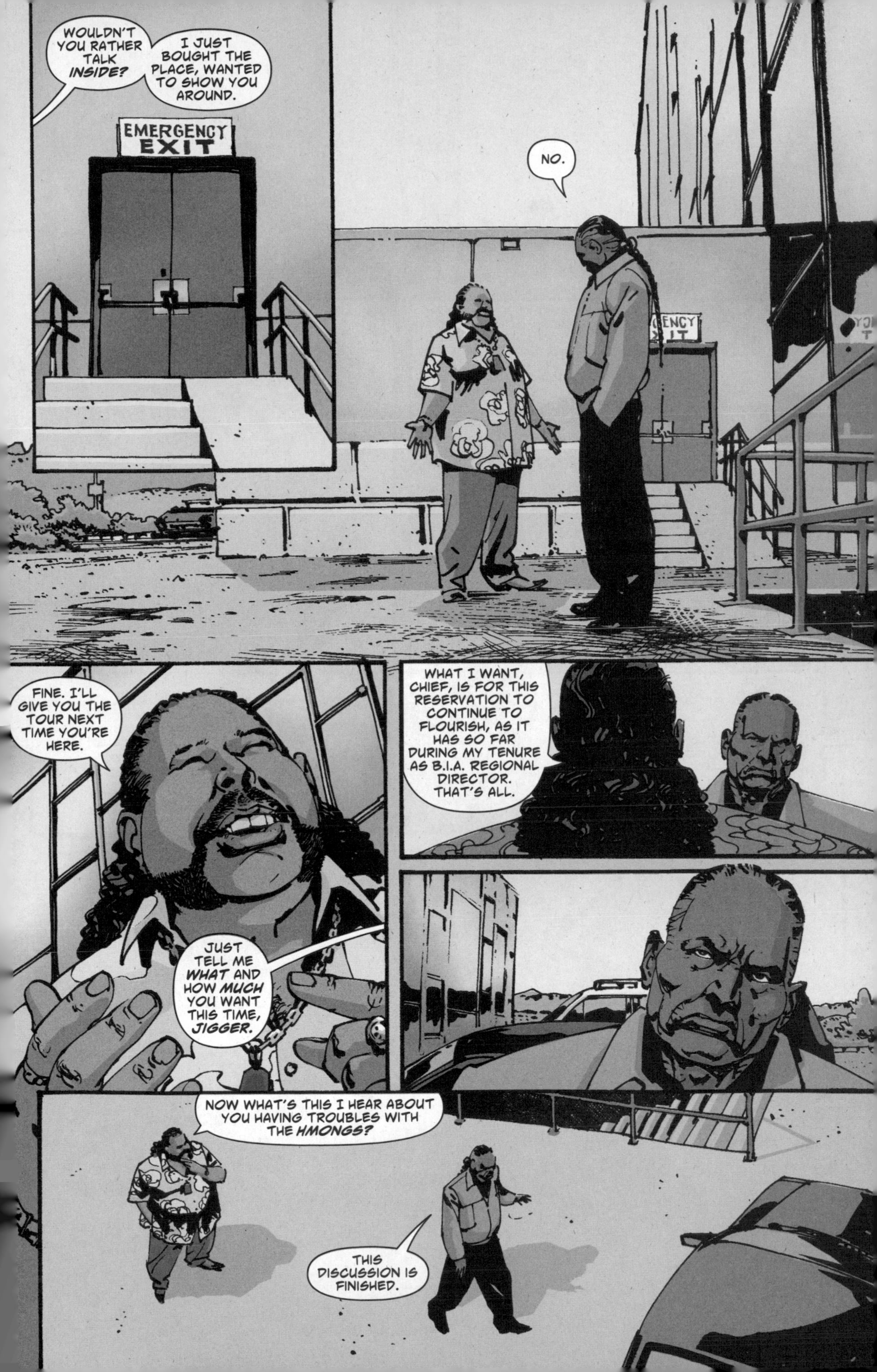
WOULDN'T YOU RATHER TALK *INSIDE?*
I JUST BOUGHT THE PLACE, WANTED TO SHOW YOU AROUND.
EMERGENCY EXIT
NO.
FINE. I'LL GIVE YOU THE TOUR NEXT TIME YOU'RE HERE.
JUST TELL ME *WHAT* AND HOW *MUCH* YOU WANT THIS TIME, *JIGGER.*
WHAT I WANT, CHIEF, IS FOR THIS RESERVATION TO CONTINUE TO FLOURISH, AS IT HAS SO FAR DURING MY TENURE AS B.I.A. REGIONAL DIRECTOR. THAT'S ALL.
NOW WHAT'S THIS I HEAR ABOUT YOU HAVING TROUBLES WITH THE *HMONGS?*
THIS DISCUSSION IS FINISHED.

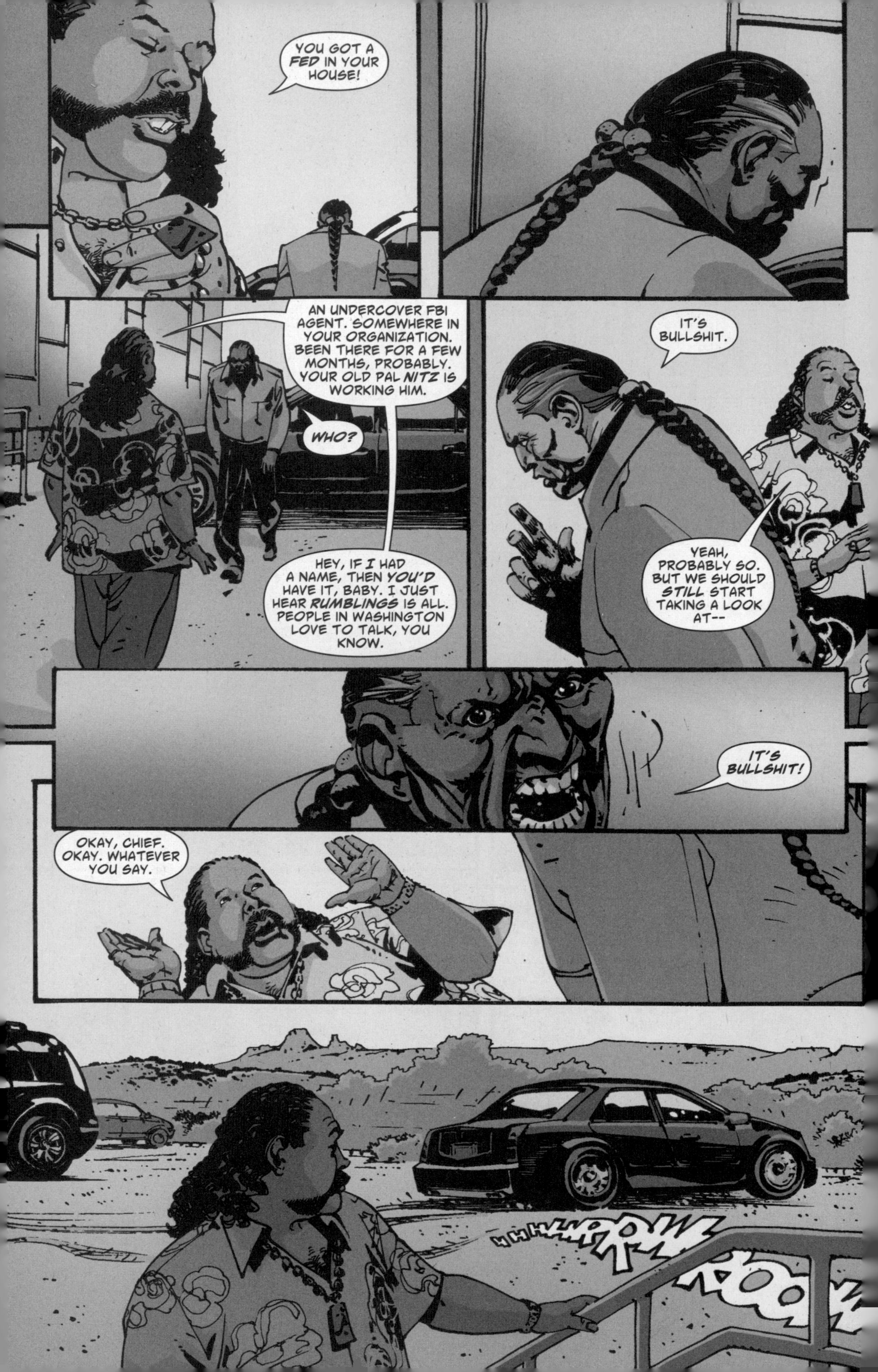

YOU GOT A FED IN YOUR HOUSE!
AN UNDERCOVER FBI AGENT. SOMEWHERE IN YOUR ORGANIZATION. BEEN THERE FOR A FEW MONTHS, PROBABLY. YOUR OLD PAL NITZ IS WORKING HIM.
WHO?
HEY, IF I HAD A NAME, THEN YOU'D HAVE IT, BABY. I JUST HEAR RUMBLINGS IS ALL. PEOPLE IN WASHINGTON LOVE TO TALK, YOU KNOW.
IT'S BULLSHIT.
YEAH, PROBABLY SO. BUT WE SHOULD STILL START TAKING A LOOK AT--
IT'S BULLSHIT!
OKAY, CHIEF. OKAY. WHATEVER YOU SAY.
HHHWROOM
BROOM

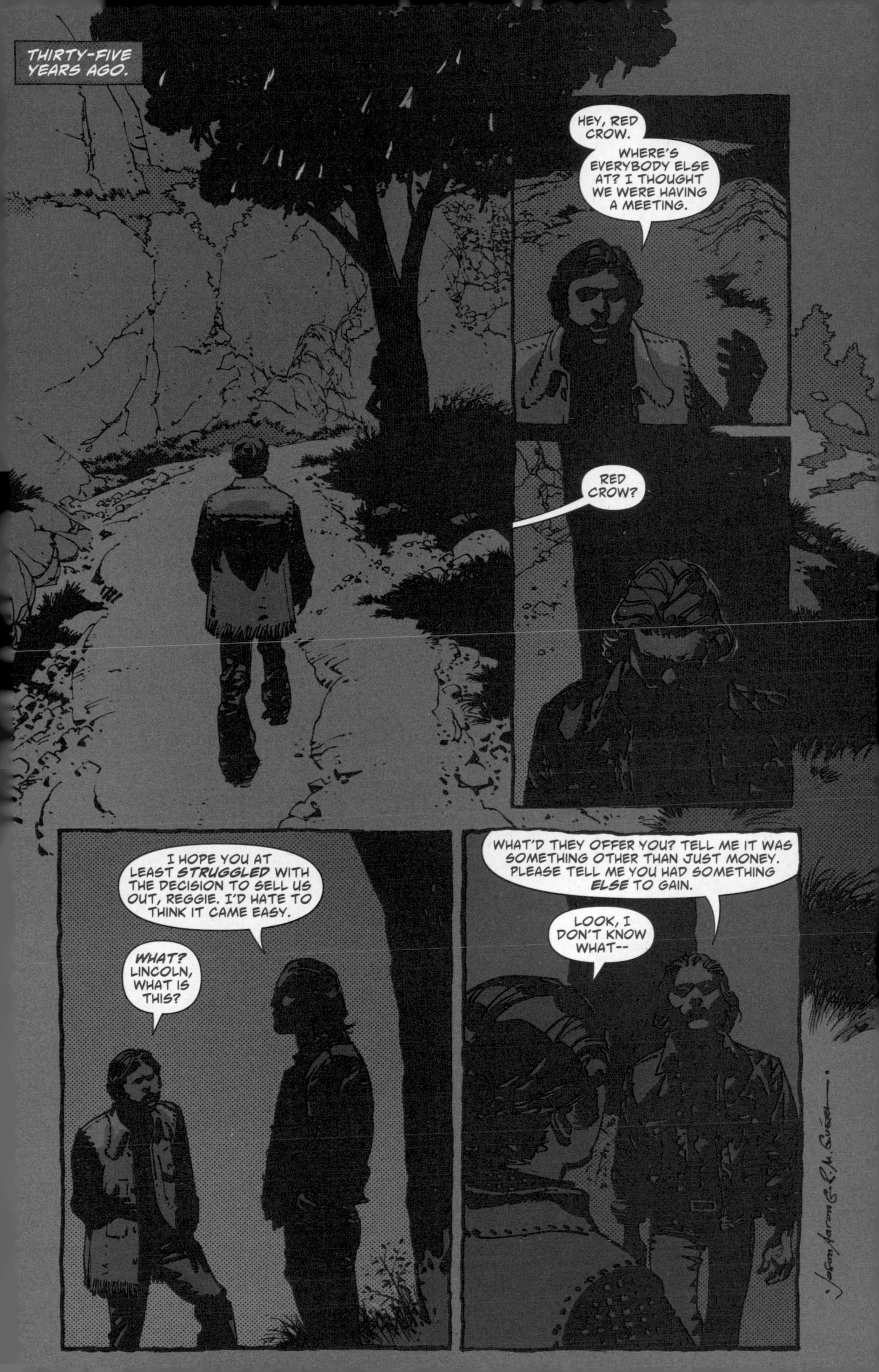
THIRTY-FIVE YEARS AGO.
HEY, RED CROW.
WHERE'S EVERYBODY ELSE AT? I THOUGHT WE WERE HAVING A MEETING.
RED CROW?
I HOPE YOU AT LEAST *STRUGGLED* WITH THE DECISION TO SELL US OUT, REGGIE. I'D HATE TO THINK IT CAME EASY.
WHAT? LINCOLN, WHAT IS THIS?
WHAT'D THEY OFFER YOU? TELL ME IT WAS SOMETHING OTHER THAN JUST MONEY. PLEASE TELL ME YOU HAD SOMETHING *ELSE* TO GAIN.
LOOK, I DON'T KNOW WHAT--

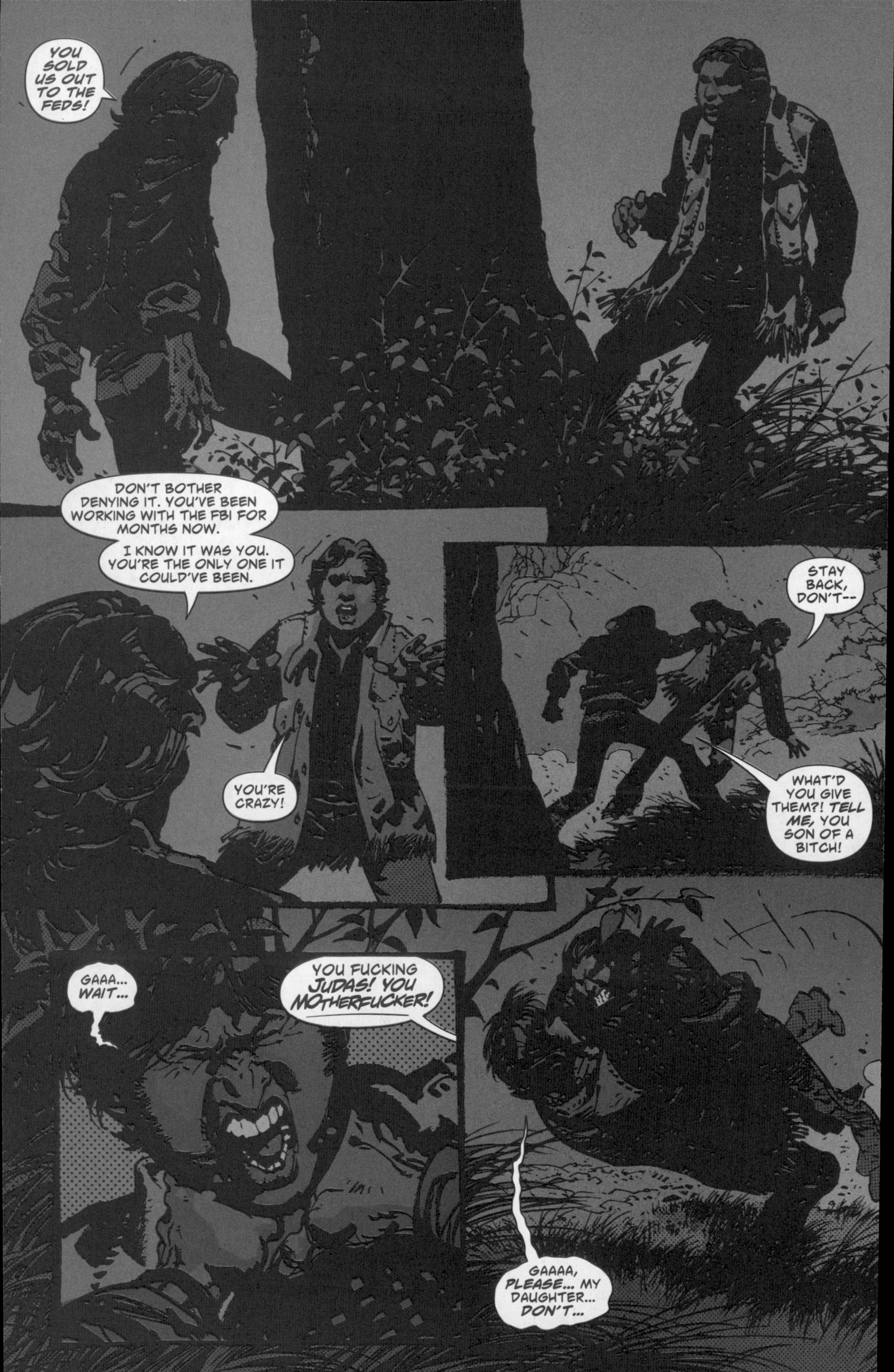
YOU SOLD US OUT TO THE FEDS!
DON'T BOTHER DENYING IT. YOU'VE BEEN WORKING WITH THE FBI FOR MONTHS NOW.
I KNOW IT WAS YOU. YOU'RE THE ONLY ONE IT COULD'VE BEEN.
YOU'RE CRAZY!
STAY BACK, DON'T--
WHAT'D YOU GIVE THEM?! TELL ME, YOU SON OF A BITCH!
GAAA... WAIT...
YOU FUCKING JUDAS! YOU MOTHERFUCKER!
GAAAA, PLEASE... MY DAUGHTER... DON'T...

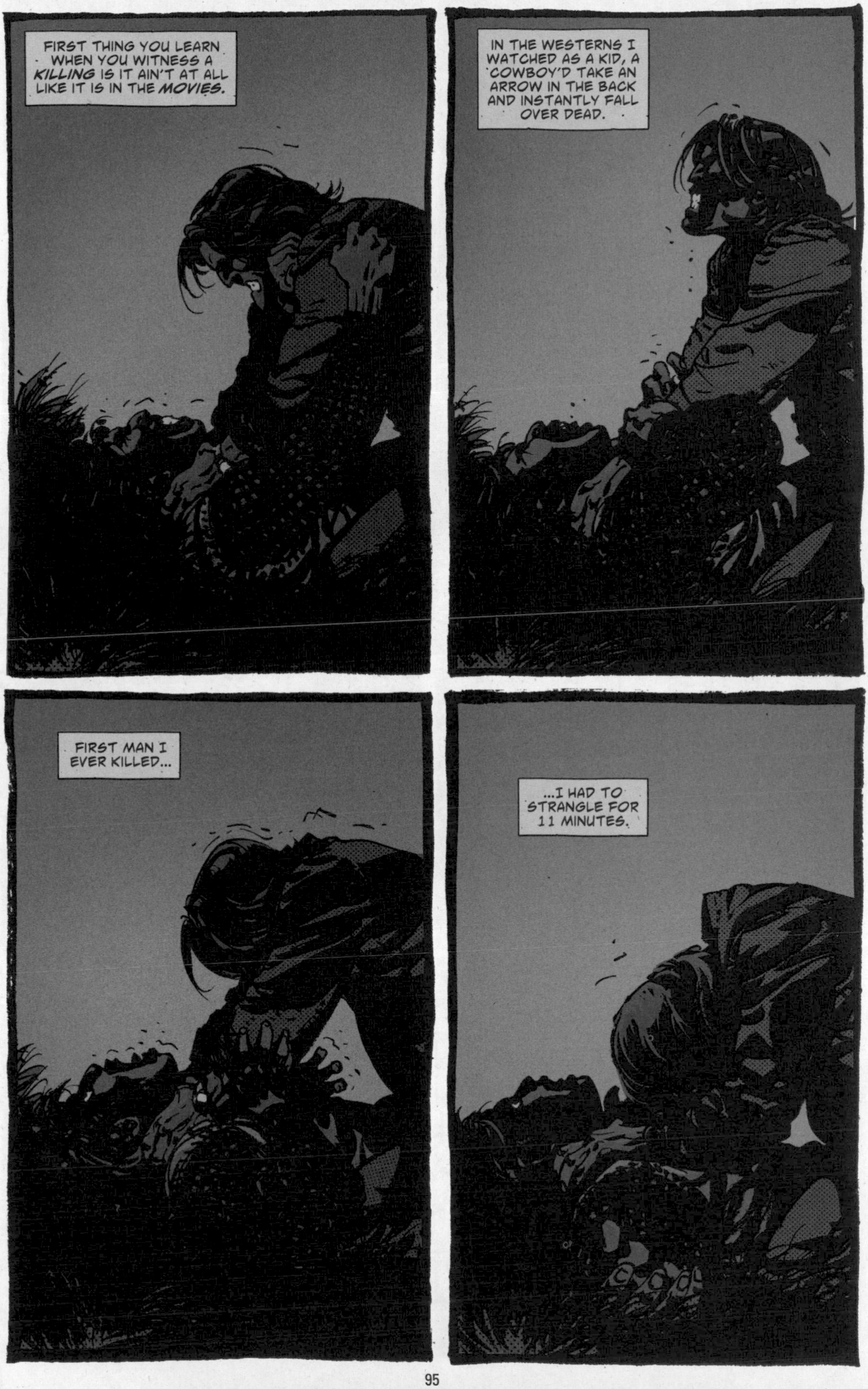
FIRST THING YOU LEARN WHEN YOU WITNESS A KILLING IS IT AIN'T AT ALL LIKE IT IS IN THE MOVIES.
IN THE WESTERNS I WATCHED AS A KID, A COWBOY'D TAKE AN ARROW IN THE BACK AND INSTANTLY FALL OVER DEAD.
FIRST MAN I EVER KILLED...
...I HAD TO STRANGLE FOR 11 MINUTES.

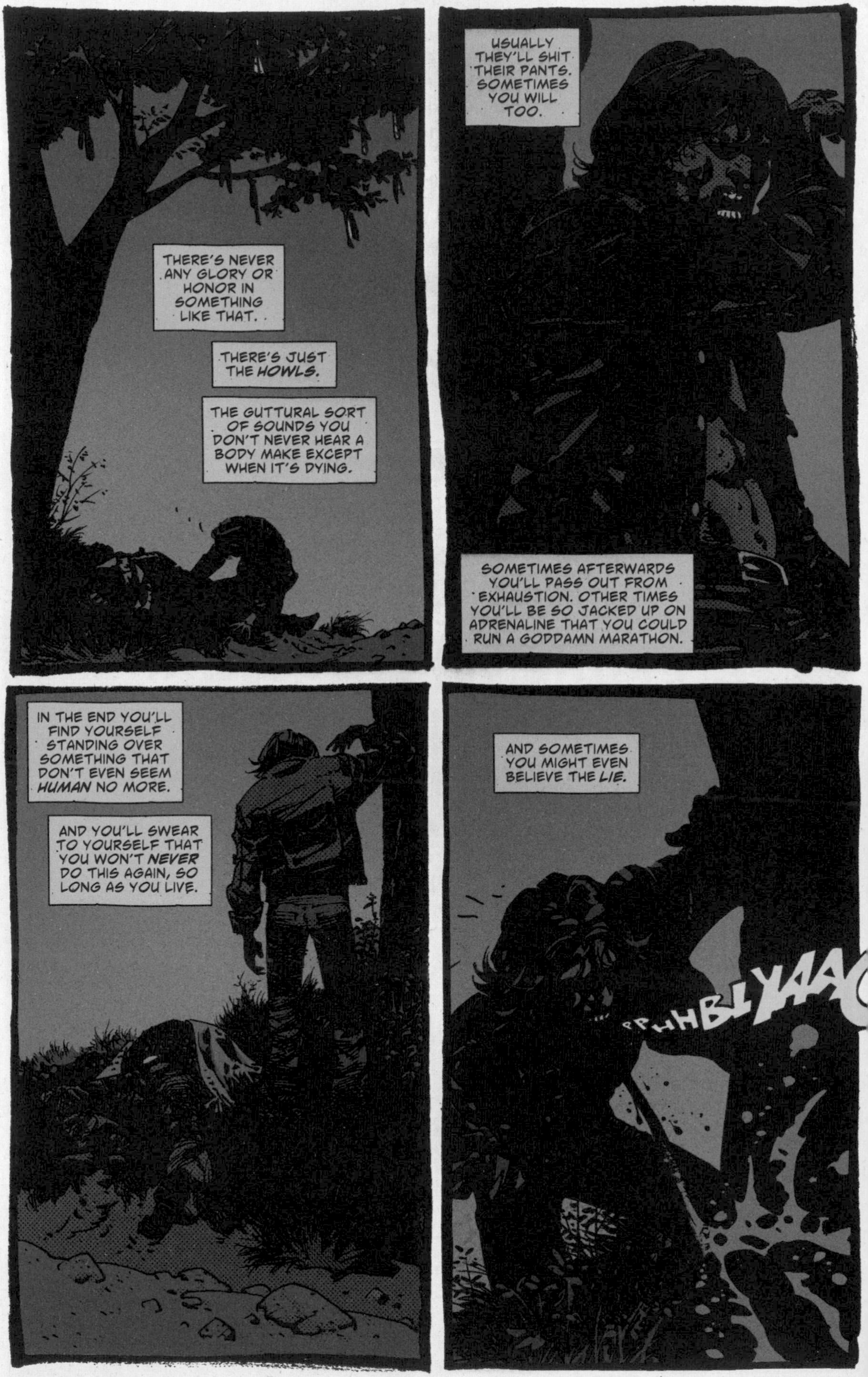
THERE'S NEVER ANY GLORY OR HONOR IN SOMETHING LIKE THAT.
THERE'S JUST THE *HOWLS*.
THE GUTTURAL SORT OF SOUNDS YOU DON'T NEVER HEAR A BODY MAKE EXCEPT WHEN IT'S DYING.
USUALLY THEY'LL SHIT THEIR PANTS. SOMETIMES YOU WILL TOO.
SOMETIMES AFTERWARDS YOU'LL PASS OUT FROM EXHAUSTION. OTHER TIMES YOU'LL BE SO JACKED UP ON ADRENALINE THAT YOU COULD RUN A GODDAMN MARATHON.
IN THE END YOU'LL FIND YOURSELF STANDING OVER SOMETHING THAT DON'T EVEN SEEM *HUMAN* NO MORE.
AND YOU'LL SWEAR TO YOURSELF THAT YOU WON'T *NEVER* DO THIS AGAIN, SO LONG AS YOU LIVE.
AND SOMETIMES YOU MIGHT EVEN BELIEVE THE *LIE*.
PPHHBLYAA

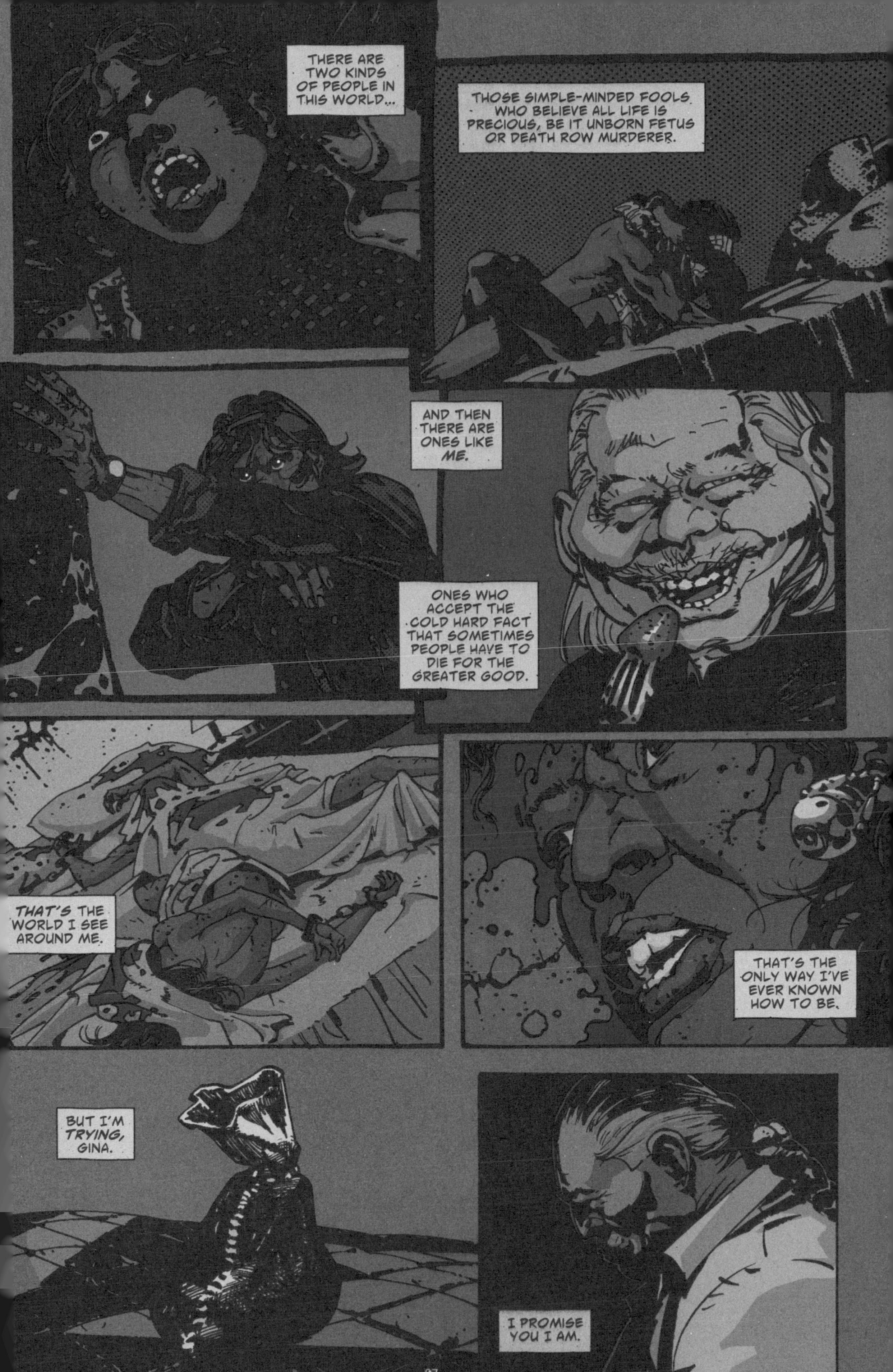
THERE ARE TWO KINDS OF PEOPLE IN THIS WORLD...
THOSE SIMPLE-MINDED FOOLS WHO BELIEVE ALL LIFE IS PRECIOUS, BE IT UNBORN FETUS OR DEATH ROW MURDERER.
AND THEN THERE ARE ONES LIKE *ME.*
ONES WHO ACCEPT THE COLD HARD FACT THAT SOMETIMES PEOPLE HAVE TO DIE FOR THE GREATER GOOD.
THAT'S THE WORLD I SEE AROUND ME.
THAT'S THE ONLY WAY I'VE EVER KNOWN HOW TO BE.
BUT I'M *TRYING,* GINA.
I PROMISE YOU I AM.

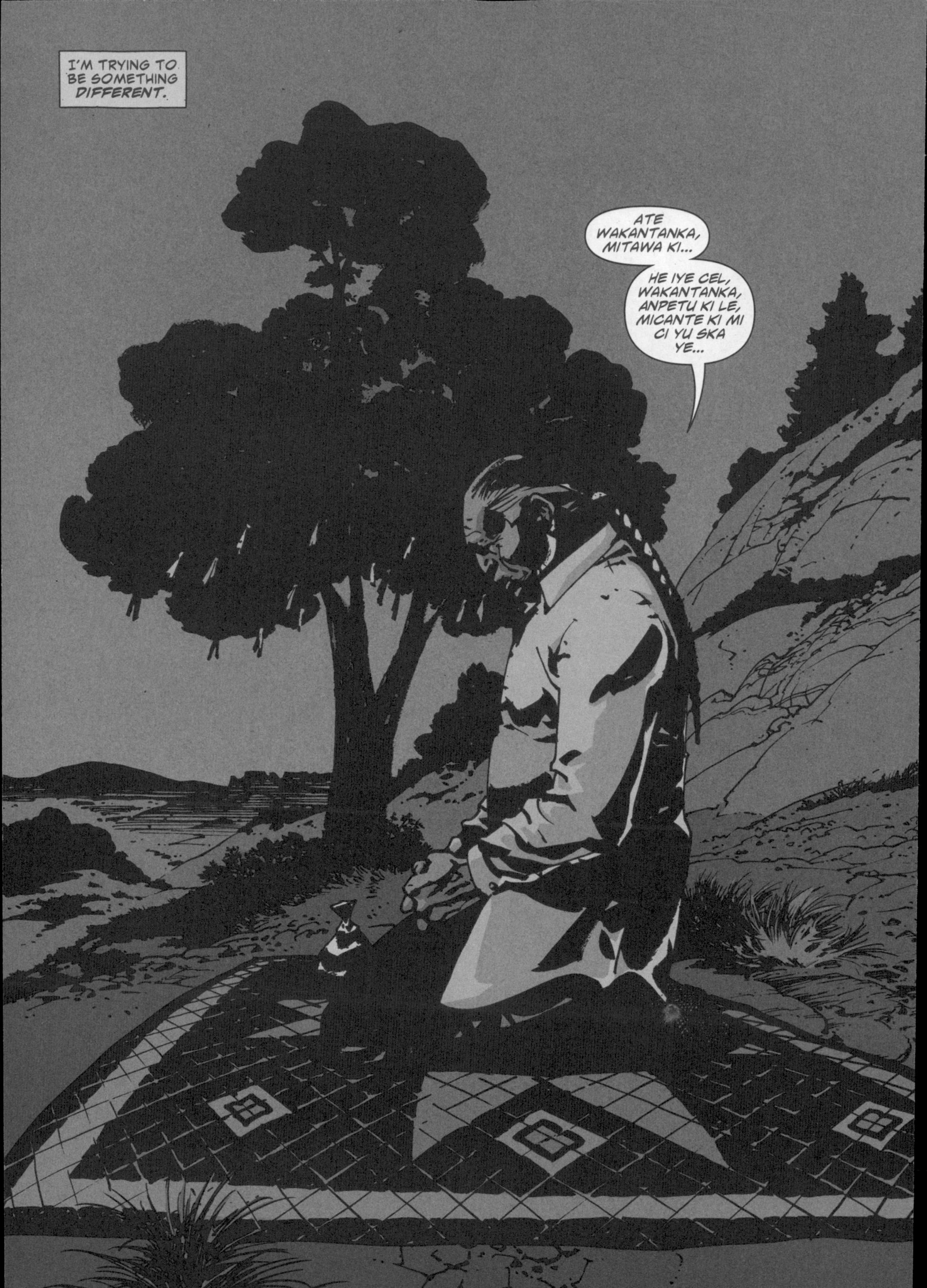
I'M TRYING TO BE SOMETHING DIFFERENT.
ATE WAKANTANKA, MITAWA KI...
HE IYE CEL, WAKANTANKA, ANPETU KI LE, MICANTE KI MI CI YU SKA YE...

THE GRAVEL IN YOUR GUTS PART 3

COVER ART BY JOCK

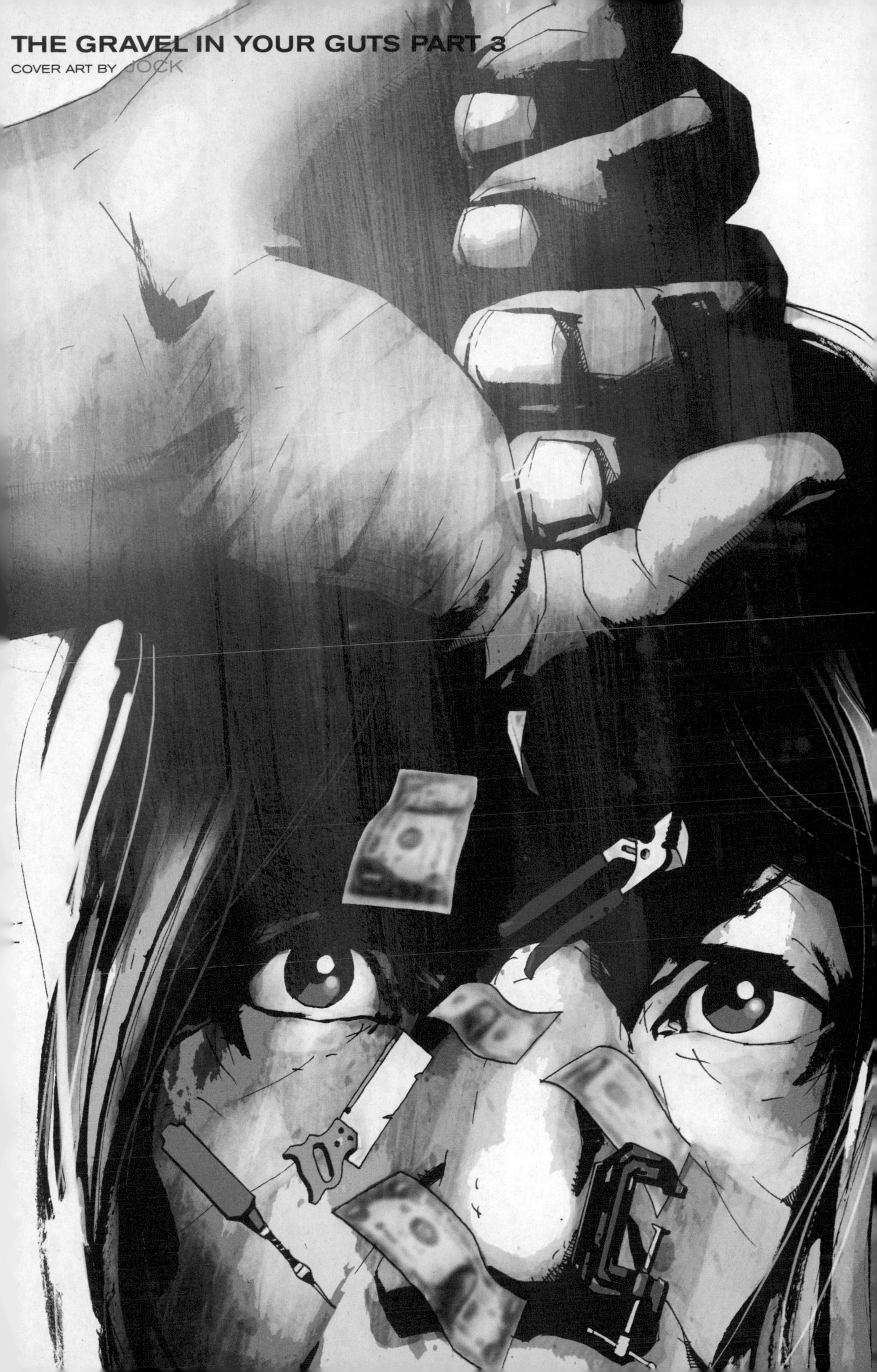

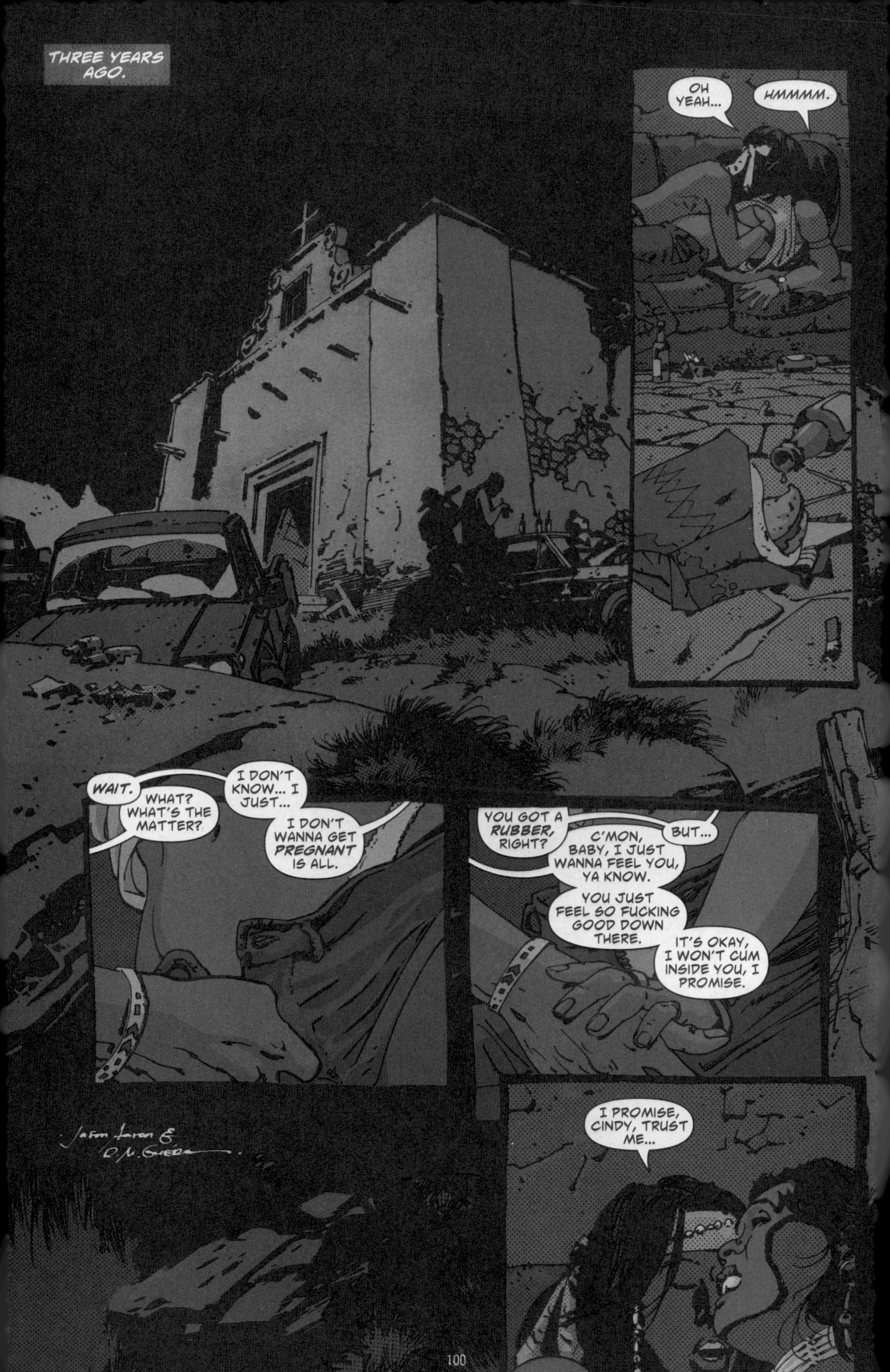

THREE YEARS AGO.
OH YEAH...
HMMMM.
WAIT.
WHAT? WHAT'S THE MATTER?
I DON'T KNOW... I JUST...
I DON'T WANNA GET PREGNANT IS ALL.
YOU GOT A RUBBER, RIGHT?
BUT...
C'MON, BABY, I JUST WANNA FEEL YOU, YA KNOW.
YOU JUST FEEL SO FUCKING GOOD DOWN THERE.
IT'S OKAY, I WON'T CUM INSIDE YOU, I PROMISE.
I PROMISE, CINDY, TRUST ME...

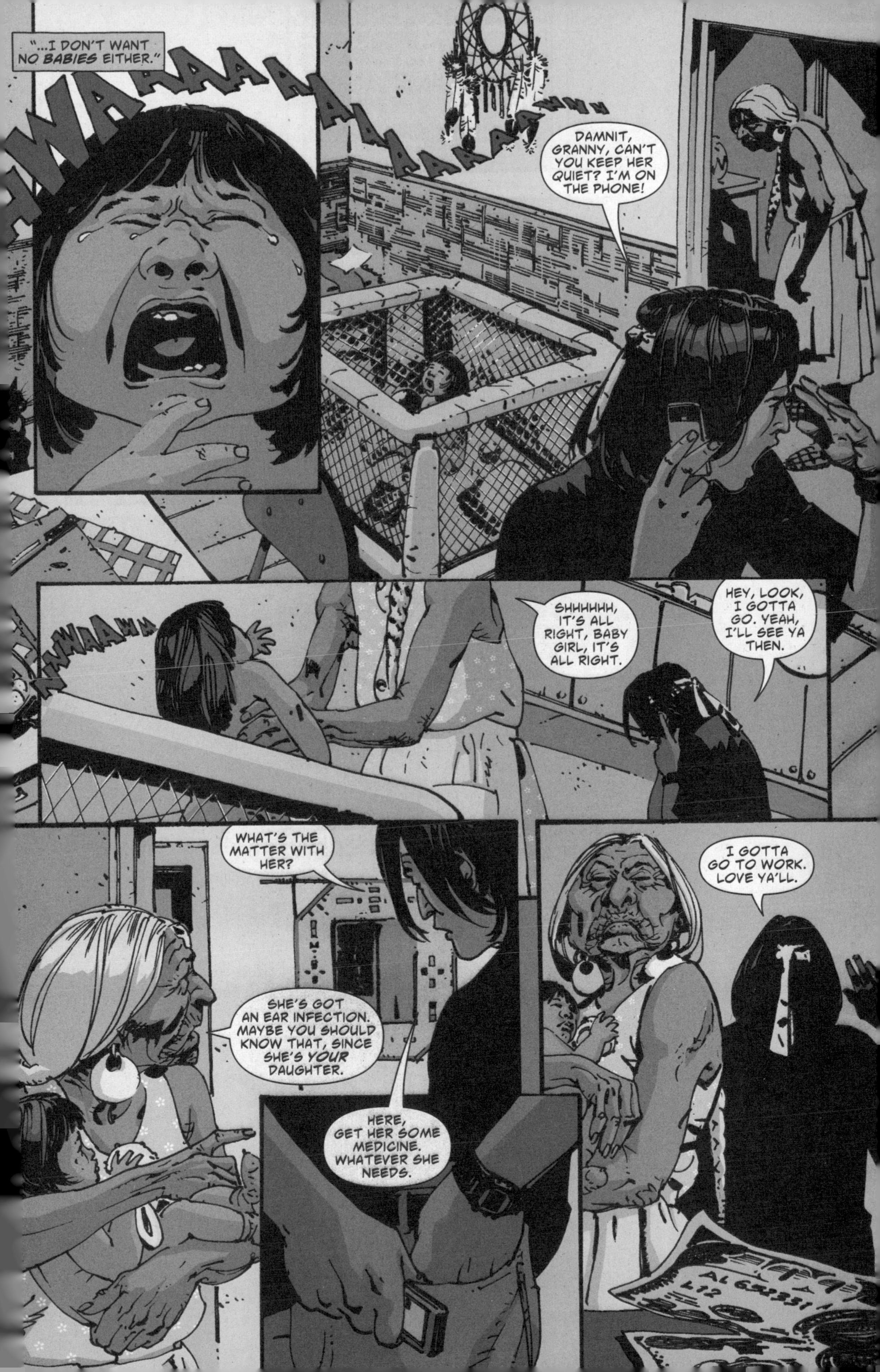
"...I DON'T WANT NO *BABIES* EITHER."
HWAAAAAAAAAAAAAAAWWW
DAMNIT, GRANNY, CAN'T YOU KEEP HER QUIET? I'M ON THE PHONE!
NWAAWW
SHHHHHH, IT'S ALL RIGHT, BABY GIRL, IT'S ALL RIGHT.
HEY, LOOK, I GOTTA GO. YEAH, I'LL SEE YA THEN.
WHAT'S THE MATTER WITH HER?
SHE'S GOT AN EAR INFECTION. MAYBE YOU SHOULD KNOW THAT, SINCE SHE'S *YOUR* DAUGHTER.
HERE, GET HER SOME MEDICINE. WHATEVER SHE NEEDS.
I GOTTA GO TO WORK. LOVE YA'LL.

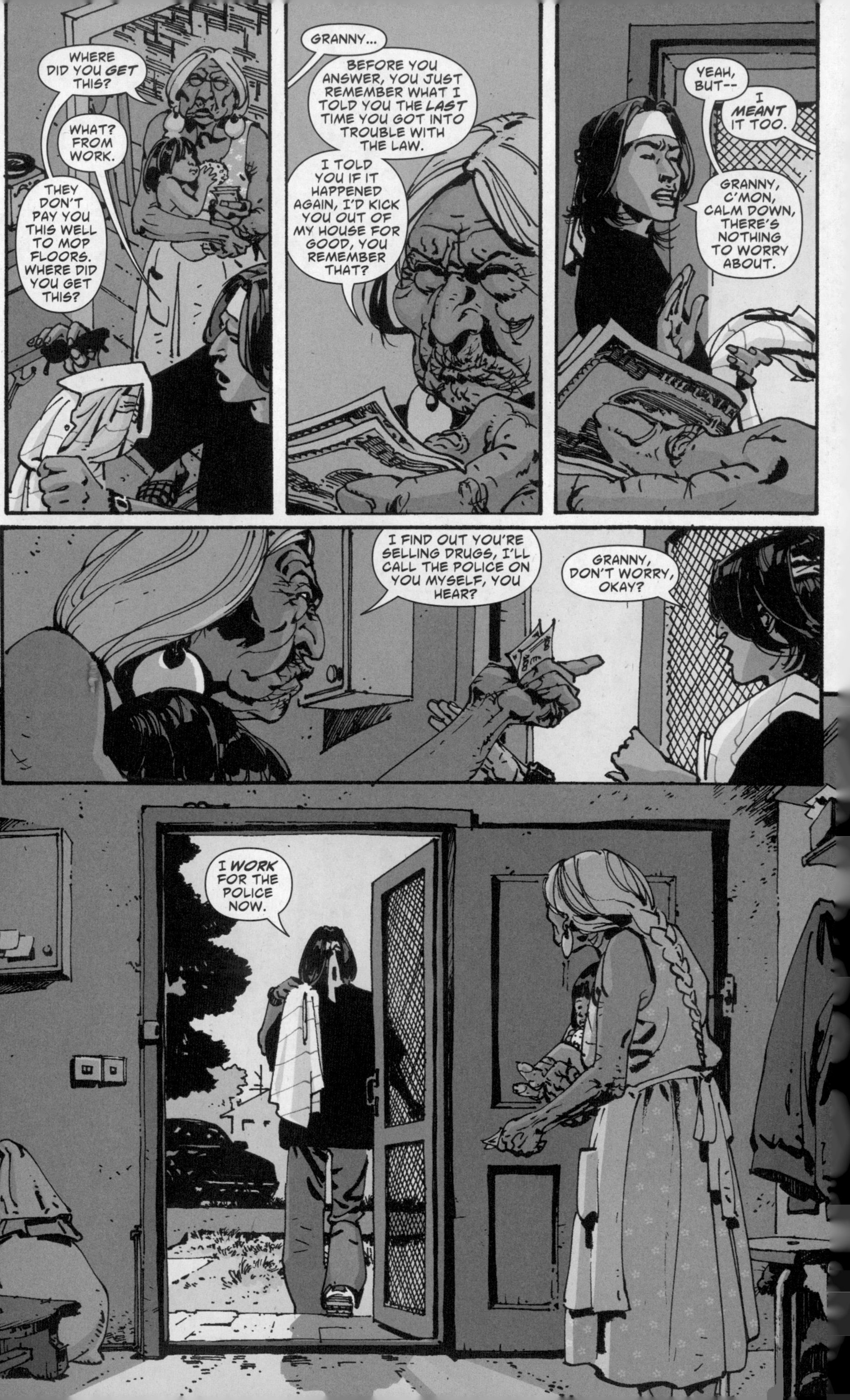
WHERE DID YOU GET THIS?
WHAT? FROM WORK.
THEY DON'T PAY YOU THIS WELL TO MOP FLOORS. WHERE DID YOU GET THIS?
GRANNY...
BEFORE YOU ANSWER, YOU JUST REMEMBER WHAT I TOLD YOU THE LAST TIME YOU GOT INTO TROUBLE WITH THE LAW.
I TOLD YOU IF IT HAPPENED AGAIN, I'D KICK YOU OUT OF MY HOUSE FOR GOOD, YOU REMEMBER THAT?
YEAH, BUT--
I MEANT IT TOO.
GRANNY, C'MON, CALM DOWN, THERE'S NOTHING TO WORRY ABOUT.
I FIND OUT YOU'RE SELLING DRUGS, I'LL CALL THE POLICE ON YOU MYSELF, YOU HEAR?
GRANNY, DON'T WORRY, OKAY?
I WORK FOR THE POLICE NOW.

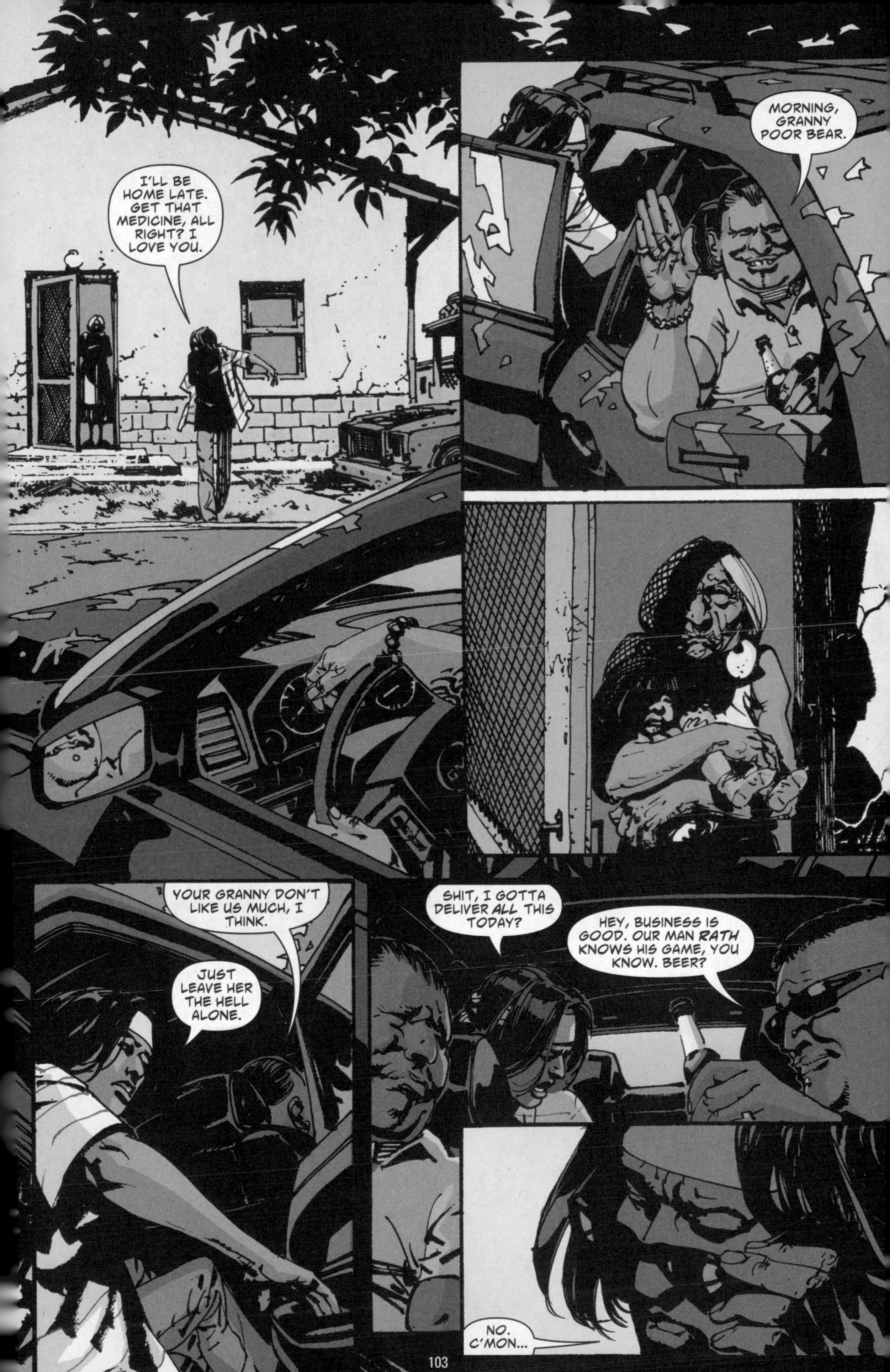
I'LL BE HOME LATE. GET THAT MEDICINE, ALL RIGHT? I LOVE YOU.
MORNING, GRANNY POOR BEAR.
YOUR GRANNY DON'T LIKE US MUCH, I THINK.
JUST LEAVE HER THE HELL ALONE.
SHIT, I GOTTA DELIVER ALL THIS TODAY?
HEY, BUSINESS IS GOOD. OUR MAN RATH KNOWS HIS GAME, YOU KNOW. BEER?
NO. C'MON...

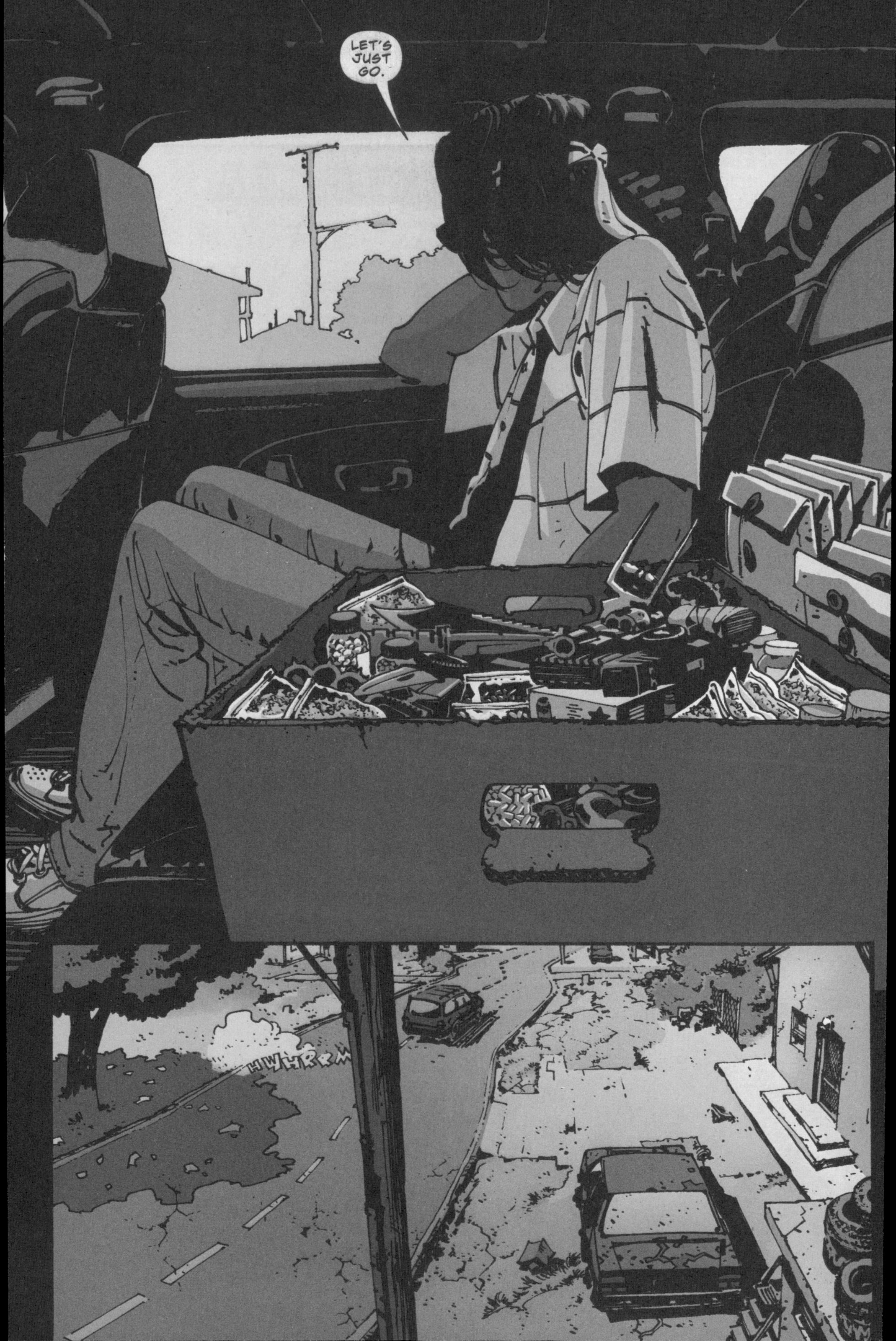
LET'S JUST GO.
HWHRRM

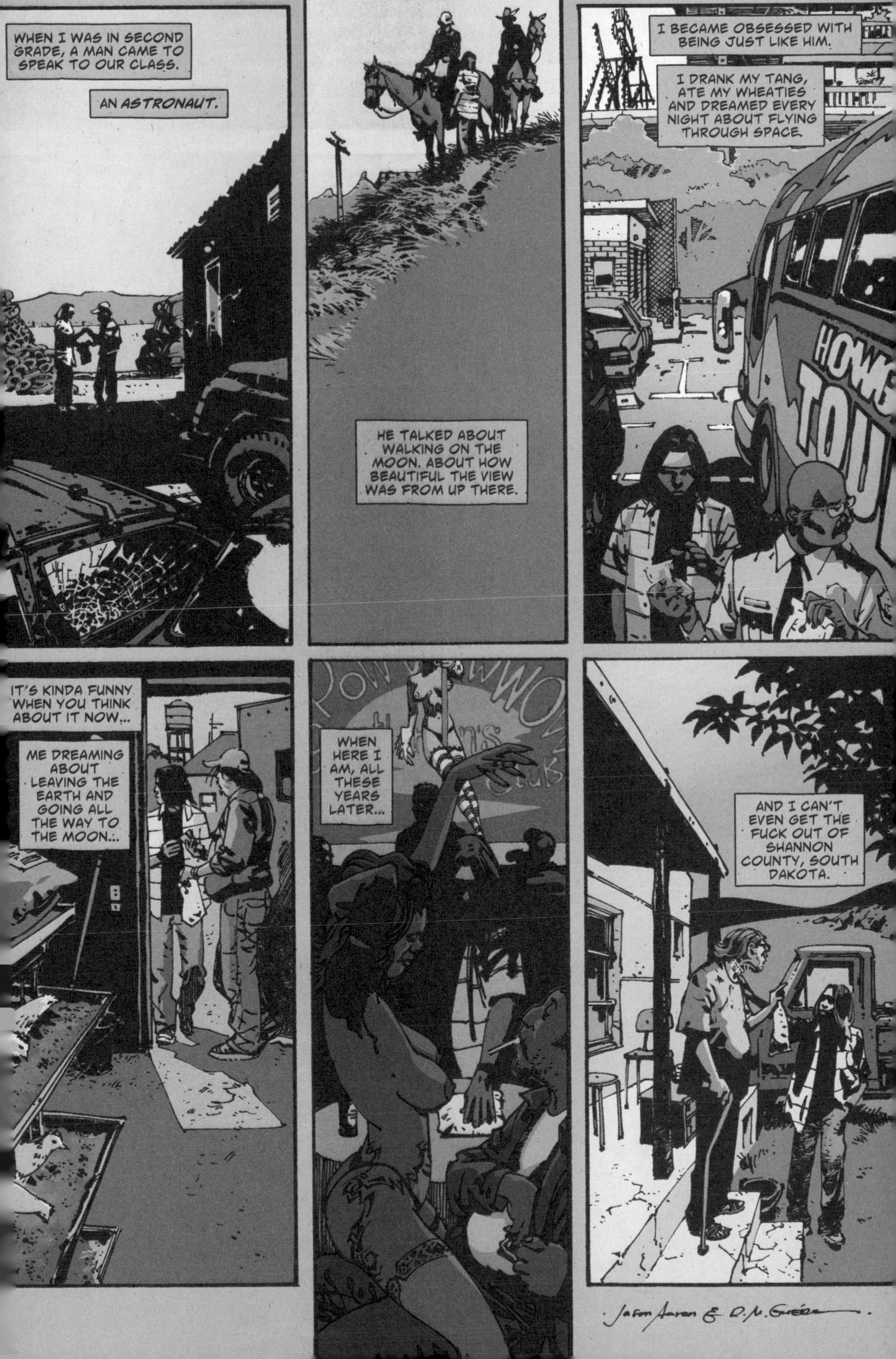

WHEN I WAS IN SECOND GRADE, A MAN CAME TO SPEAK TO OUR CLASS.
AN *ASTRONAUT*.
HE TALKED ABOUT WALKING ON THE MOON. ABOUT HOW BEAUTIFUL THE VIEW WAS FROM UP THERE.
I BECAME OBSESSED WITH BEING JUST LIKE HIM.
I DRANK MY TANG, ATE MY WHEATIES AND DREAMED EVERY NIGHT ABOUT FLYING THROUGH SPACE.
IT'S KINDA FUNNY WHEN YOU THINK ABOUT IT NOW...
ME DREAMING ABOUT LEAVING THE EARTH AND GOING ALL THE WAY TO THE MOON...
WHEN HERE I AM, ALL THESE YEARS LATER...
AND I CAN'T EVEN GET THE FUCK OUT OF SHANNON COUNTY, SOUTH DAKOTA.

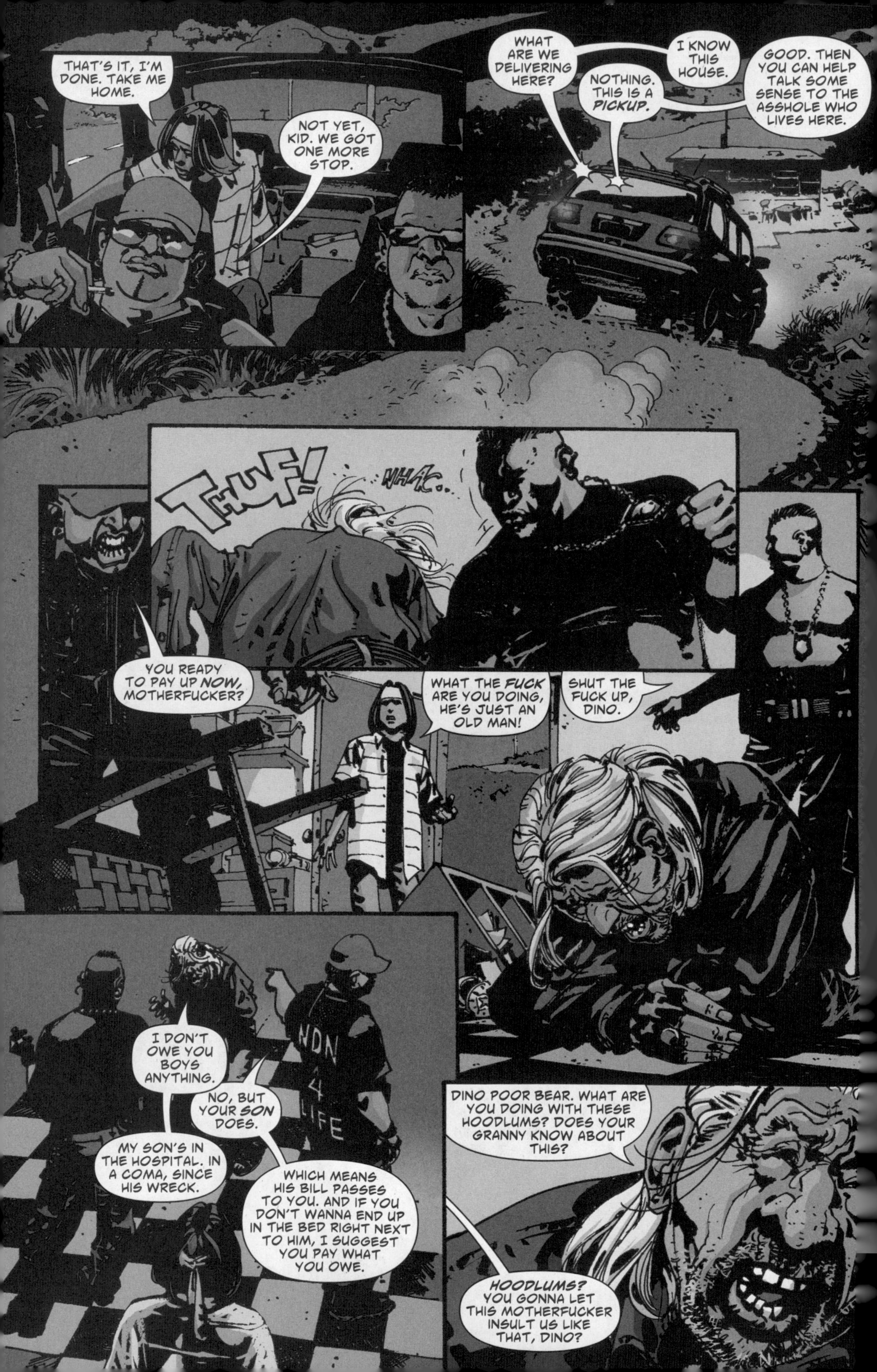
THAT'S IT, I'M DONE. TAKE ME HOME.
NOT YET, KID. WE GOT ONE MORE STOP.
WHAT ARE WE DELIVERING HERE?
NOTHING. THIS IS A *PICKUP.*
I KNOW THIS HOUSE.
GOOD. THEN YOU CAN HELP TALK SOME SENSE TO THE ASSHOLE WHO LIVES HERE.
THUF!
WHAC..
YOU READY TO PAY UP *NOW,* MOTHERFUCKER?
WHAT THE *FUCK* ARE YOU DOING, HE'S JUST AN OLD MAN!
SHUT THE FUCK UP, DINO.
I DON'T OWE YOU BOYS ANYTHING.
NO, BUT YOUR *SON* DOES.
MY SON'S IN THE HOSPITAL. IN A COMA, SINCE HIS WRECK.
WHICH MEANS HIS BILL PASSES TO YOU. AND IF YOU DON'T WANNA END UP IN THE BED RIGHT NEXT TO HIM, I SUGGEST YOU PAY WHAT YOU OWE.
NDN 4 LIFE
DINO POOR BEAR. WHAT ARE YOU DOING WITH THESE HOODLUMS? DOES YOUR GRANNY KNOW ABOUT THIS?
HOODLUMS? YOU GONNA LET THIS MOTHERFUCKER INSULT US LIKE THAT, DINO?

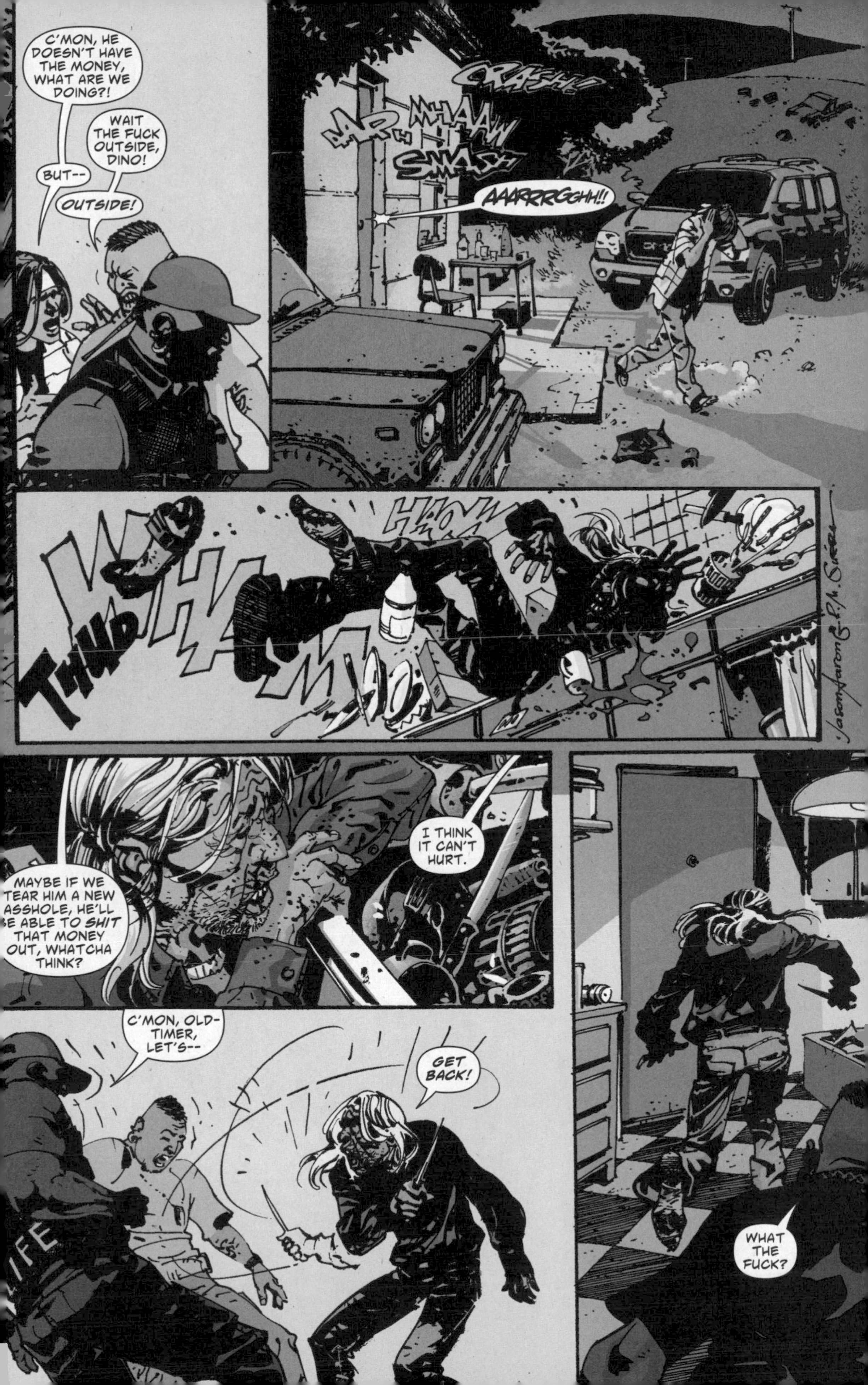
C'MON, HE DOESN'T HAVE THE MONEY, WHAT ARE WE DOING?!
WAIT THE FUCK OUTSIDE, DINO!
BUT--
OUTSIDE!
CRASH!
AARGH
WHAAAM
SMASH
AAARRRGGHH!!
THUD
WHAM
HAM
MAYBE IF WE TEAR HIM A NEW ASSHOLE, HE'LL BE ABLE TO SHIT THAT MONEY OUT, WHATCHA THINK?
I THINK IT CAN'T HURT.
C'MON, OLD-TIMER, LET'S--
GET BACK!
WHAT THE FUCK?

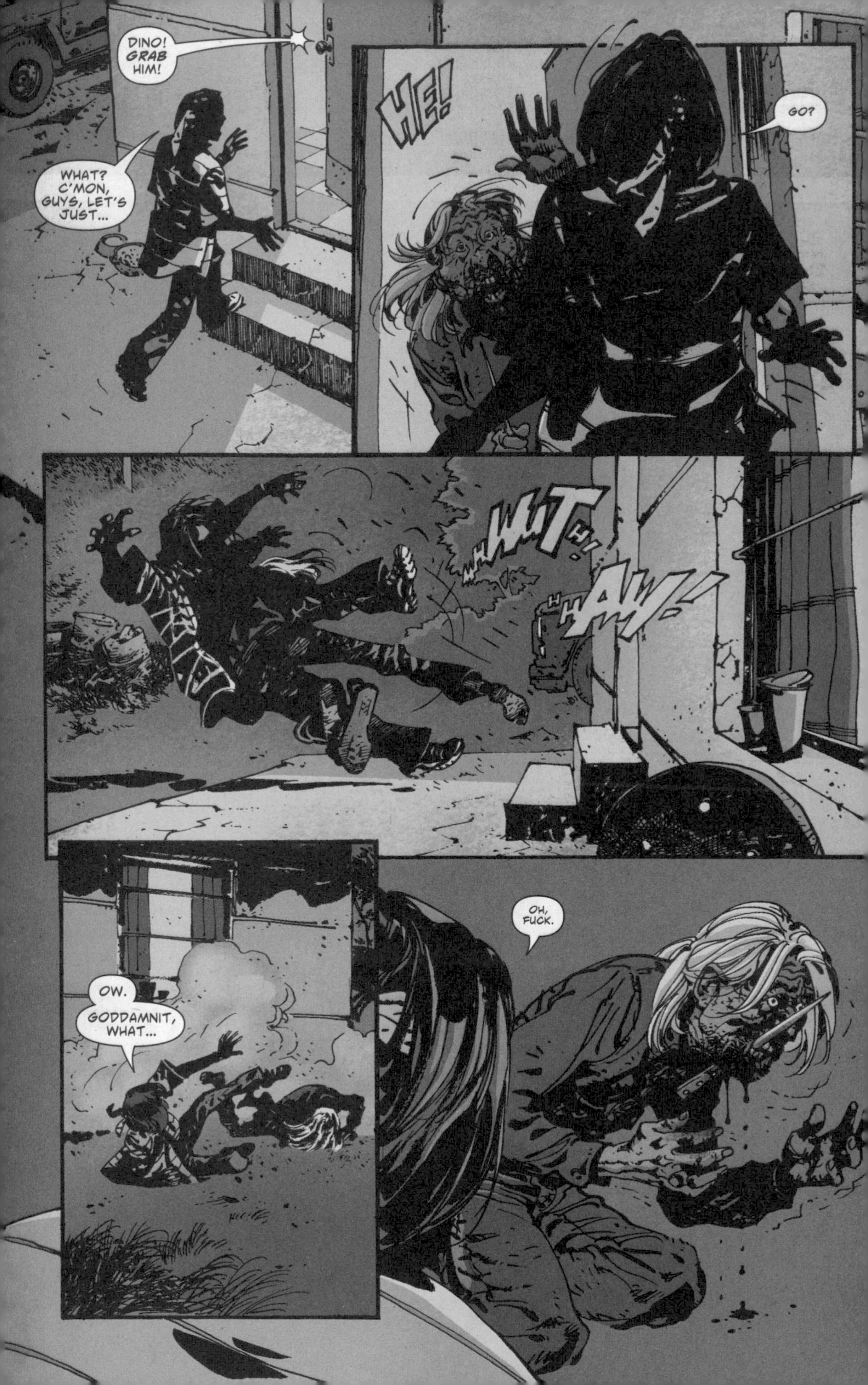
DINO! GRAB HIM!
WHAT? C'MON, GUYS, LET'S JUST...
HE!
GO?
WHHWUT
HH!
HHAW!
OH, FUCK.
OW. GODDAMNIT, WHAT...

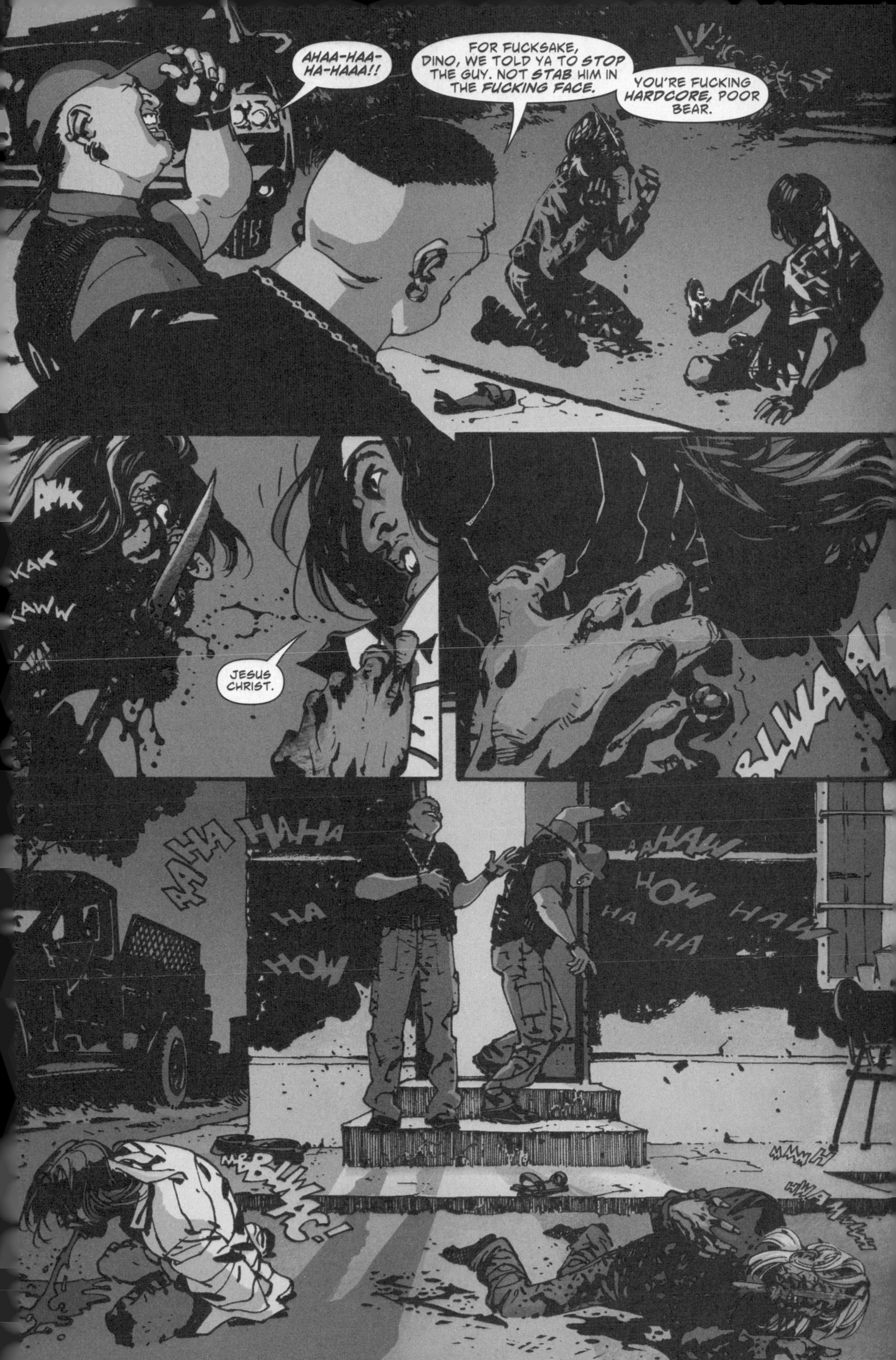
AHAA-HAA-HA-HAAA!!
FOR FUCKSAKE, DINO, WE TOLD YA TO STOP THE GUY. NOT STAB HIM IN THE FUCKING FACE.
YOU'RE FUCKING HARDCORE, POOR BEAR.
AWK
KAK
KAWW
JESUS CHRIST.
BLWAM
HAHA
HAHA
HA
HOW
HAW
HOW
HA
HA
HAW
BLWAC!

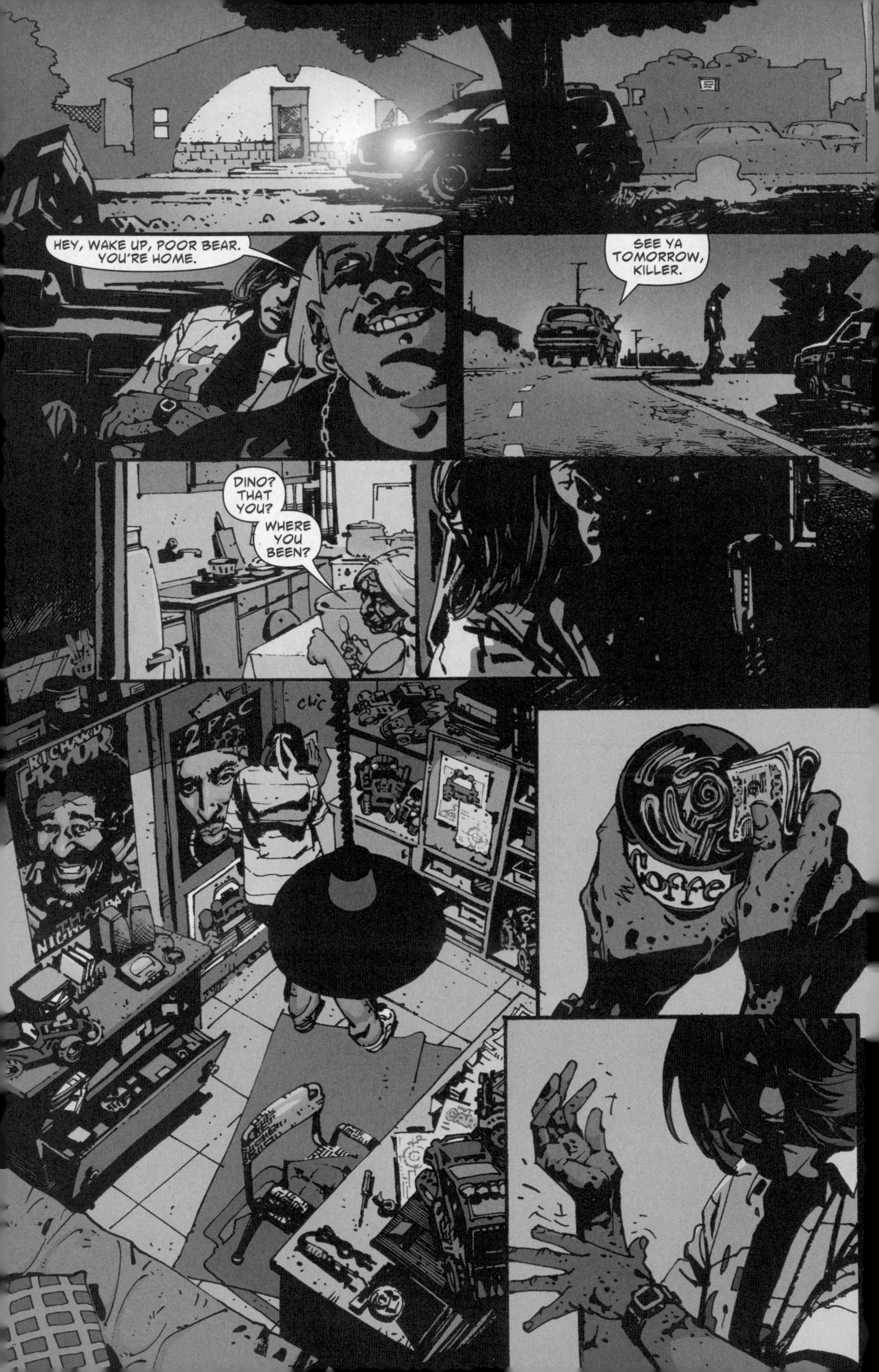
HEY, WAKE UP, POOR BEAR. YOU'RE HOME.
SEE YA TOMORROW, KILLER.
DINO? THAT YOU?
WHERE YOU BEEN?
RICHARD PRYOR
2 PAC
CLIC
COFFEE

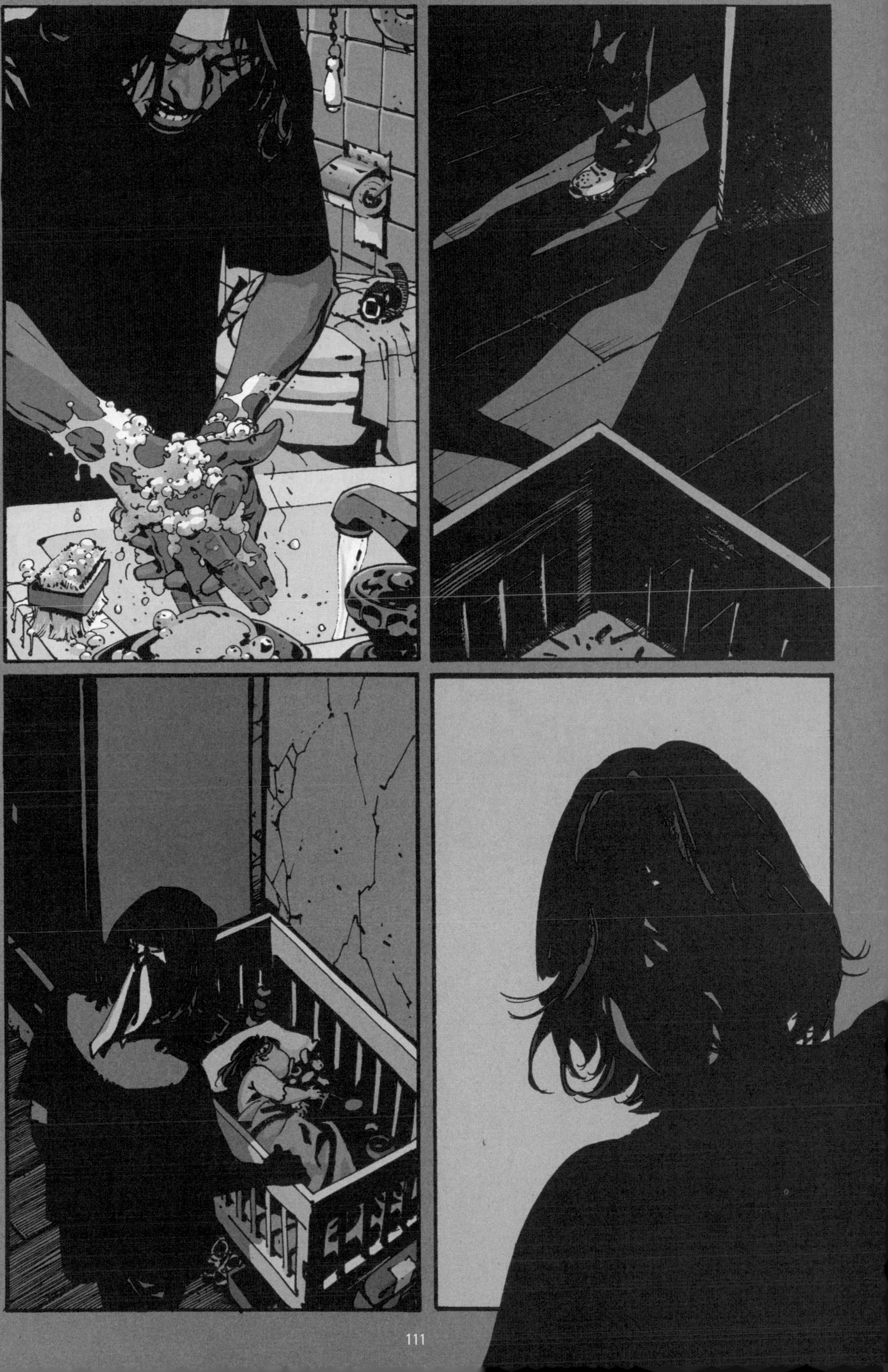

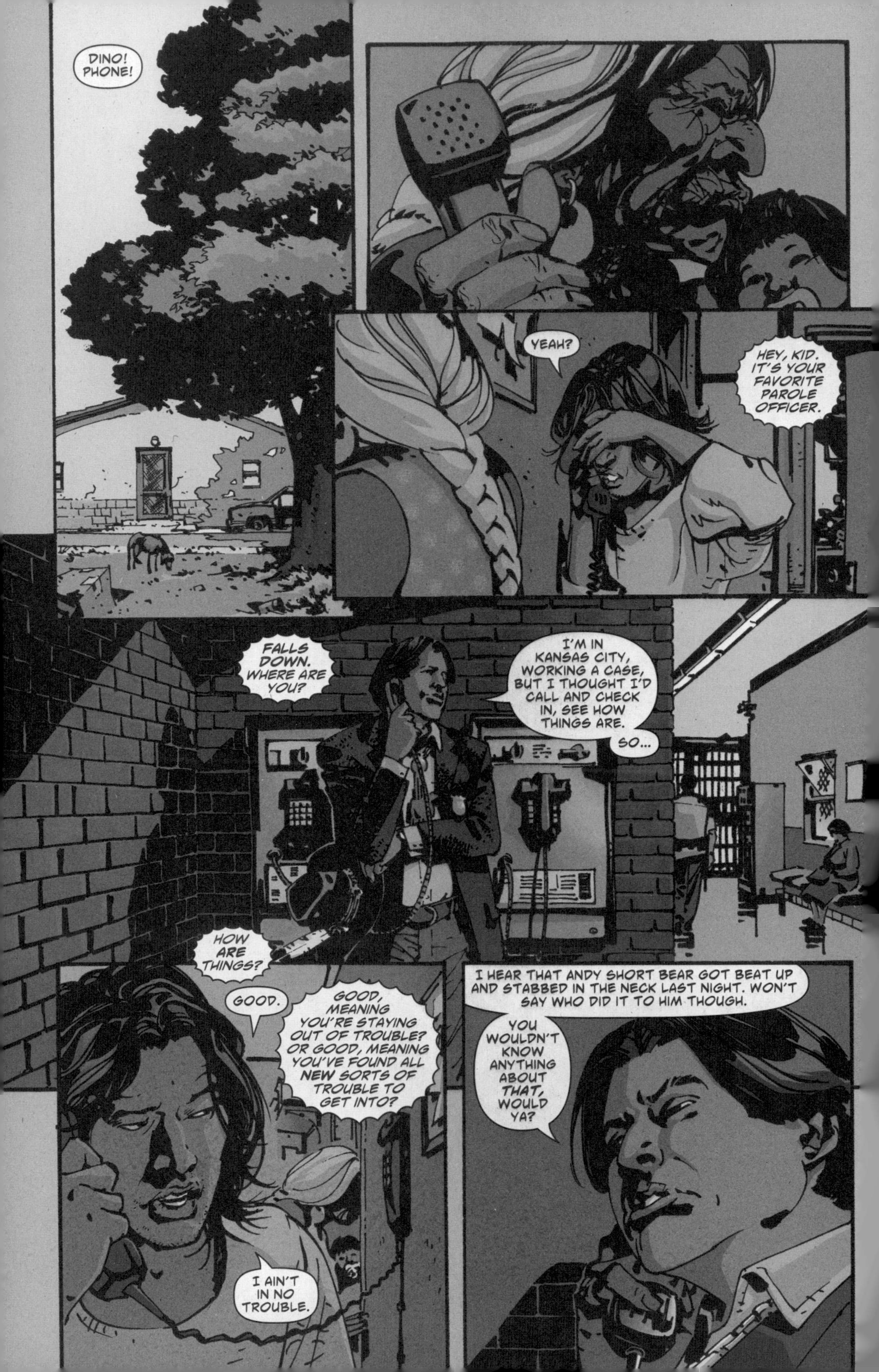
DINO! PHONE!
YEAH?
HEY, KID. IT'S YOUR FAVORITE PAROLE OFFICER.
FALLS DOWN. WHERE ARE YOU?
I'M IN KANSAS CITY, WORKING A CASE, BUT I THOUGHT I'D CALL AND CHECK IN, SEE HOW THINGS ARE.
SO...
HOW ARE THINGS?
GOOD.
GOOD, MEANING YOU'RE STAYING OUT OF TROUBLE? OR GOOD, MEANING YOU'VE FOUND ALL NEW SORTS OF TROUBLE TO GET INTO?
I AIN'T IN NO TROUBLE.
I HEAR THAT ANDY SHORT BEAR GOT BEAT UP AND STABBED IN THE NECK LAST NIGHT. WON'T SAY WHO DID IT TO HIM THOUGH.
YOU WOULDN'T KNOW ANYTHING ABOUT THAT, WOULD YA?

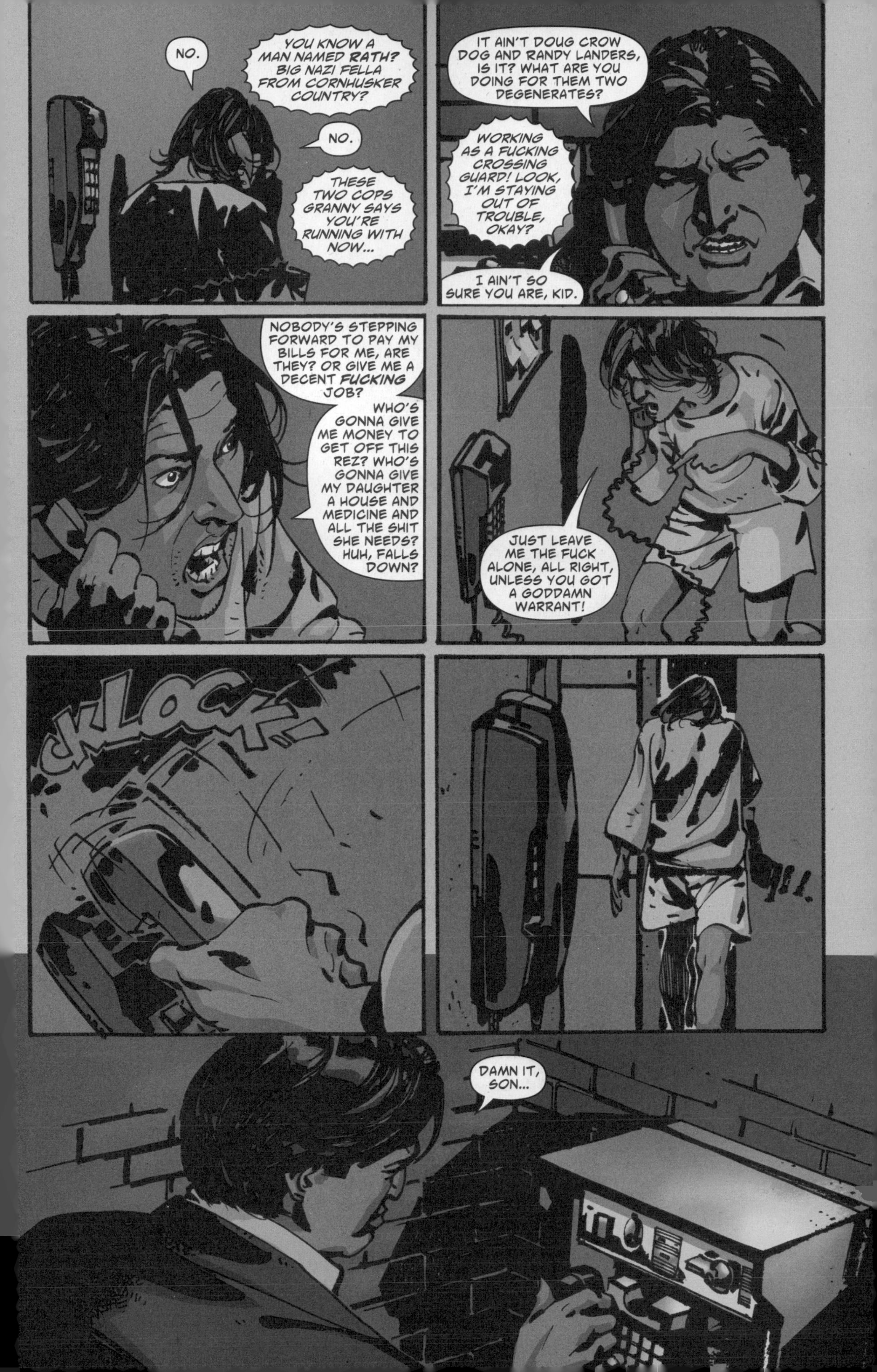
NO.
YOU KNOW A MAN NAMED RATH? BIG NAZI FELLA FROM CORNHUSKER COUNTRY?
NO.
THESE TWO COPS GRANNY SAYS YOU'RE RUNNING WITH NOW...
IT AIN'T DOUG CROW DOG AND RANDY LANDERS, IS IT? WHAT ARE YOU DOING FOR THEM TWO DEGENERATES?
WORKING AS A FUCKING CROSSING GUARD! LOOK, I'M STAYING OUT OF TROUBLE, OKAY?
I AIN'T SO SURE YOU ARE, KID.
NOBODY'S STEPPING FORWARD TO PAY MY BILLS FOR ME, ARE THEY? OR GIVE ME A DECENT FUCKING JOB?
WHO'S GONNA GIVE ME MONEY TO GET OFF THIS REZ? WHO'S GONNA GIVE MY DAUGHTER A HOUSE AND MEDICINE AND ALL THE SHIT SHE NEEDS? HUH, FALLS DOWN?
JUST LEAVE ME THE FUCK ALONE, ALL RIGHT, UNLESS YOU GOT A GODDAMN WARRANT!
CKLOCK!
DAMN IT, SON...

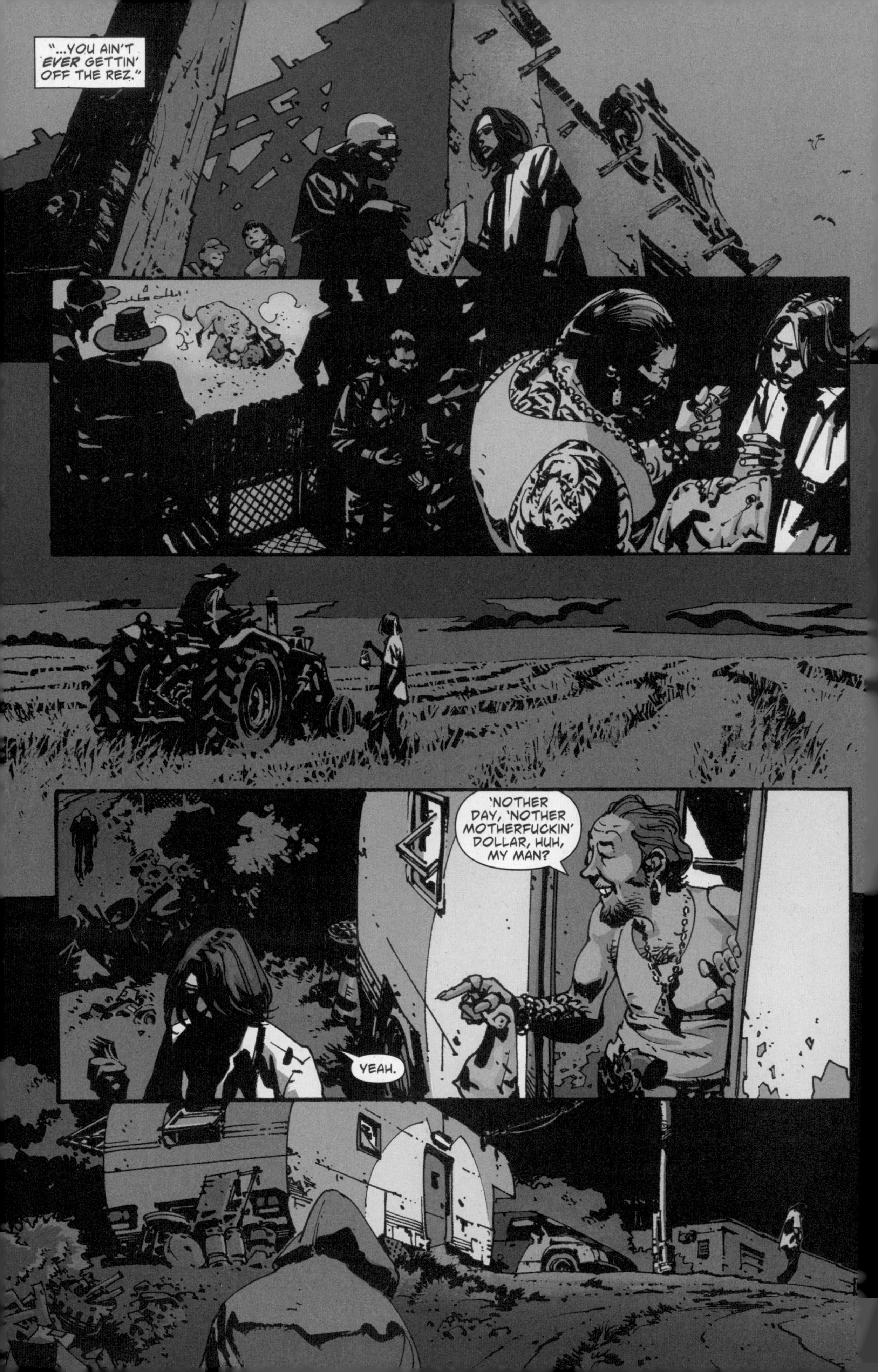
"...YOU AIN'T *EVER* GETTIN' OFF THE REZ."
'NOTHER DAY, 'NOTHER MOTHERFUCKIN' DOLLAR, HUH, MY MAN?
YEAH.

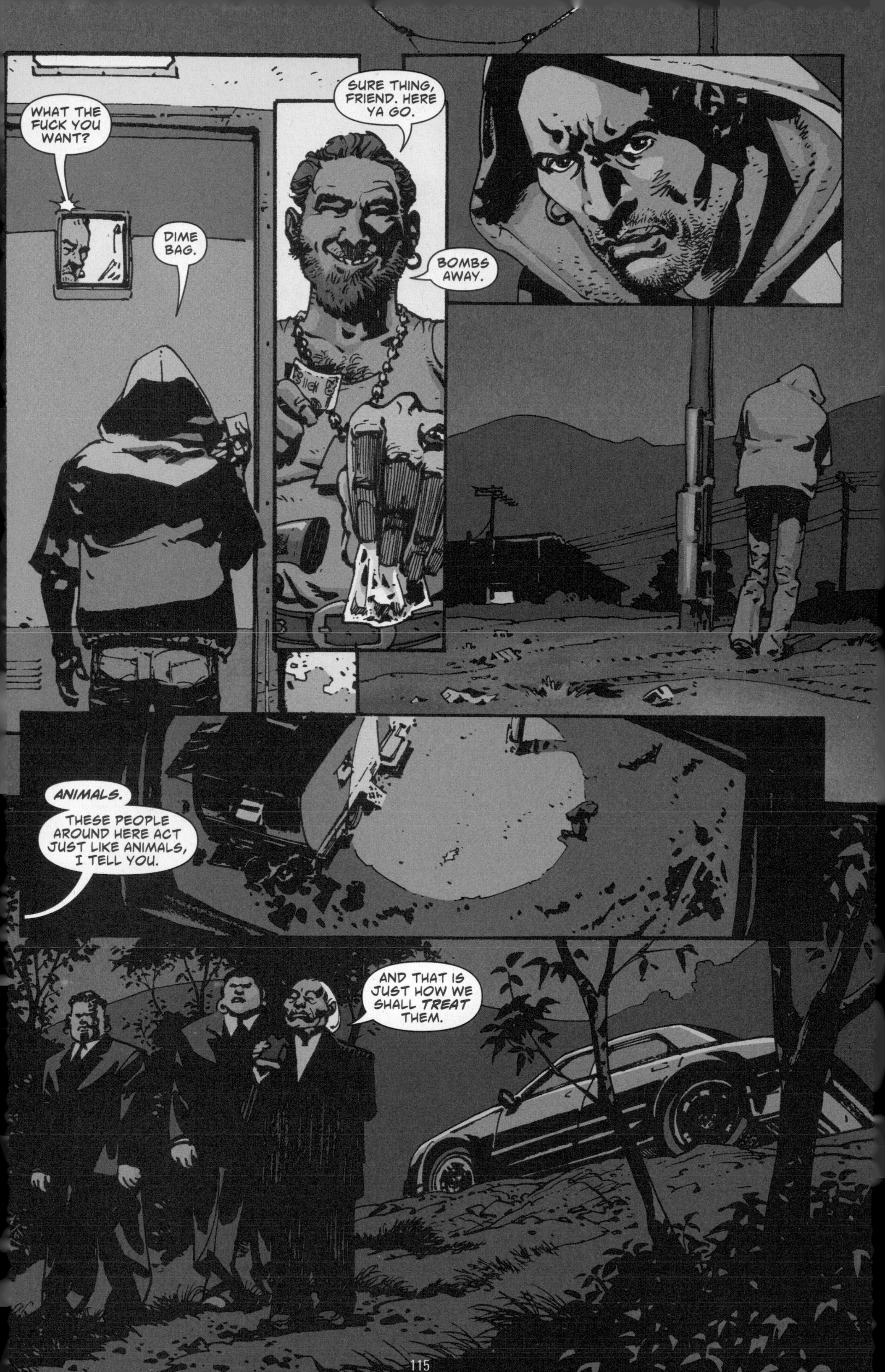
WHAT THE FUCK YOU WANT?
DIME BAG.
SURE THING, FRIEND. HERE YA GO.
BOMBS AWAY.
ANIMALS.
THESE PEOPLE AROUND HERE ACT JUST LIKE ANIMALS, I TELL YOU.
AND THAT IS JUST HOW WE SHALL TREAT THEM.

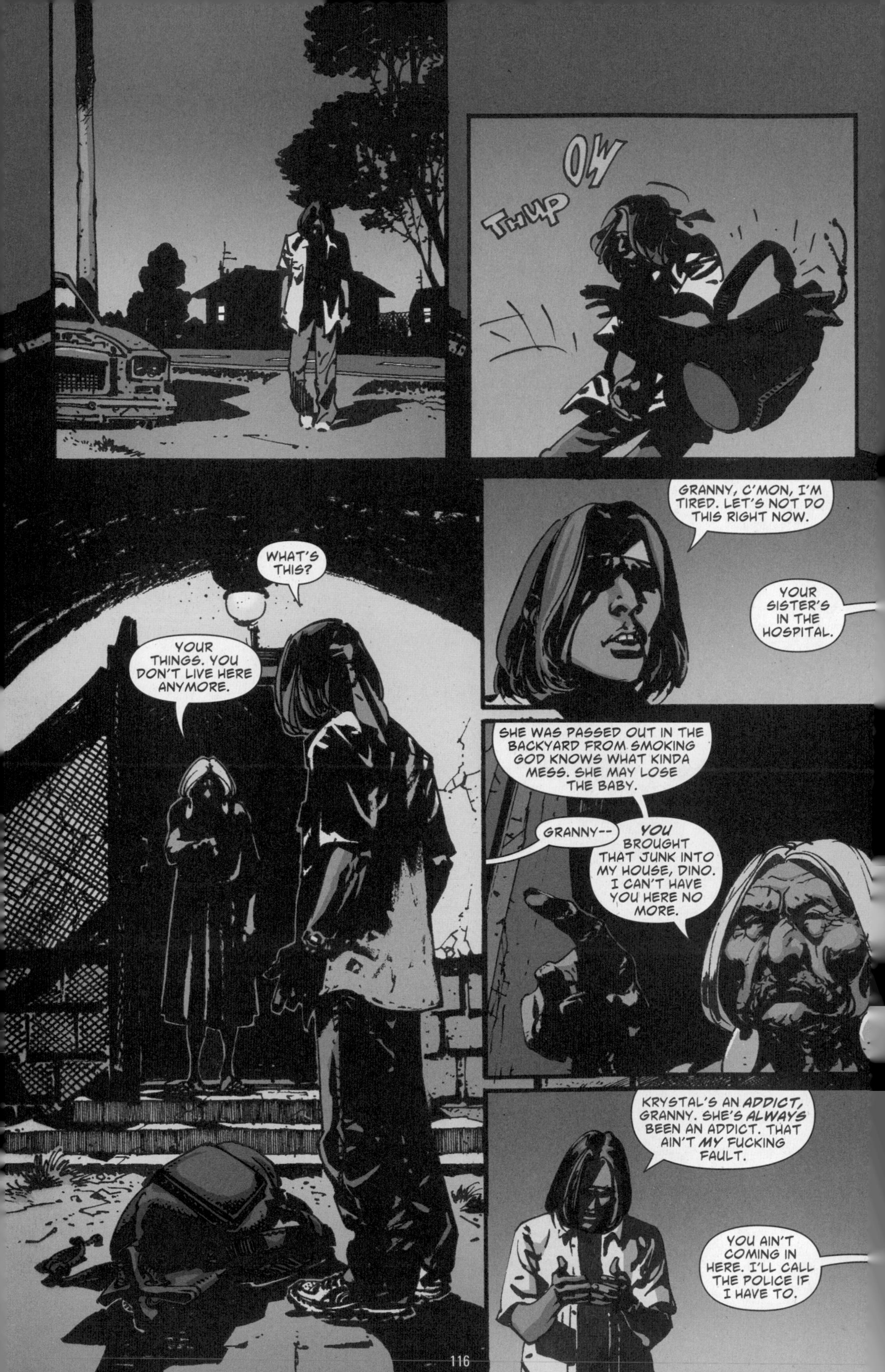
THUP
OW
WHAT'S THIS?
YOUR THINGS. YOU DON'T LIVE HERE ANYMORE.
GRANNY, C'MON, I'M TIRED. LET'S NOT DO THIS RIGHT NOW.
YOUR SISTER'S IN THE HOSPITAL.
SHE WAS PASSED OUT IN THE BACKYARD FROM SMOKING GOD KNOWS WHAT KINDA MESS. SHE MAY LOSE THE BABY.
GRANNY--
YOU BROUGHT THAT JUNK INTO MY HOUSE, DINO. I CAN'T HAVE YOU HERE NO MORE.
KRYSTAL'S AN *ADDICT*, GRANNY. SHE'S *ALWAYS* BEEN AN ADDICT. THAT AIN'T *MY* FUCKING FAULT.
YOU AIN'T COMING IN HERE. I'LL CALL THE POLICE IF I HAVE TO.

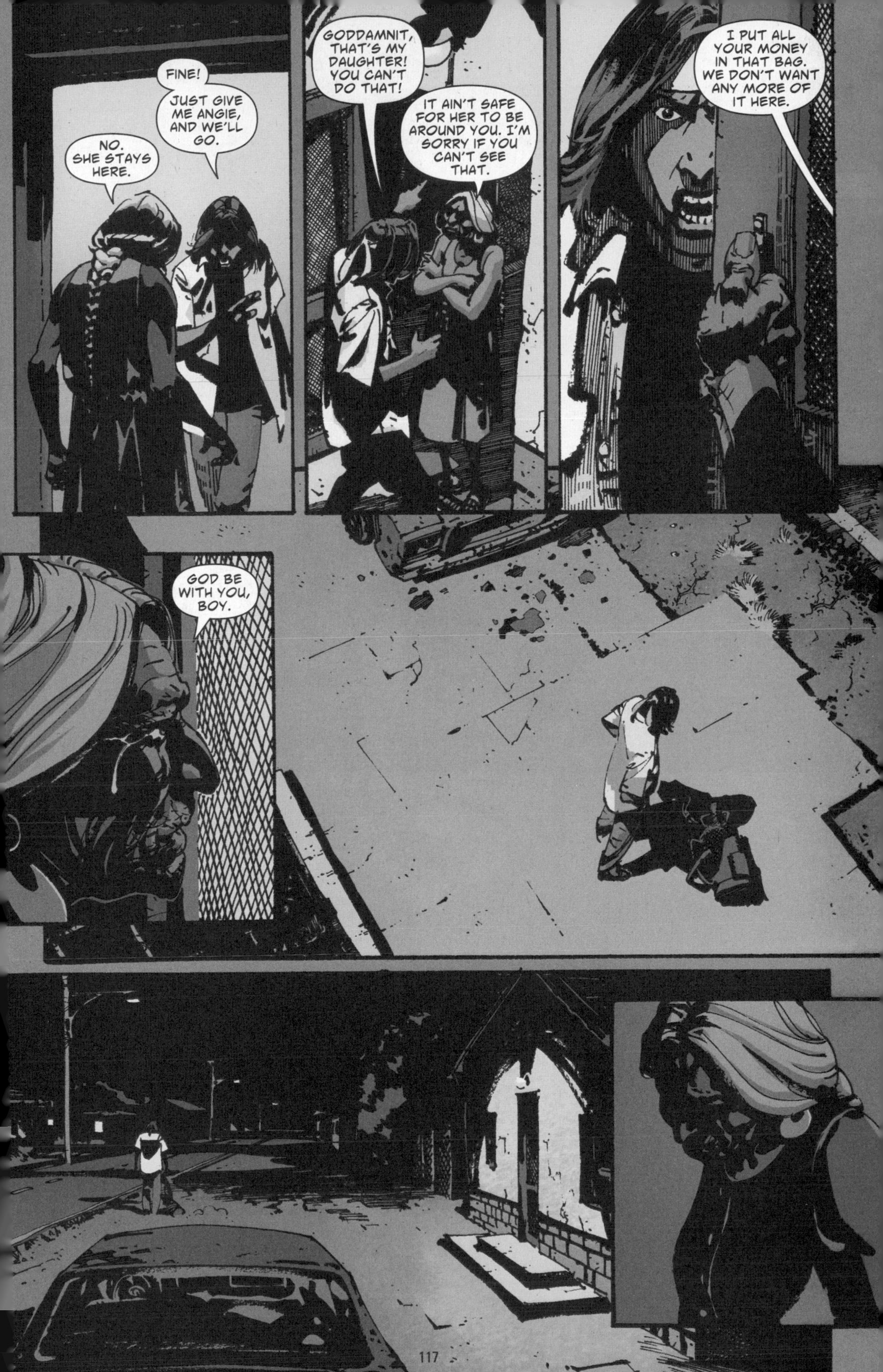
FINE!
JUST GIVE ME ANGIE, AND WE'LL GO.
NO. SHE STAYS HERE.
GODDAMNIT, THAT'S MY DAUGHTER! YOU CAN'T DO THAT!
IT AIN'T SAFE FOR HER TO BE AROUND YOU. I'M SORRY IF YOU CAN'T SEE THAT.
I PUT ALL YOUR MONEY IN THAT BAG. WE DON'T WANT ANY MORE OF IT HERE.
GOD BE WITH YOU, BOY.

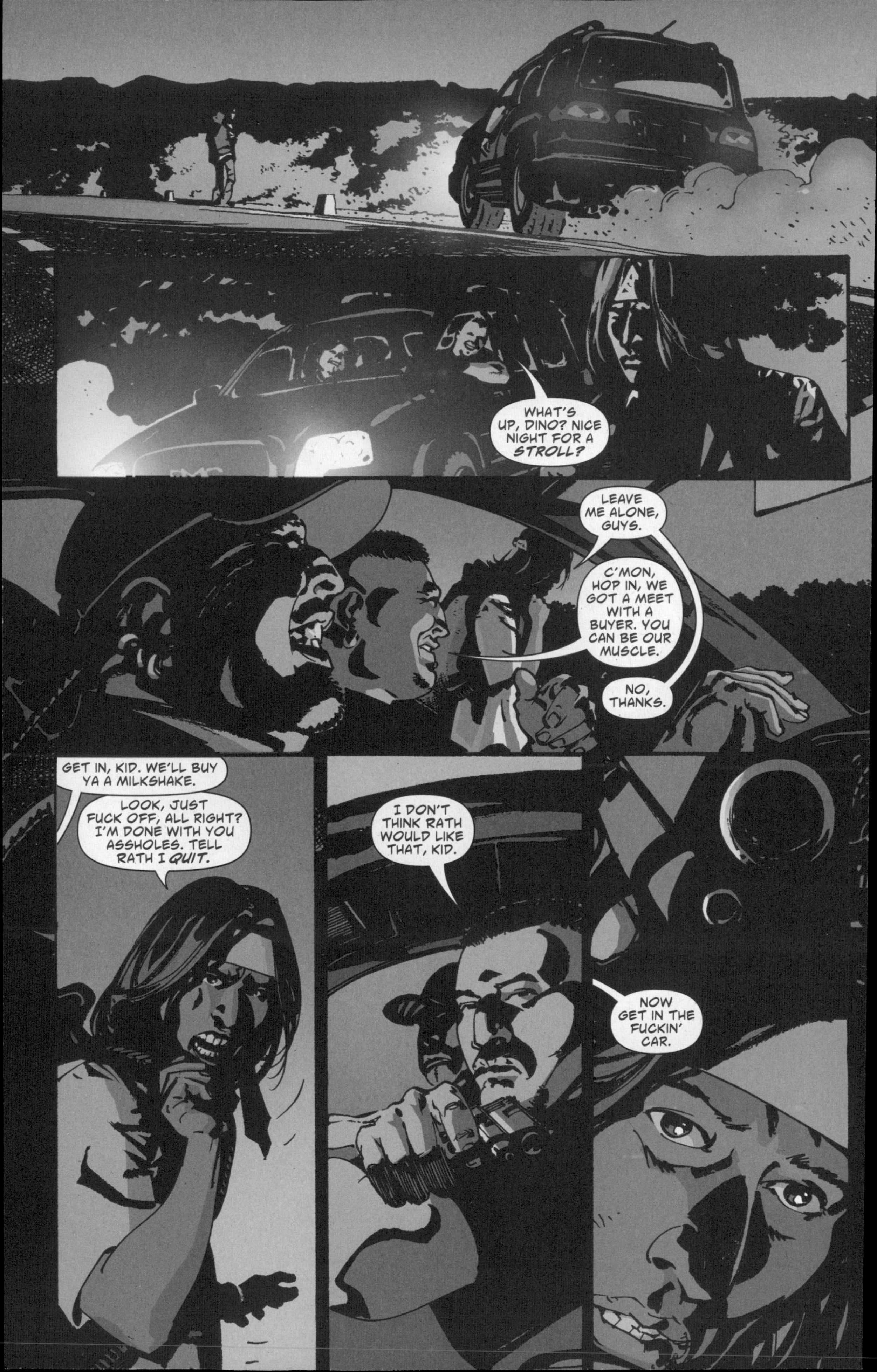
WHAT'S UP, DINO? NICE NIGHT FOR A STROLL?
LEAVE ME ALONE, GUYS.
C'MON, HOP IN, WE GOT A MEET WITH A BUYER. YOU CAN BE OUR MUSCLE.
NO, THANKS.
GET IN, KID. WE'LL BUY YA A MILKSHAKE.
LOOK, JUST FUCK OFF, ALL RIGHT? I'M DONE WITH YOU ASSHOLES. TELL RATH I QUIT.
I DON'T THINK RATH WOULD LIKE THAT, KID.
NOW GET IN THE FUCKIN' CAR.

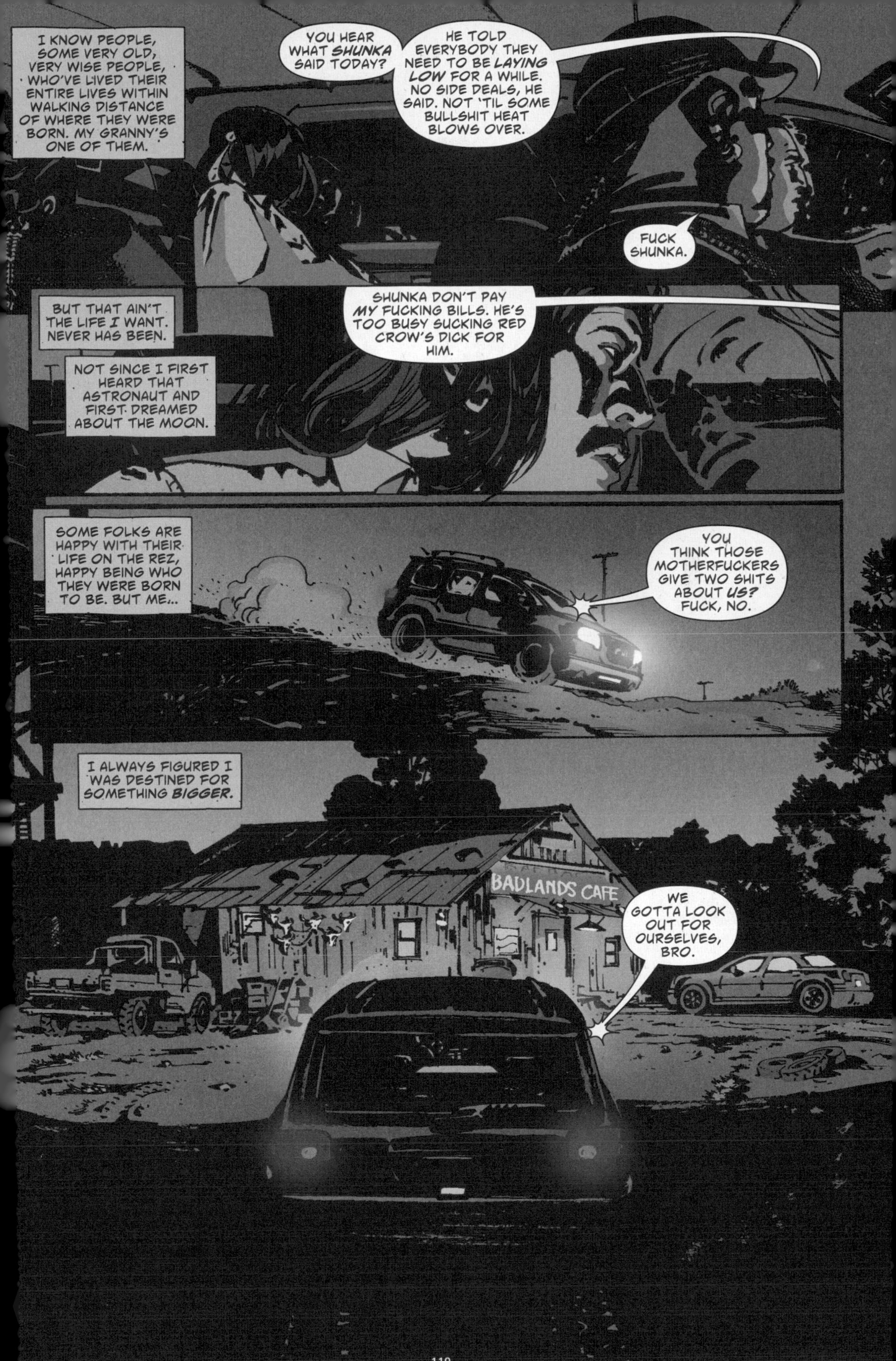

I KNOW PEOPLE, SOME VERY OLD, VERY WISE PEOPLE, WHO'VE LIVED THEIR ENTIRE LIVES WITHIN WALKING DISTANCE OF WHERE THEY WERE BORN. MY GRANNY'S ONE OF THEM.
YOU HEAR WHAT *SHUNKA* SAID TODAY?
HE TOLD EVERYBODY THEY NEED TO BE *LAYING LOW* FOR A WHILE. NO SIDE DEALS, HE SAID. NOT 'TIL SOME BULLSHIT HEAT BLOWS OVER.
FUCK SHUNKA.
BUT THAT AIN'T THE LIFE *I* WANT. NEVER HAS BEEN.
SHUNKA DON'T PAY *MY* FUCKING BILLS. HE'S TOO BUSY SUCKING RED CROW'S DICK FOR HIM.
NOT SINCE I FIRST HEARD THAT ASTRONAUT AND FIRST DREAMED ABOUT THE MOON.
SOME FOLKS ARE HAPPY WITH THEIR LIFE ON THE REZ, HAPPY BEING WHO THEY WERE BORN TO BE. BUT ME...
YOU THINK THOSE MOTHERFUCKERS GIVE TWO SHITS ABOUT *US?* FUCK, NO.
I ALWAYS FIGURED I WAS DESTINED FOR SOMETHING *BIGGER*.
BADLANDS CAFE
WE GOTTA LOOK OUT FOR OURSELVES, BRO.

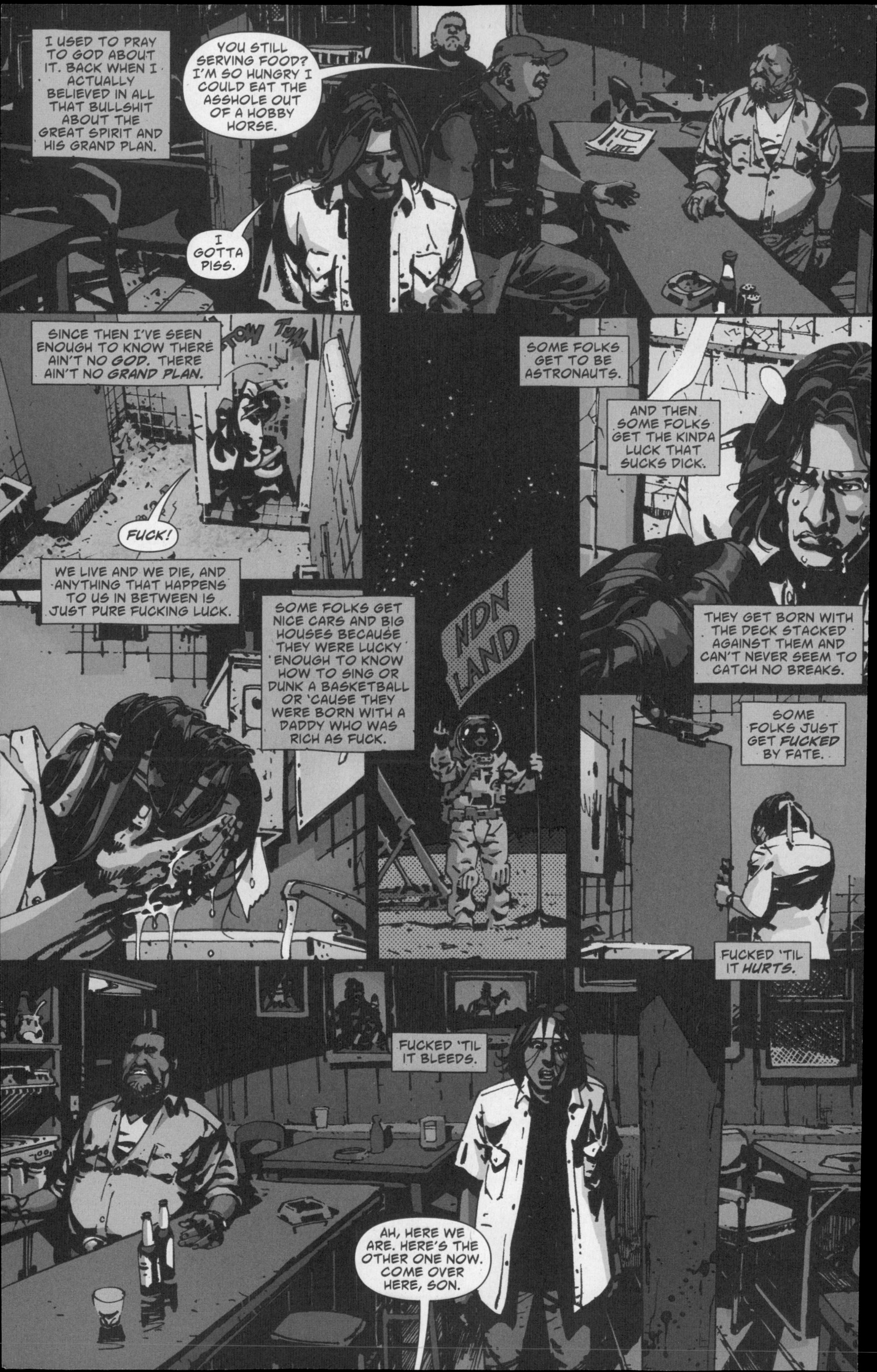
I USED TO PRAY TO GOD ABOUT IT. BACK WHEN I ACTUALLY BELIEVED IN ALL THAT BULLSHIT ABOUT THE GREAT SPIRIT AND HIS GRAND PLAN.
YOU STILL SERVING FOOD? I'M SO HUNGRY I COULD EAT THE ASSHOLE OUT OF A HOBBY HORSE.
I GOTTA PISS.
SINCE THEN I'VE SEEN ENOUGH TO KNOW THERE AIN'T NO GOD. THERE AIN'T NO GRAND PLAN.
FUCK!
WE LIVE AND WE DIE, AND ANYTHING THAT HAPPENS TO US IN BETWEEN IS JUST PURE FUCKING LUCK.
SOME FOLKS GET NICE CARS AND BIG HOUSES BECAUSE THEY WERE LUCKY ENOUGH TO KNOW HOW TO SING OR DUNK A BASKETBALL OR 'CAUSE THEY WERE BORN WITH A DADDY WHO WAS RICH AS FUCK.
NDN LAND
SOME FOLKS GET TO BE ASTRONAUTS.
AND THEN SOME FOLKS GET THE KINDA LUCK THAT SUCKS DICK.
THEY GET BORN WITH THE DECK STACKED AGAINST THEM AND CAN'T NEVER SEEM TO CATCH NO BREAKS.
SOME FOLKS JUST GET FUCKED BY FATE.
FUCKED 'TIL IT HURTS.
FUCKED 'TIL IT BLEEDS.
AH, HERE WE ARE. HERE'S THE OTHER ONE NOW. COME OVER HERE, SON.

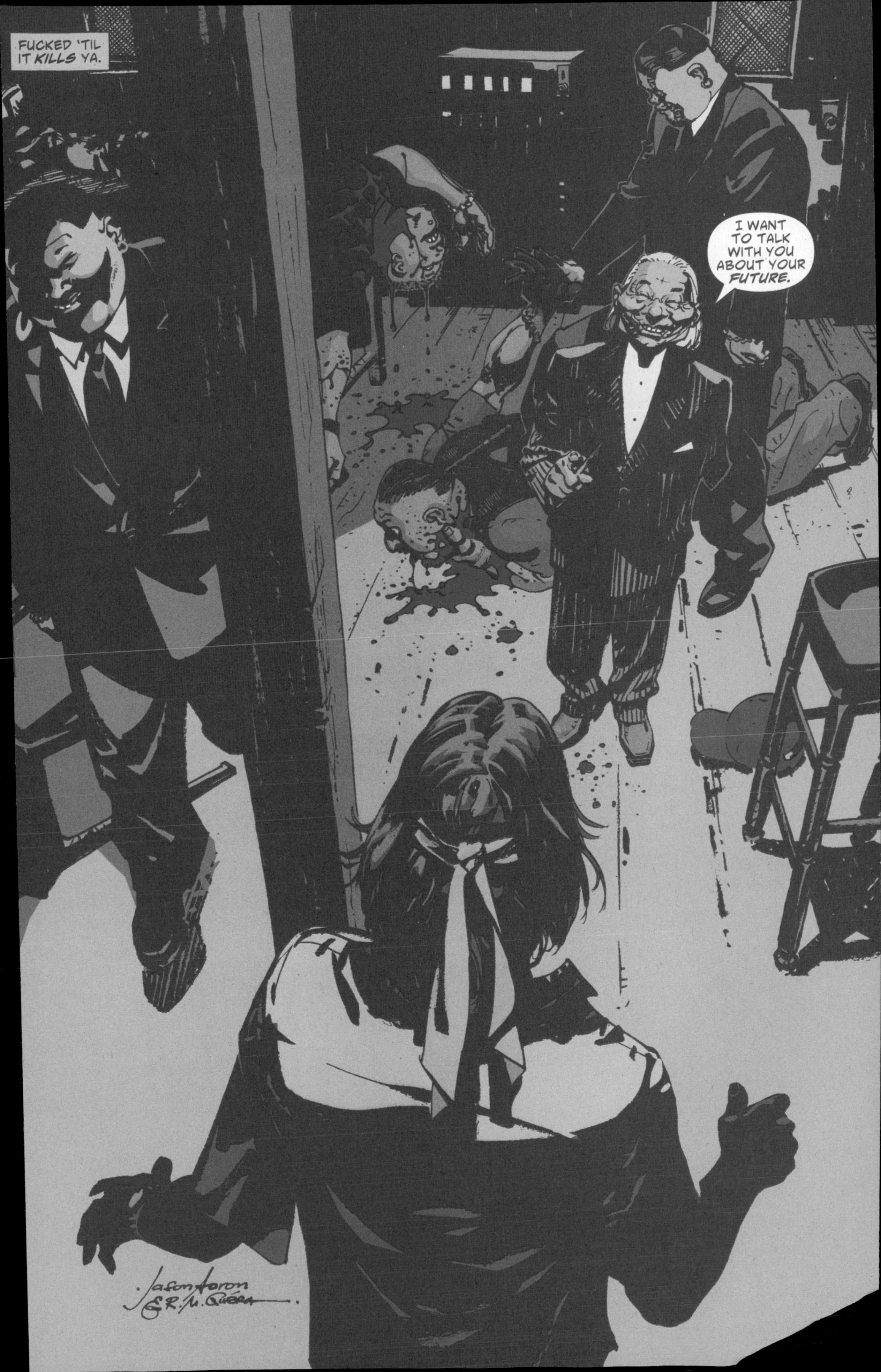
FUCKED 'TIL IT KILLS YA.
I WANT TO TALK WITH YOU ABOUT YOUR FUTURE.
Jason Aaron
E.R.M. Guéra

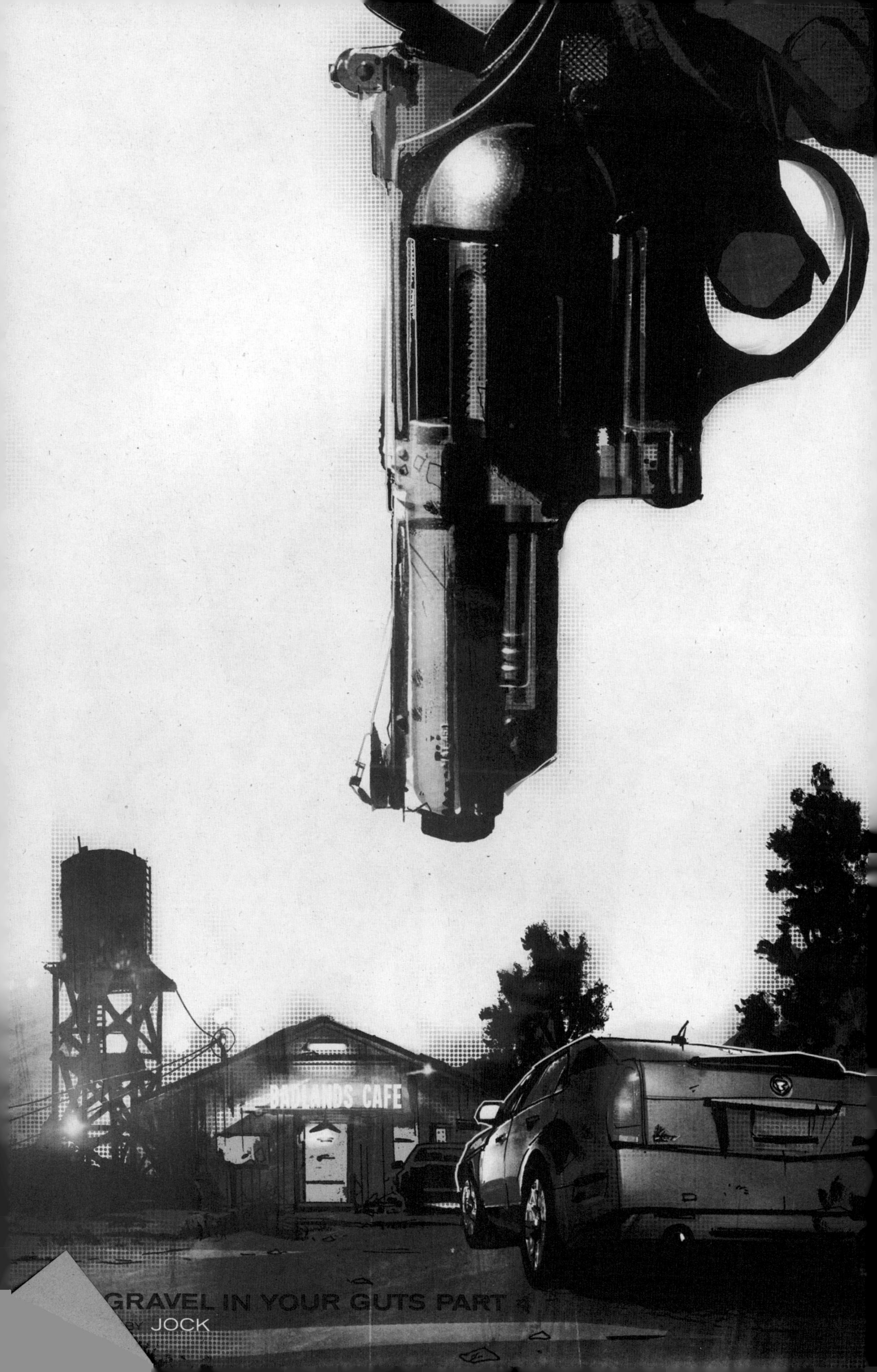
BADLANDS CAFE
GRAVEL IN YOUR GUTS PART 4
BY JOCK

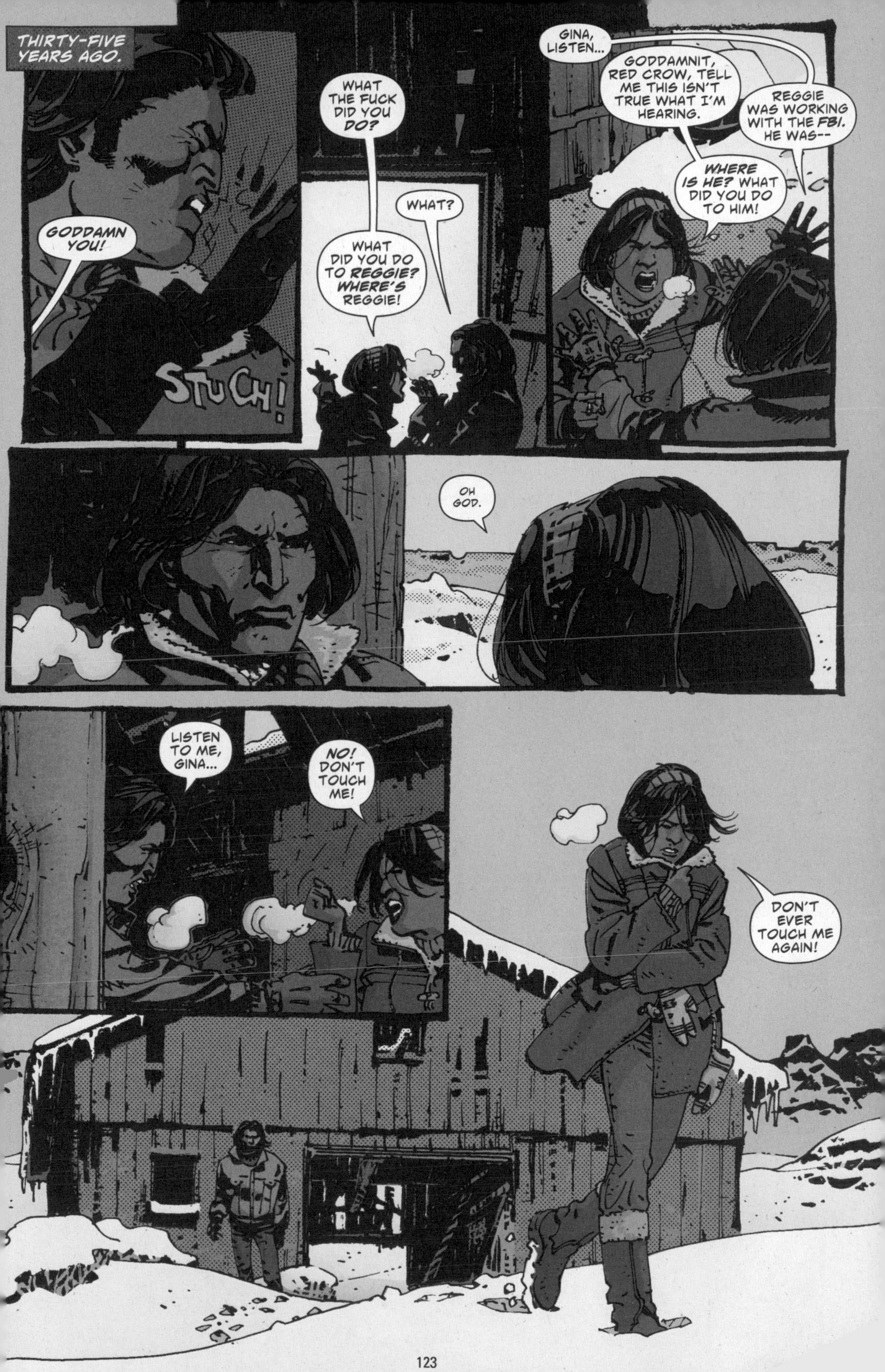

THIRTY-FIVE YEARS AGO.
GODDAMN YOU!
STUCH!
WHAT THE FUCK DID YOU DO?
WHAT?
WHAT DID YOU DO TO REGGIE? WHERE'S REGGIE!
GINA, LISTEN...
GODDAMNIT, RED CROW, TELL ME THIS ISN'T TRUE WHAT I'M HEARING.
REGGIE WAS WORKING WITH THE FBI. HE WAS--
WHERE IS HE? WHAT DID YOU DO TO HIM!
OH GOD.
LISTEN TO ME, GINA...
NO! DON'T TOUCH ME!
DON'T EVER TOUCH ME AGAIN!

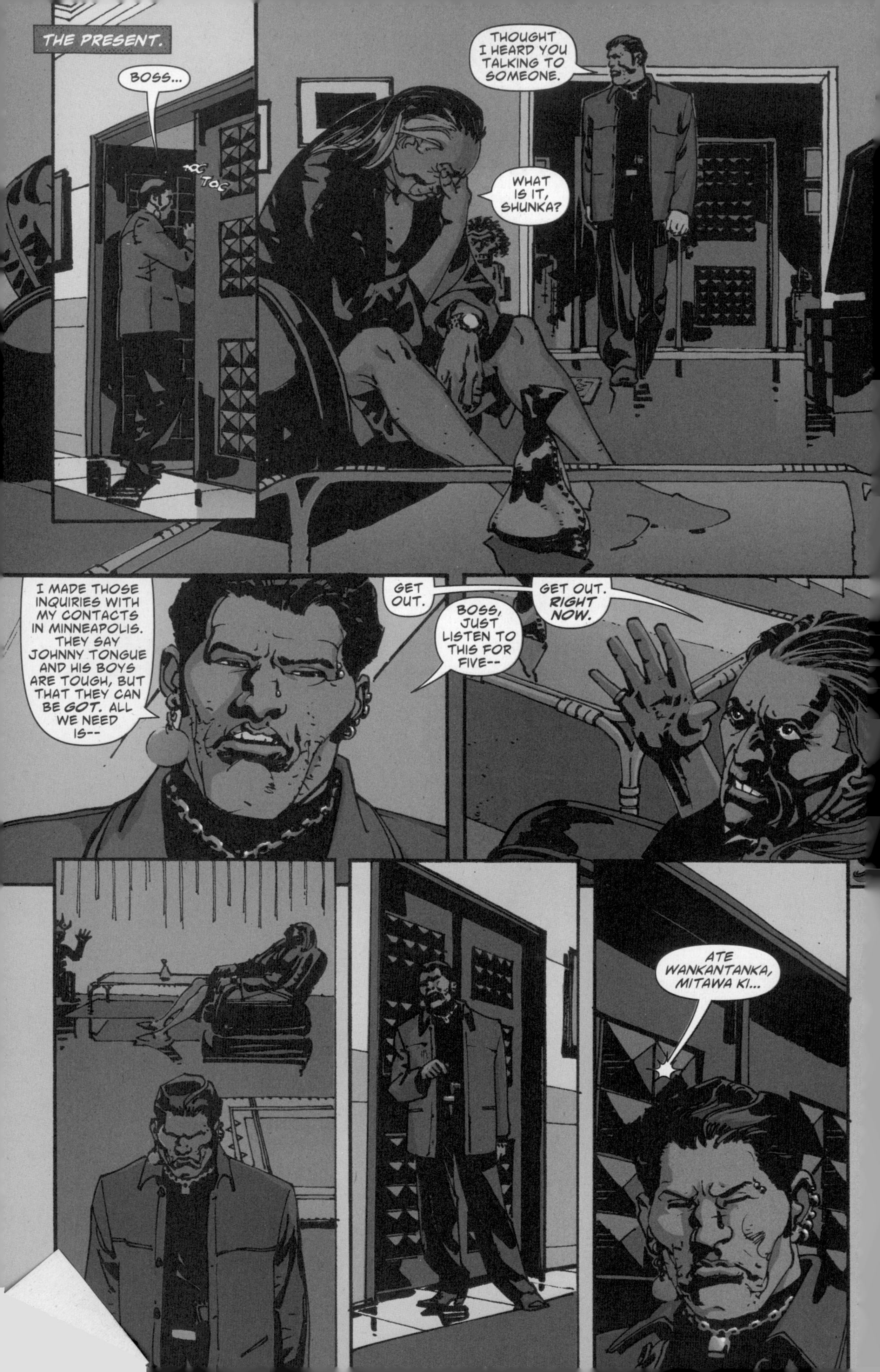
THE PRESENT.
BOSS...
TOC TOC
THOUGHT I HEARD YOU TALKING TO SOMEONE.
WHAT IS IT, SHUNKA?
I MADE THOSE INQUIRIES WITH MY CONTACTS IN MINNEAPOLIS. THEY SAY JOHNNY TONGUE AND HIS BOYS ARE TOUGH, BUT THAT THEY CAN BE *GOT*. ALL WE NEED IS--
GET OUT.
BOSS, JUST LISTEN TO THIS FOR FIVE--
GET OUT. *RIGHT NOW.*
ATE WANKANTANKA, MITAWA KI...

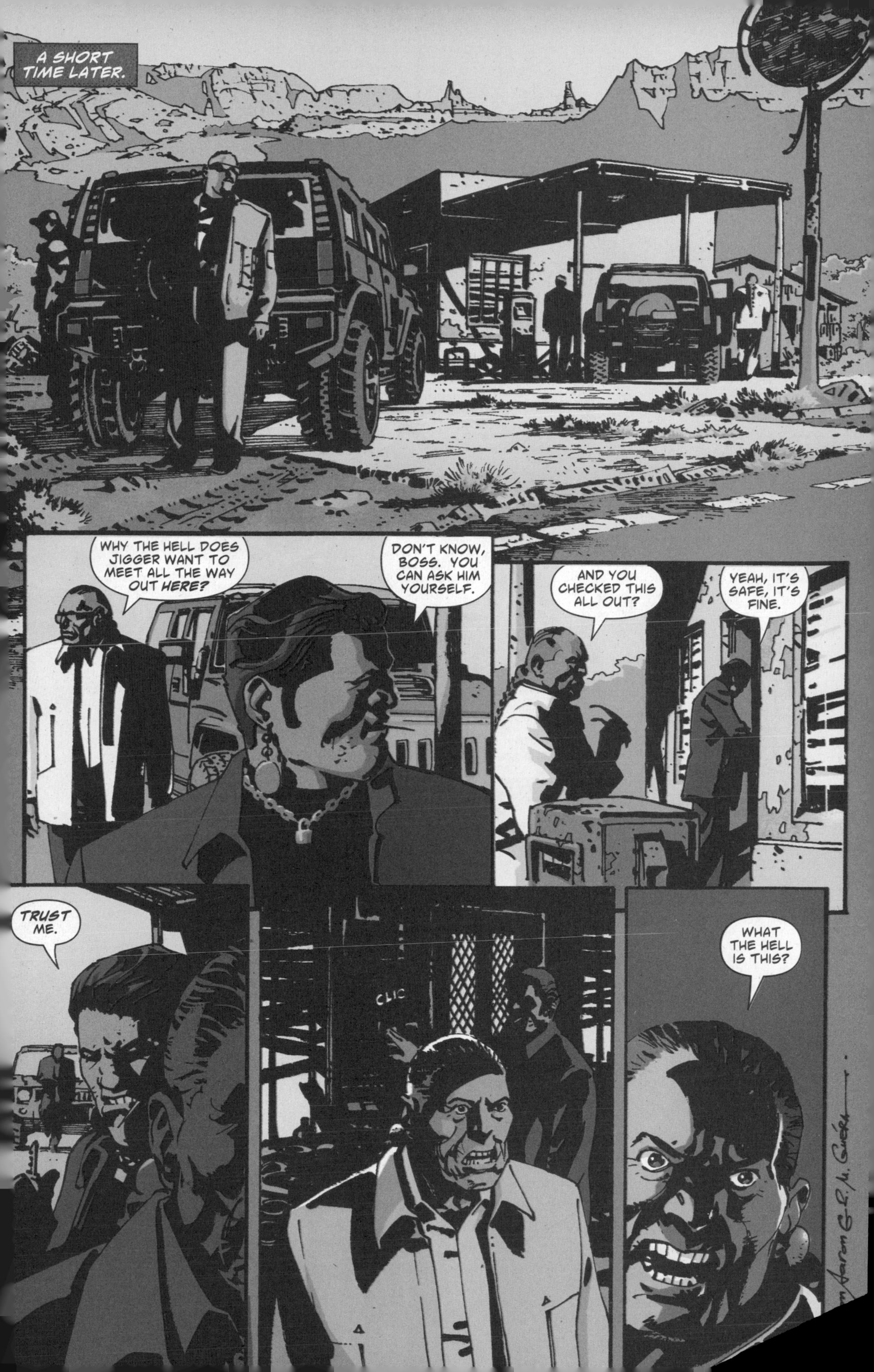
A SHORT TIME LATER.
WHY THE HELL DOES JIGGER WANT TO MEET ALL THE WAY OUT HERE?
DON'T KNOW, BOSS. YOU CAN ASK HIM YOURSELF.
AND YOU CHECKED THIS ALL OUT?
YEAH, IT'S SAFE, IT'S FINE.
TRUST ME.
CLIC
WHAT THE HELL IS THIS?

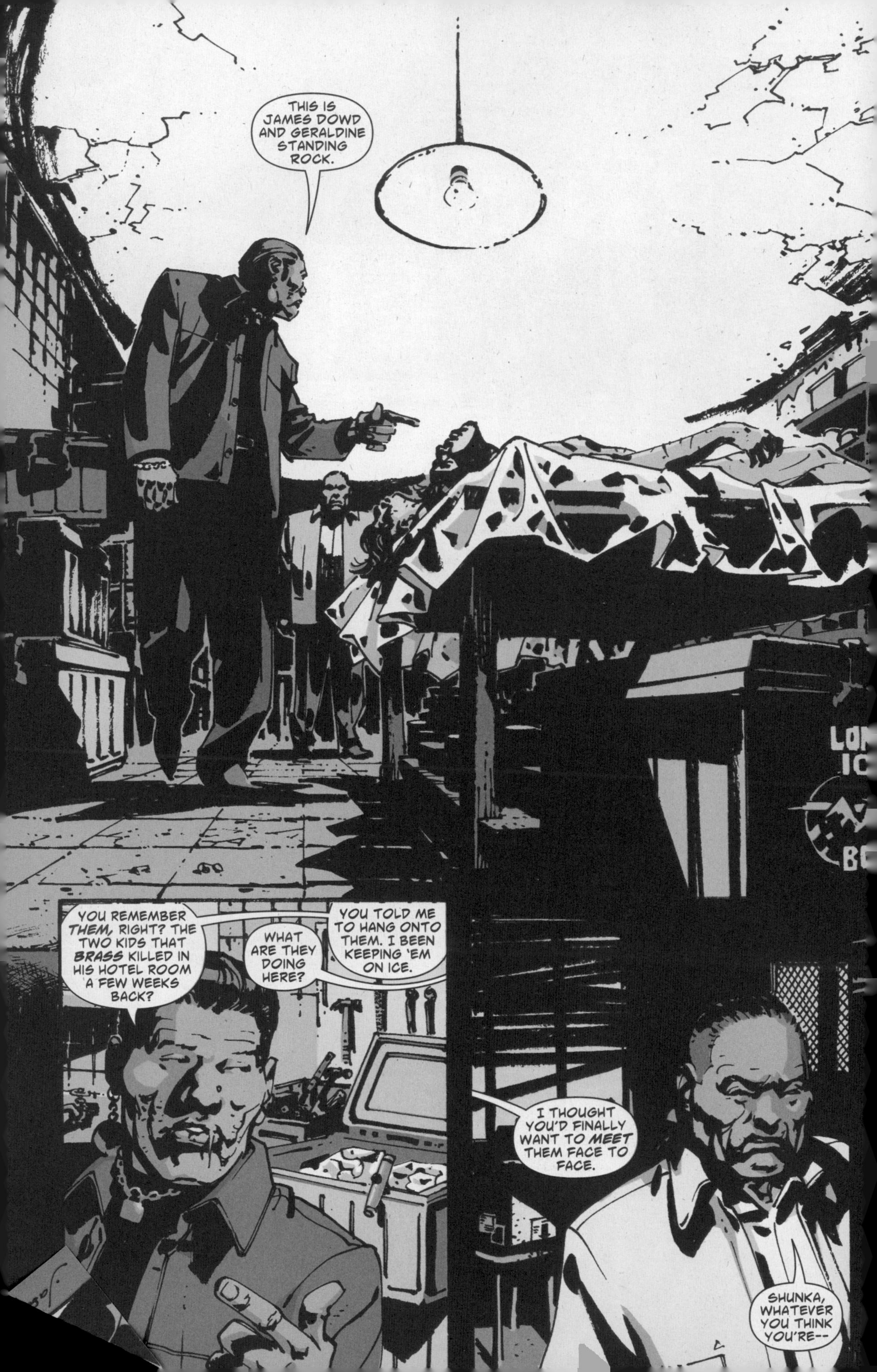
THIS IS JAMES DOWD AND GERALDINE STANDING ROCK.
YOU REMEMBER *THEM,* RIGHT? THE TWO KIDS THAT *BRASS* KILLED IN HIS HOTEL ROOM A FEW WEEKS BACK?
WHAT ARE THEY DOING HERE?
YOU TOLD ME TO HANG ONTO THEM. I BEEN KEEPING 'EM ON ICE.
I THOUGHT YOU'D FINALLY WANT TO *MEET* THEM FACE TO FACE.
SHUNKA, WHATEVER YOU THINK YOU'RE--

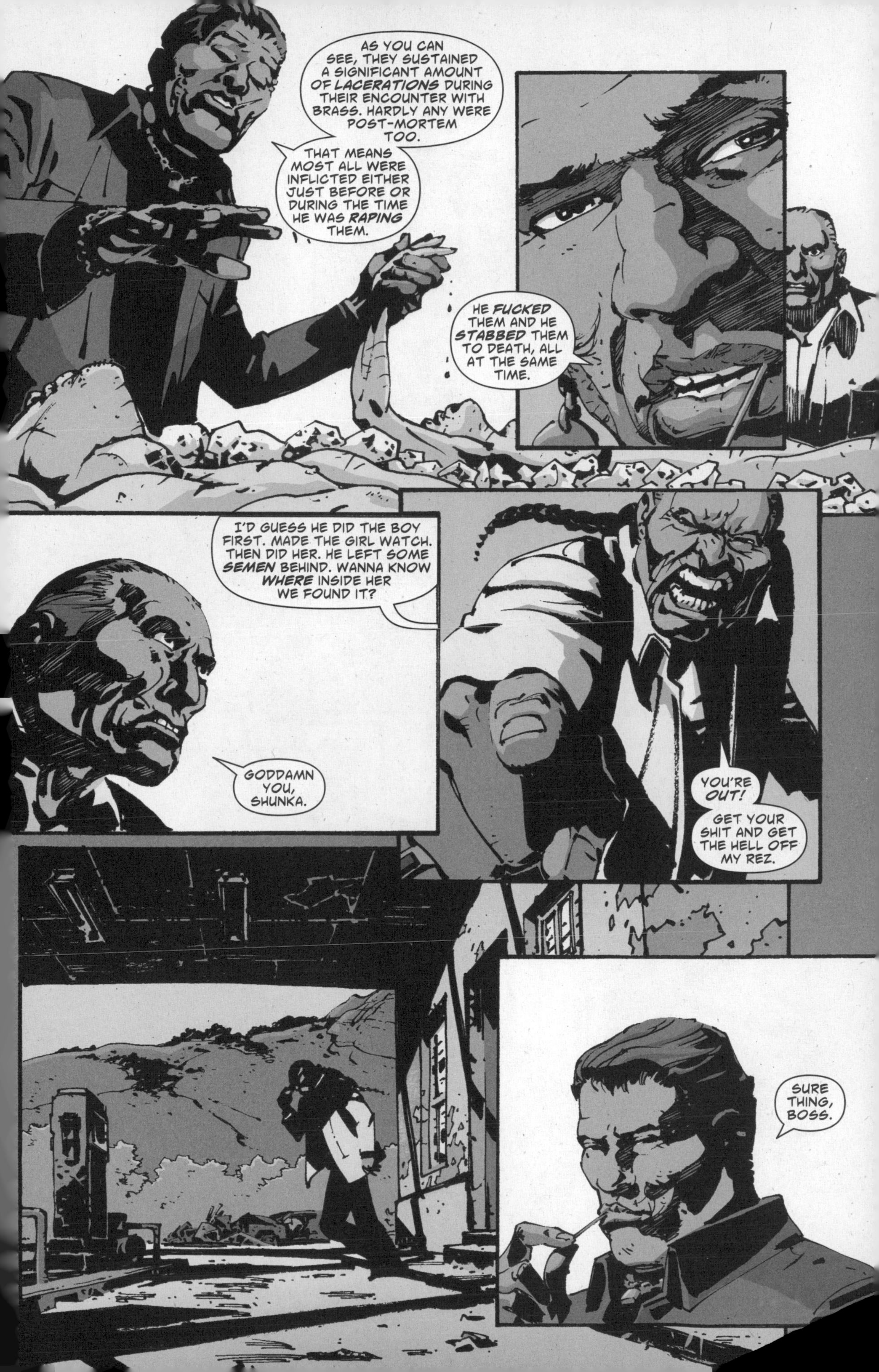
AS YOU CAN SEE, THEY SUSTAINED A SIGNIFICANT AMOUNT OF LACERATIONS DURING THEIR ENCOUNTER WITH BRASS. HARDLY ANY WERE POST-MORTEM TOO.
THAT MEANS MOST ALL WERE INFLICTED EITHER JUST BEFORE OR DURING THE TIME HE WAS RAPING THEM.
HE FUCKED THEM AND HE STABBED THEM TO DEATH, ALL AT THE SAME TIME.
I'D GUESS HE DID THE BOY FIRST. MADE THE GIRL WATCH. THEN DID HER. HE LEFT SOME SEMEN BEHIND. WANNA KNOW WHERE INSIDE HER WE FOUND IT?
GODDAMN YOU, SHUNKA.
YOU'RE OUT!
GET YOUR SHIT AND GET THE HELL OFF MY REZ.
SURE THING, BOSS.

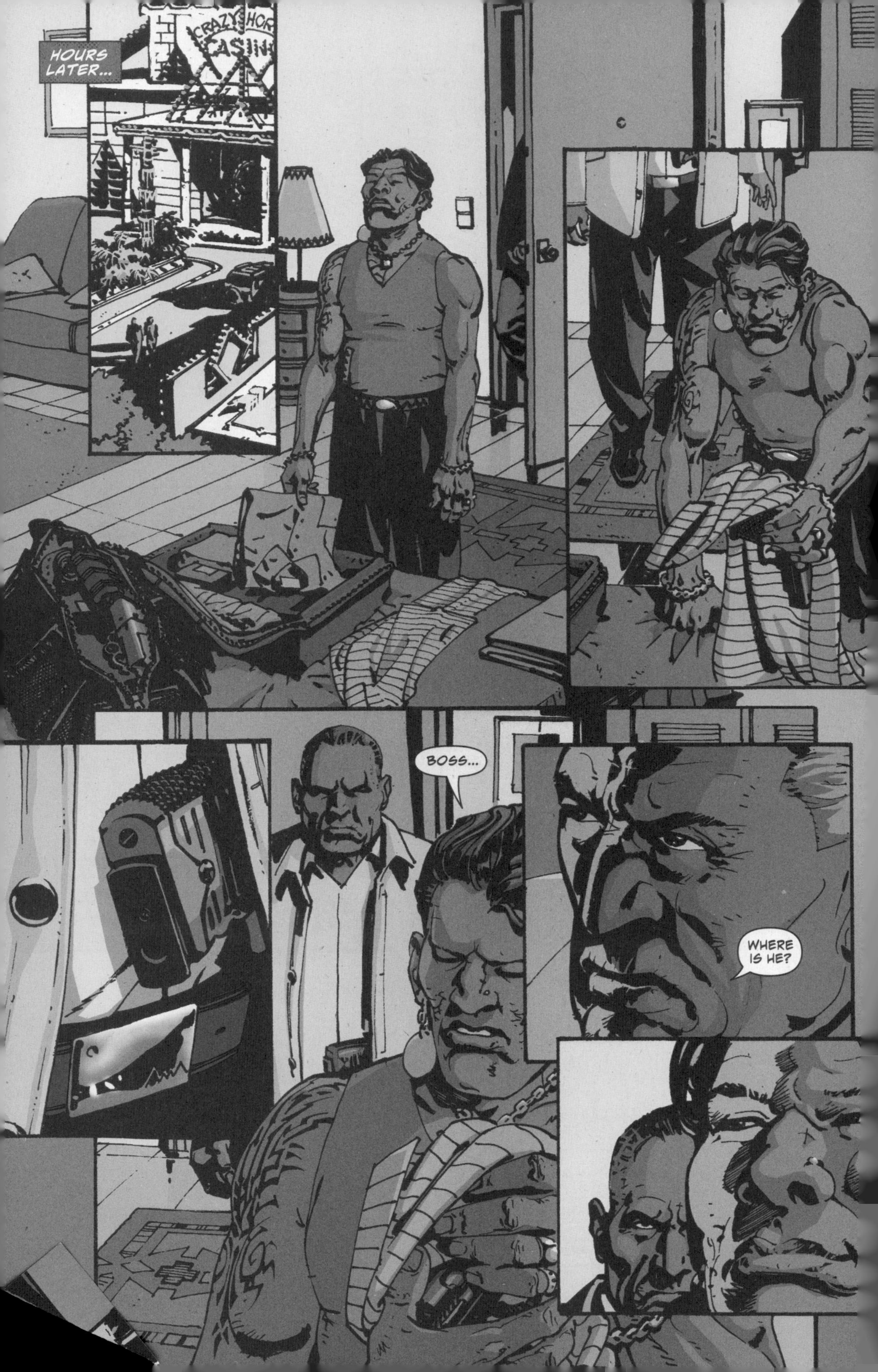
HOURS LATER...
CRAZY HORSE CASINO
BOSS...
WHERE IS HE?

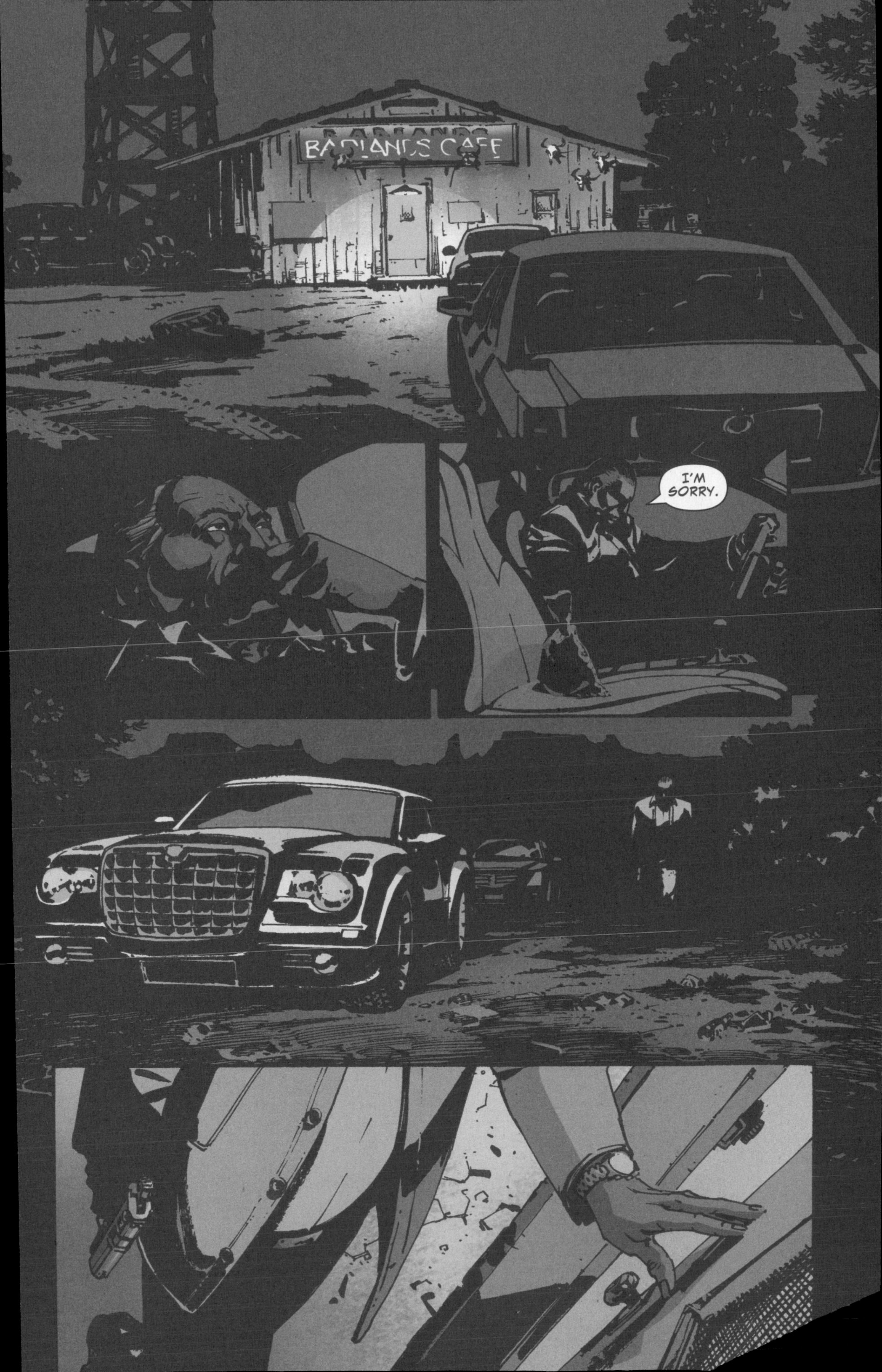
BADLANDS CAFE
I'M SORRY.

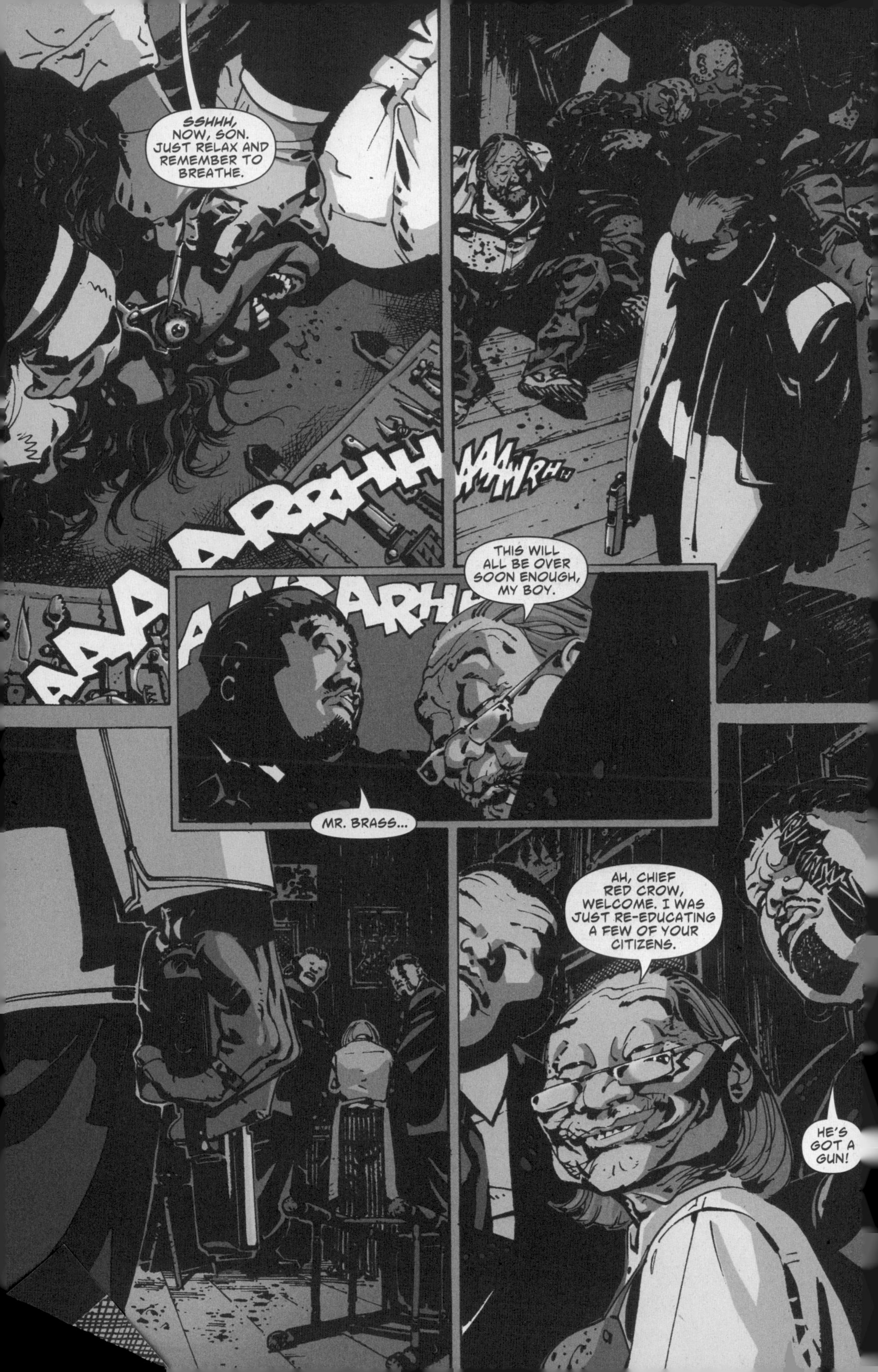
SSHHH, NOW, SON. JUST RELAX AND REMEMBER TO BREATHE.
ARRRAHHAAAARH!!
AAAAAARH!!
THIS WILL ALL BE OVER SOON ENOUGH, MY BOY.
MR. BRASS...
AH, CHIEF RED CROW, WELCOME. I WAS JUST RE-EDUCATING A FEW OF YOUR CITIZENS.
HE'S GOT A GUN!

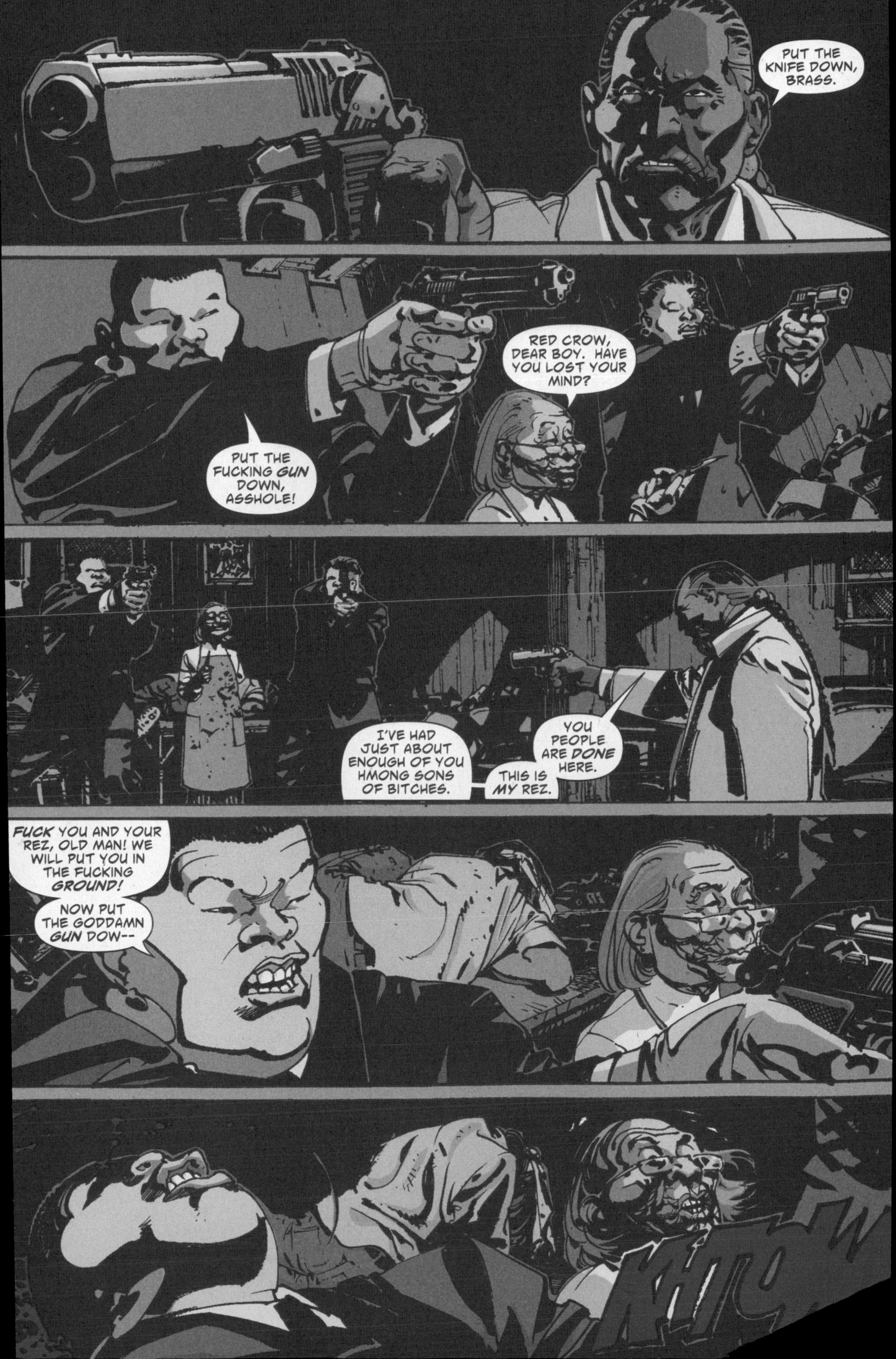
PUT THE KNIFE DOWN, BRASS.
RED CROW, DEAR BOY. HAVE YOU LOST YOUR MIND?
PUT THE FUCKING *GUN* DOWN, ASSHOLE!
YOU PEOPLE ARE *DONE* HERE.
I'VE HAD JUST ABOUT ENOUGH OF YOU HMONG SONS OF BITCHES.
THIS IS *MY* REZ.
FUCK YOU AND YOUR REZ, OLD MAN! WE WILL PUT YOU IN THE FUCKING *GROUND!*
NOW PUT THE GODDAMN *GUN* DOW--

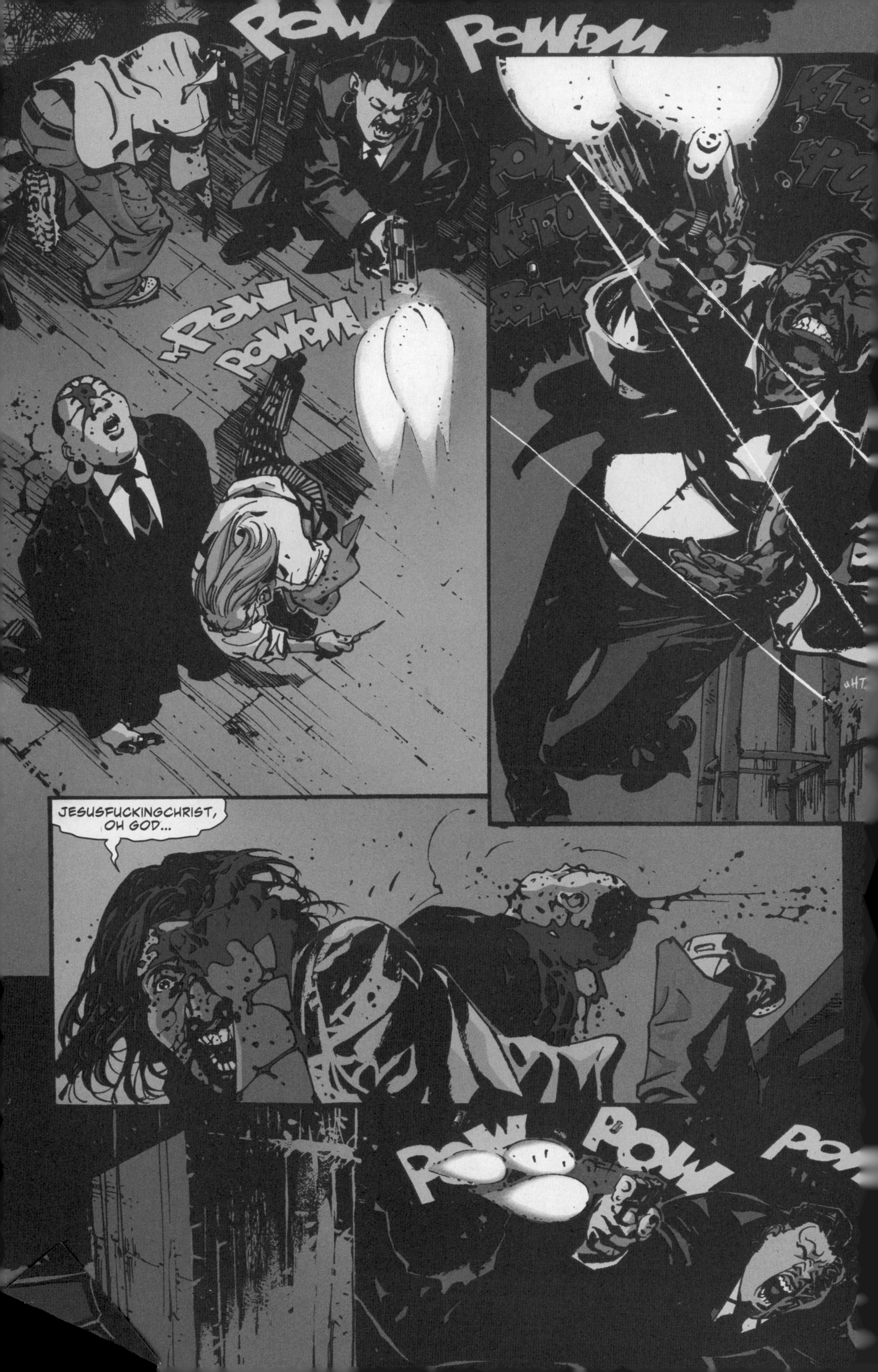
POW
POWPOW
POW
POWPOW
JESUSFUCKINGCHRIST, OH GOD...
POW
POW

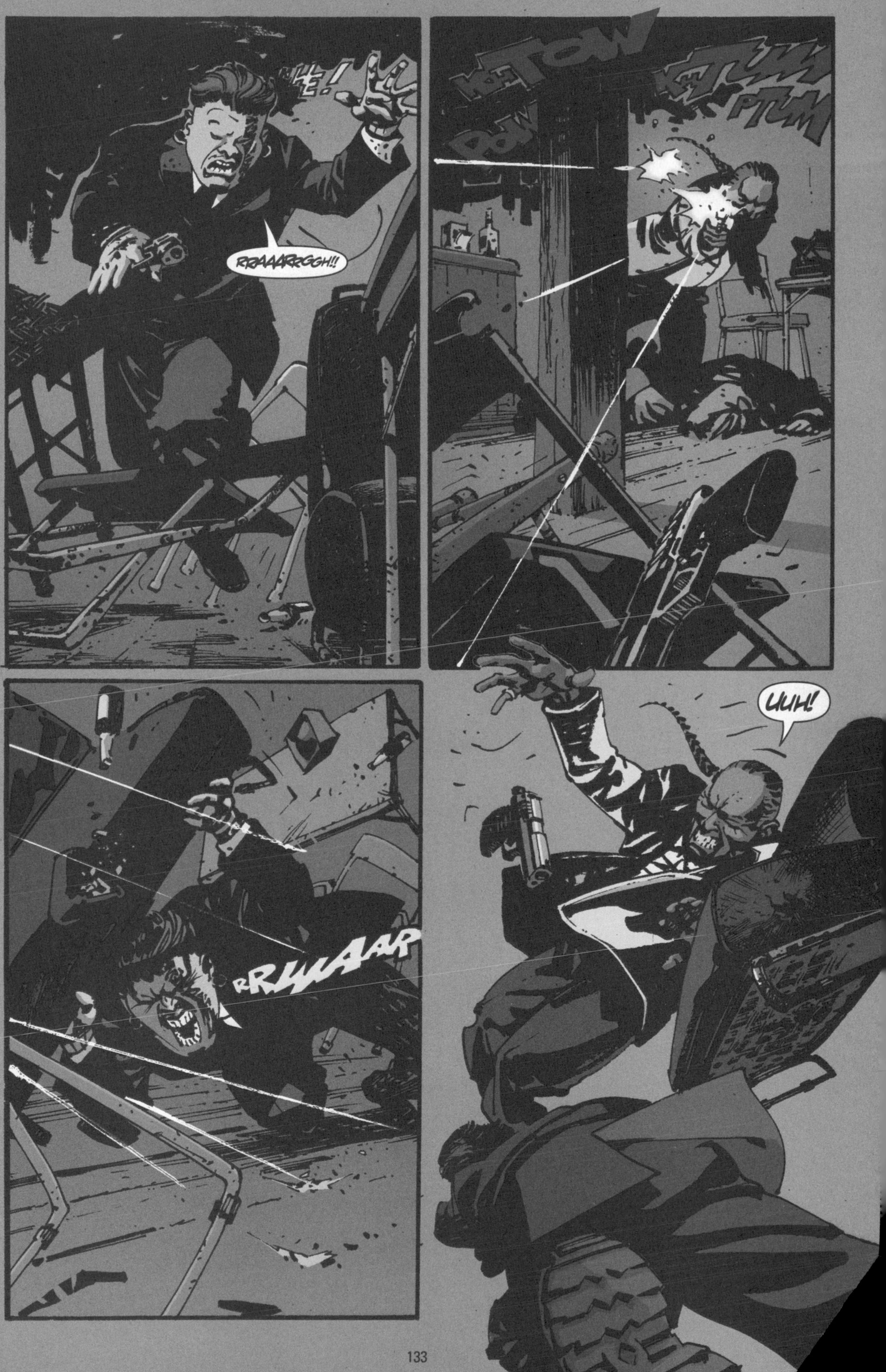
RRAAARRGGH!!
KATOW
KATUMM
PTUM
RRWAAR
UUH!

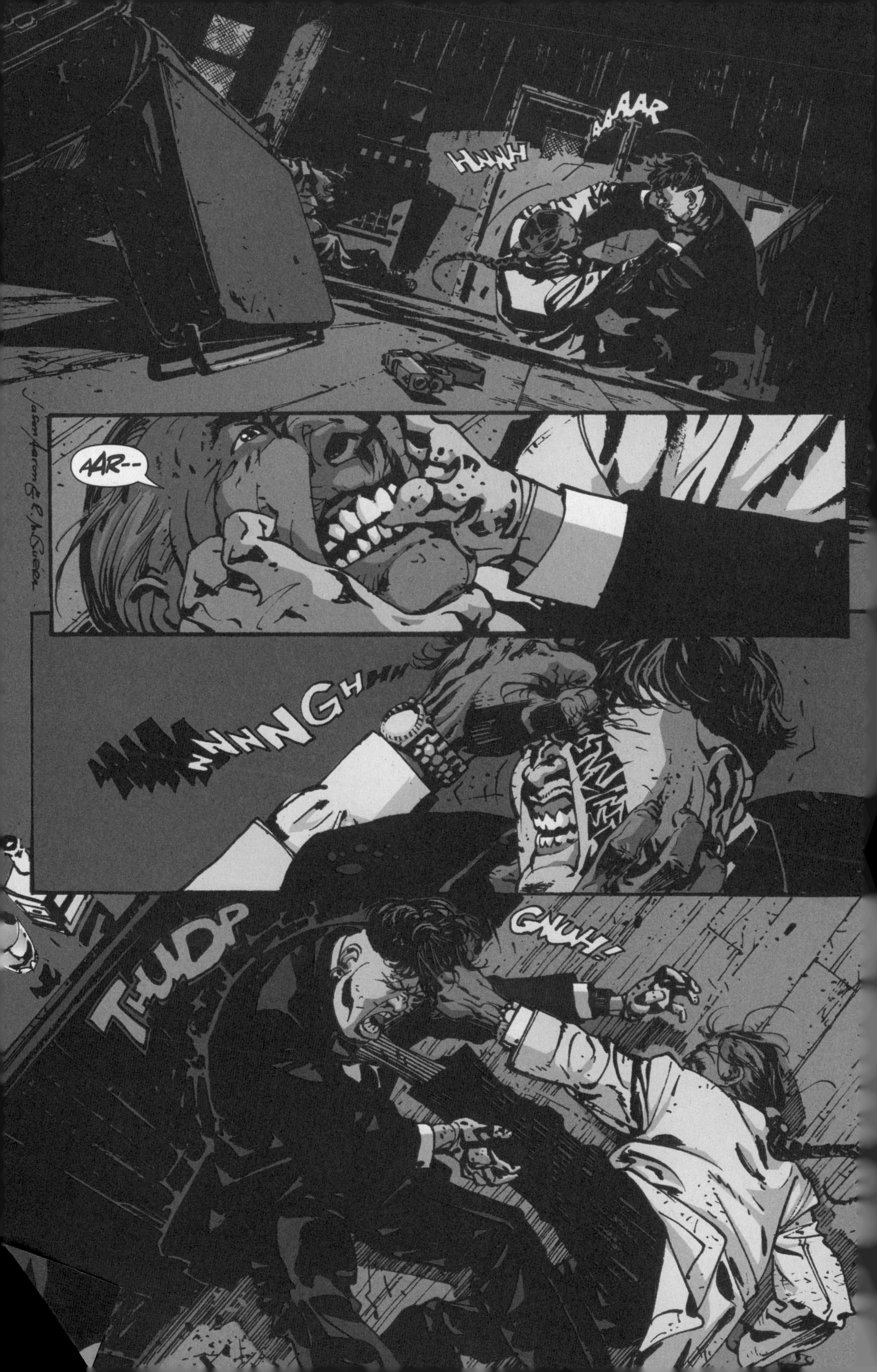
HANH
AAAAR
AAR--
NNNNGH
THUDP
GNUH!

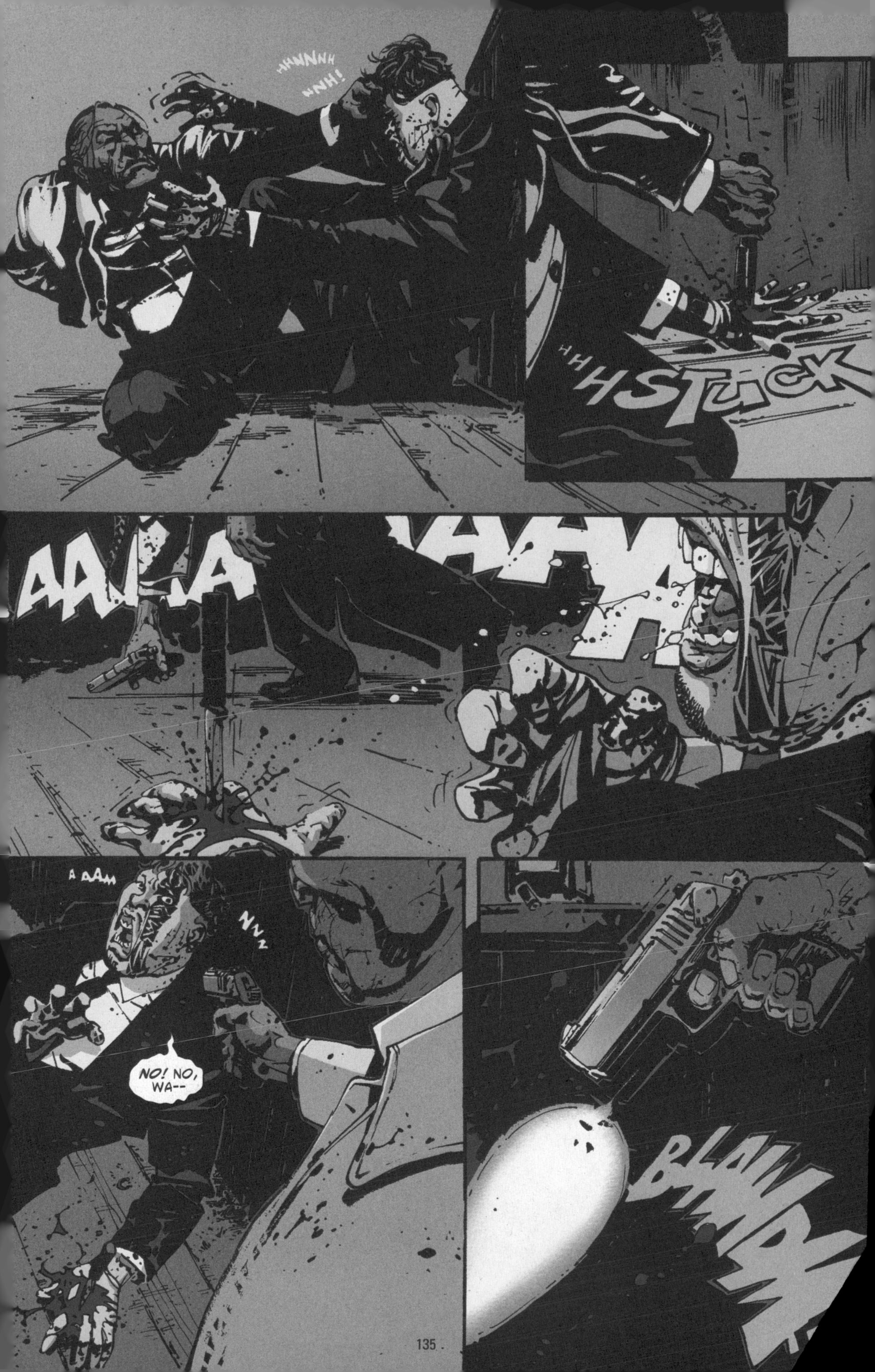

HHNNNH NNH!
HHHSTUCK
AAAAAAAAH
A AAAH
NN N
NO! NO, WA--
BLAM

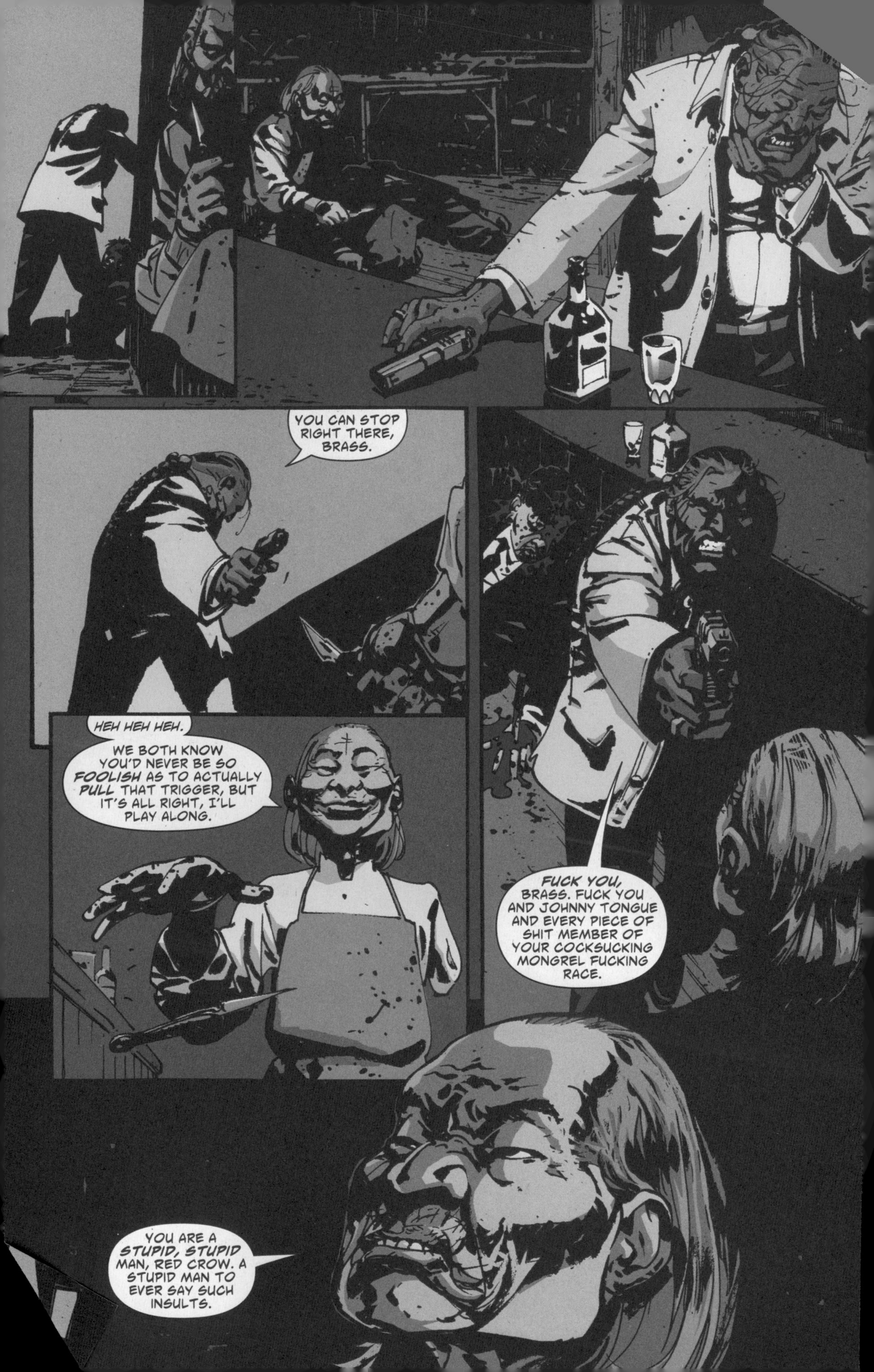
YOU CAN STOP RIGHT THERE, BRASS.
FUCK YOU, BRASS. FUCK YOU AND JOHNNY TONGUE AND EVERY PIECE OF SHIT MEMBER OF YOUR COCKSUCKING MONGREL FUCKING RACE.
HEH HEH HEH.
WE BOTH KNOW YOU'D NEVER BE SO FOOLISH AS TO ACTUALLY PULL THAT TRIGGER, BUT IT'S ALL RIGHT, I'LL PLAY ALONG.
YOU ARE A STUPID, STUPID MAN, RED CROW. A STUPID MAN TO EVER SAY SUCH INSULTS.

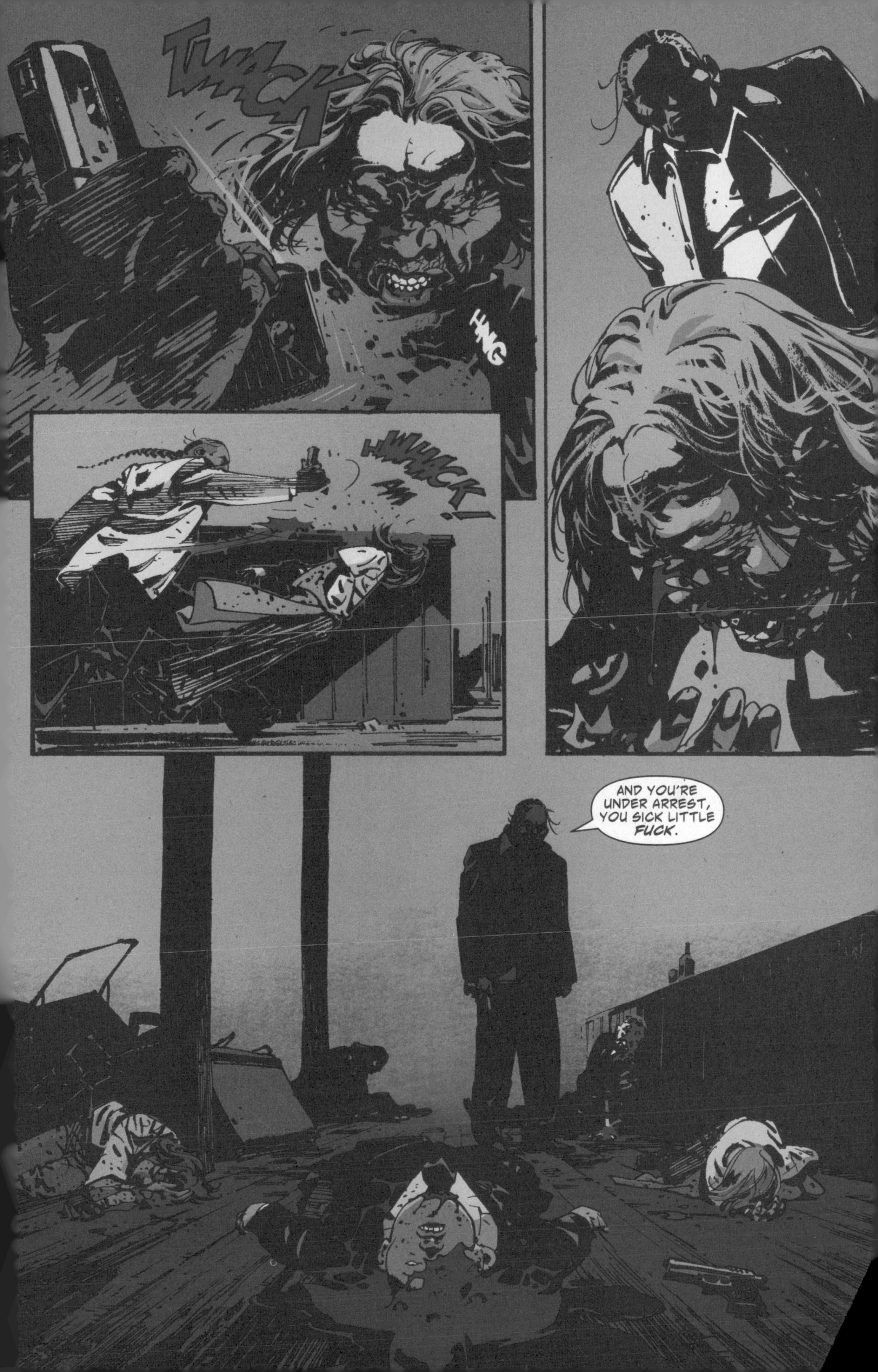
THWACK
HNG
HWHACK!
AH
AND YOU'RE UNDER ARREST, YOU SICK LITTLE FUCK.

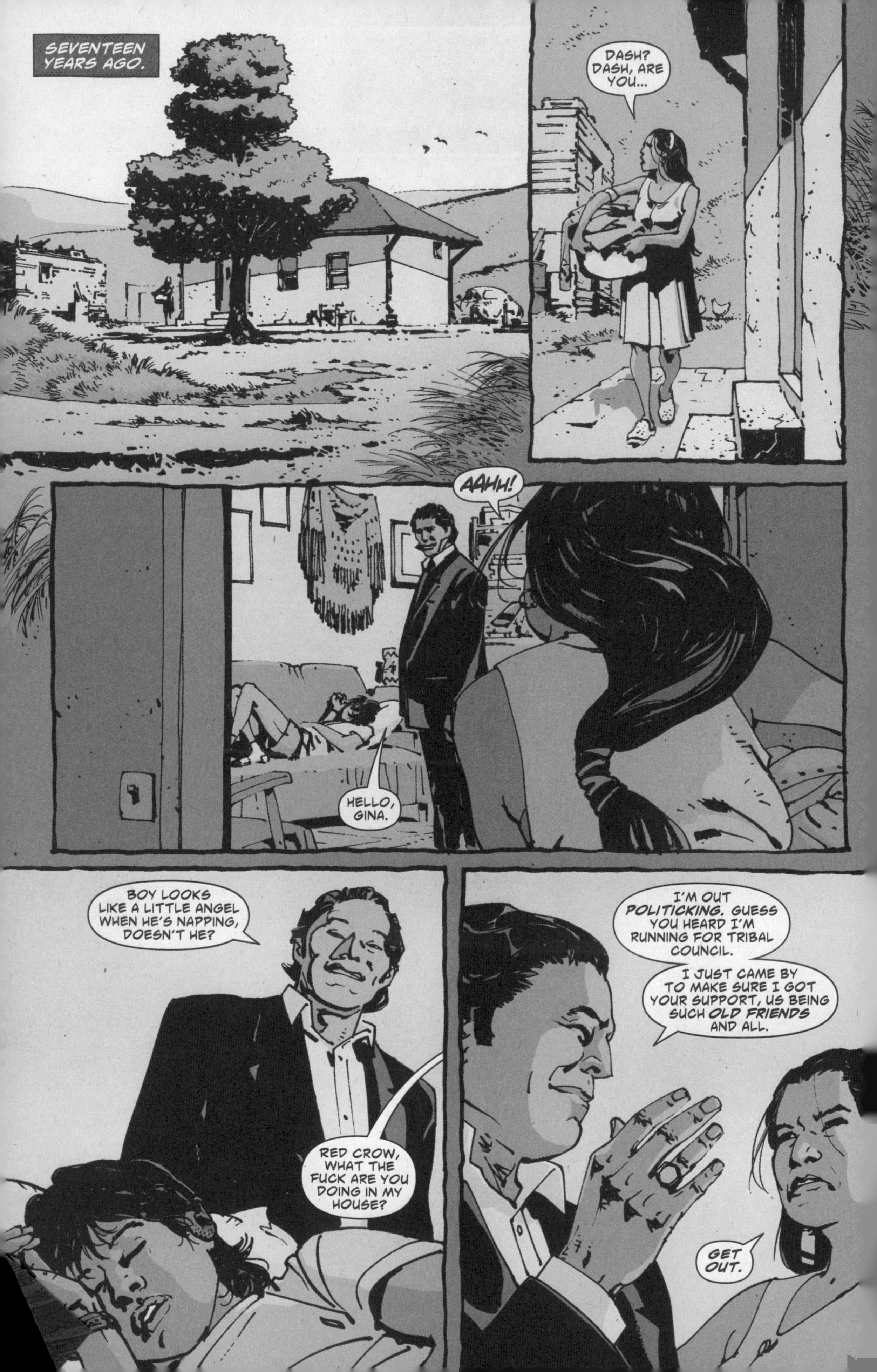
SEVENTEEN YEARS AGO.
DASH? DASH, ARE YOU...
AAHH!
HELLO, GINA.
BOY LOOKS LIKE A LITTLE ANGEL WHEN HE'S NAPPING, DOESN'T HE?
RED CROW, WHAT THE FUCK ARE YOU DOING IN MY HOUSE?
I'M OUT POLITICKING. GUESS YOU HEARD I'M RUNNING FOR TRIBAL COUNCIL.
I JUST CAME BY TO MAKE SURE I GOT YOUR SUPPORT, US BEING SUCH OLD FRIENDS AND ALL.
GET OUT.

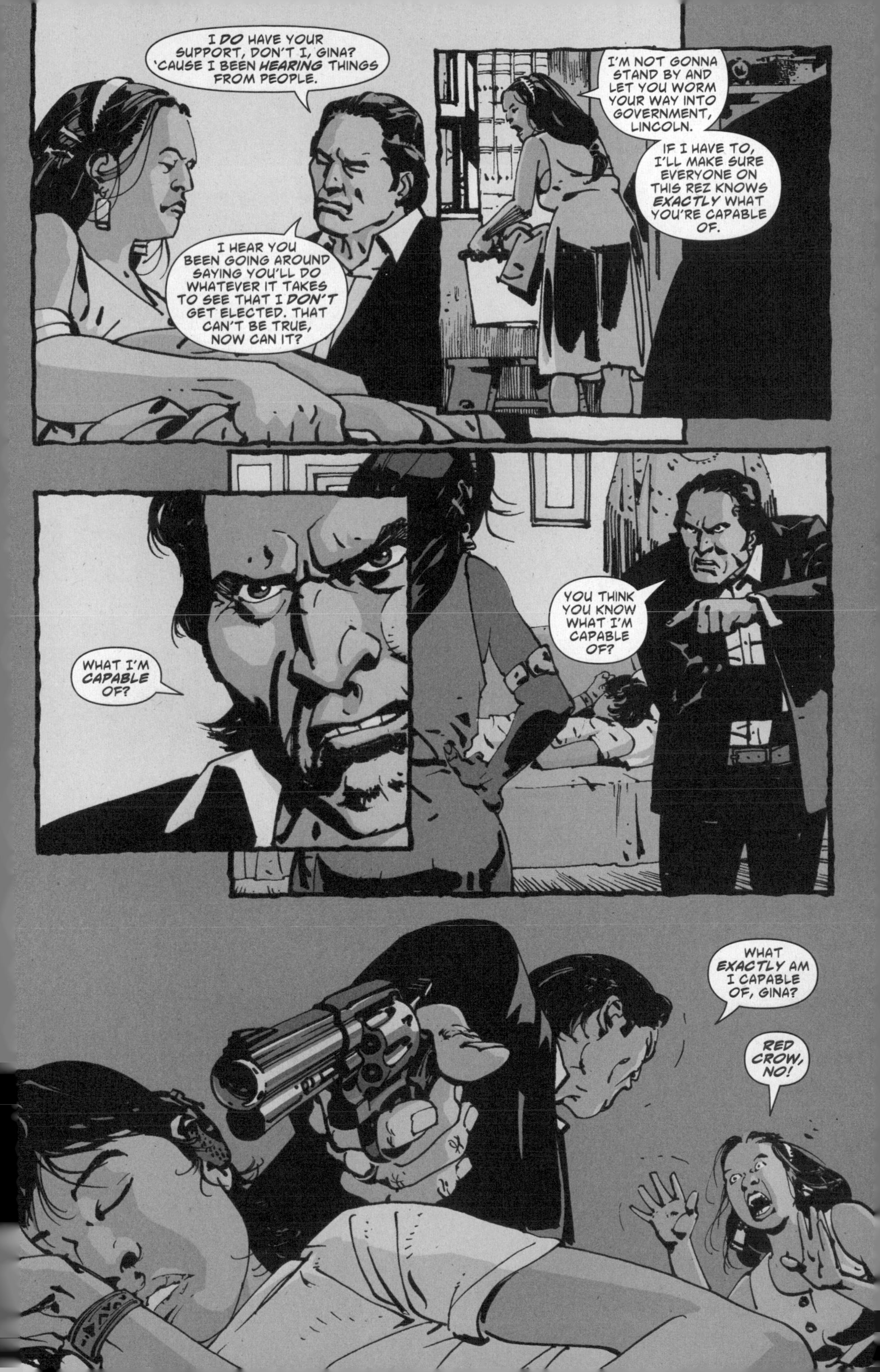
I DO HAVE YOUR SUPPORT, DON'T I, GINA? 'CAUSE I BEEN HEARING THINGS FROM PEOPLE.
I HEAR YOU BEEN GOING AROUND SAYING YOU'LL DO WHATEVER IT TAKES TO SEE THAT I DON'T GET ELECTED. THAT CAN'T BE TRUE, NOW CAN IT?
I'M NOT GONNA STAND BY AND LET YOU WORM YOUR WAY INTO GOVERNMENT, LINCOLN.
IF I HAVE TO, I'LL MAKE SURE EVERYONE ON THIS REZ KNOWS EXACTLY WHAT YOU'RE CAPABLE OF.
YOU THINK YOU KNOW WHAT I'M CAPABLE OF?
WHAT I'M CAPABLE OF?
WHAT EXACTLY AM I CAPABLE OF, GINA?
RED CROW, NO!

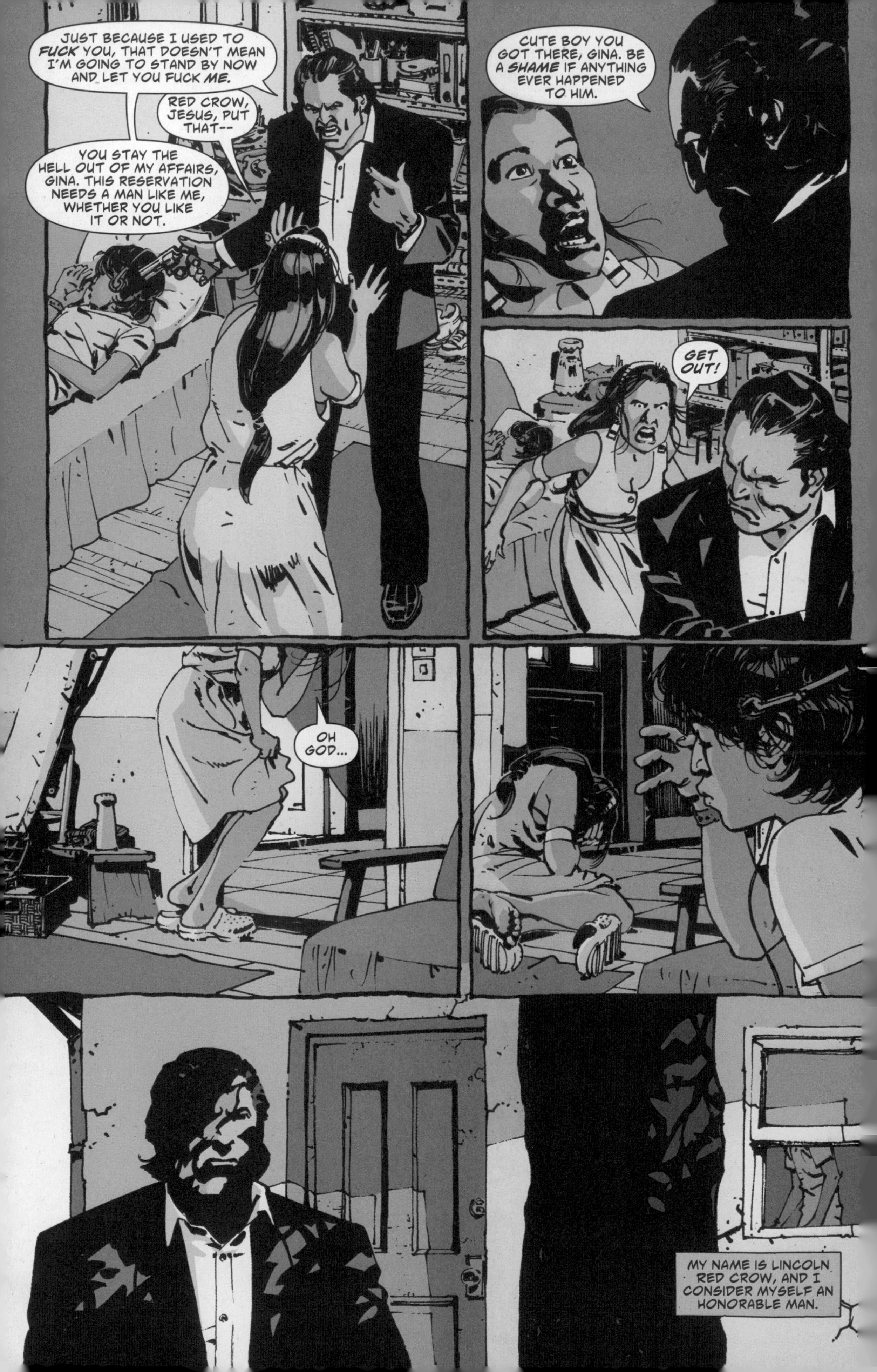
JUST BECAUSE I USED TO FUCK YOU, THAT DOESN'T MEAN I'M GOING TO STAND BY NOW AND LET YOU FUCK ME.
RED CROW, JESUS, PUT THAT--
YOU STAY THE HELL OUT OF MY AFFAIRS, GINA. THIS RESERVATION NEEDS A MAN LIKE ME, WHETHER YOU LIKE IT OR NOT.
CUTE BOY YOU GOT THERE, GINA. BE A SHAME IF ANYTHING EVER HAPPENED TO HIM.
GET OUT!
OH GOD...
MY NAME IS LINCOLN RED CROW, AND I CONSIDER MYSELF AN HONORABLE MAN.

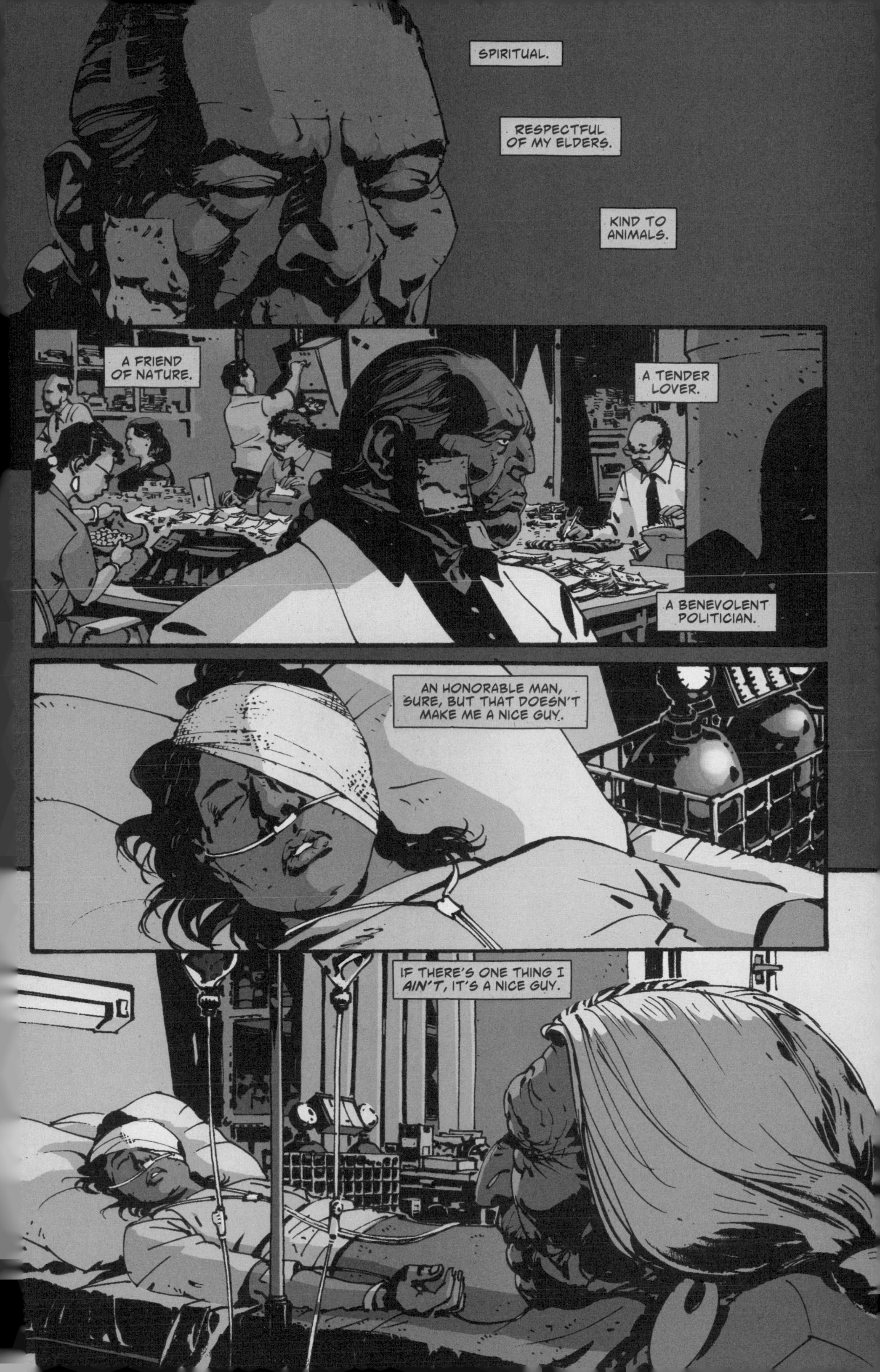
SPIRITUAL.
RESPECTFUL OF MY ELDERS.
KIND TO ANIMALS.
A FRIEND OF NATURE.
A TENDER LOVER.
A BENEVOLENT POLITICIAN.
AN HONORABLE MAN, SURE, BUT THAT DOESN'T MAKE ME A NICE GUY.
IF THERE'S ONE THING I *AIN'T*, IT'S A NICE GUY.

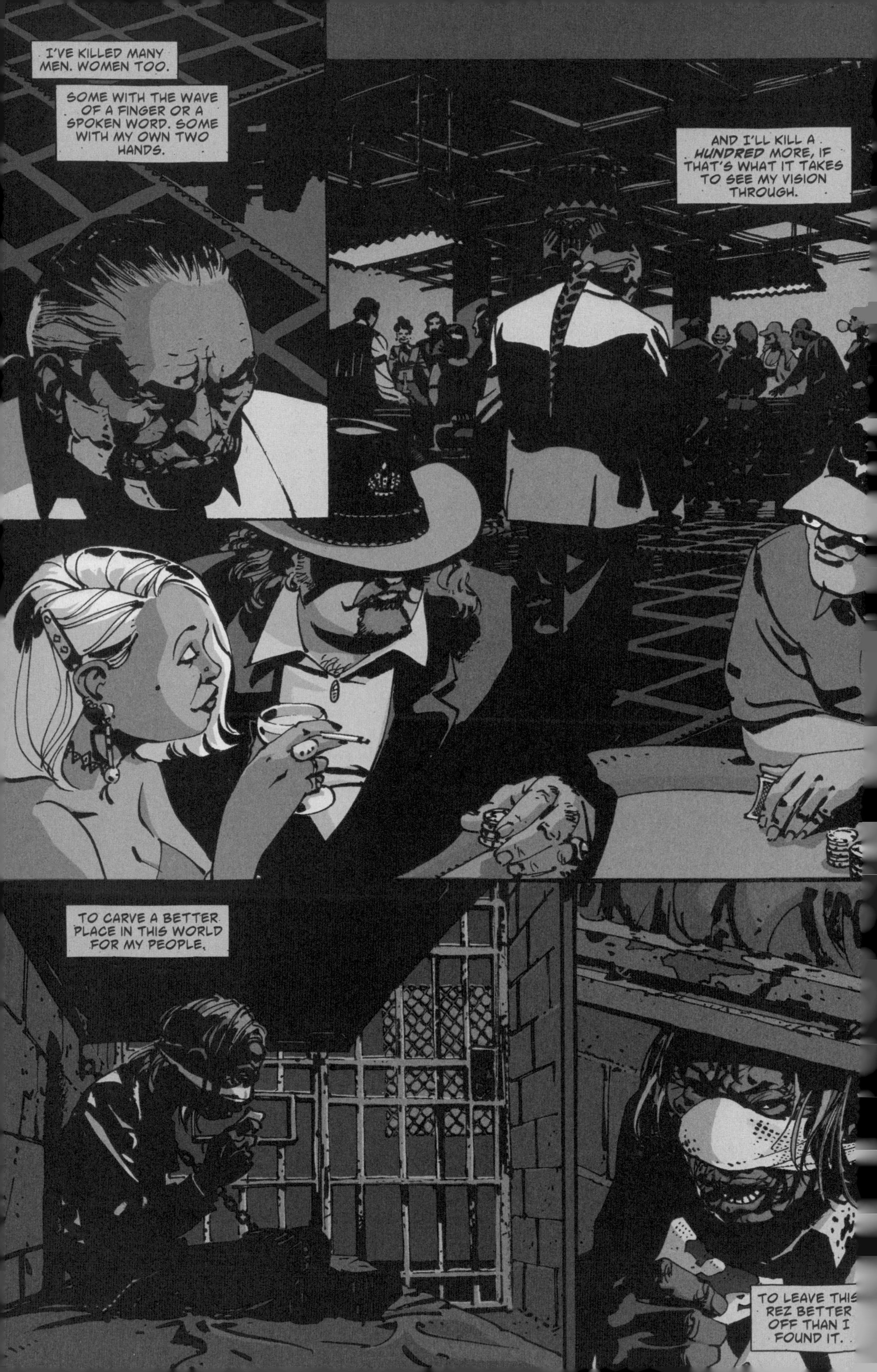
I'VE KILLED MANY MEN. WOMEN TOO.
SOME WITH THE WAVE OF A FINGER OR A SPOKEN WORD. SOME WITH MY OWN TWO HANDS.
AND I'LL KILL A *HUNDRED* MORE, IF THAT'S WHAT IT TAKES TO SEE MY VISION THROUGH.
TO CARVE A BETTER PLACE IN THIS WORLD FOR MY PEOPLE.
TO LEAVE THIS REZ BETTER OFF THAN I FOUND IT.

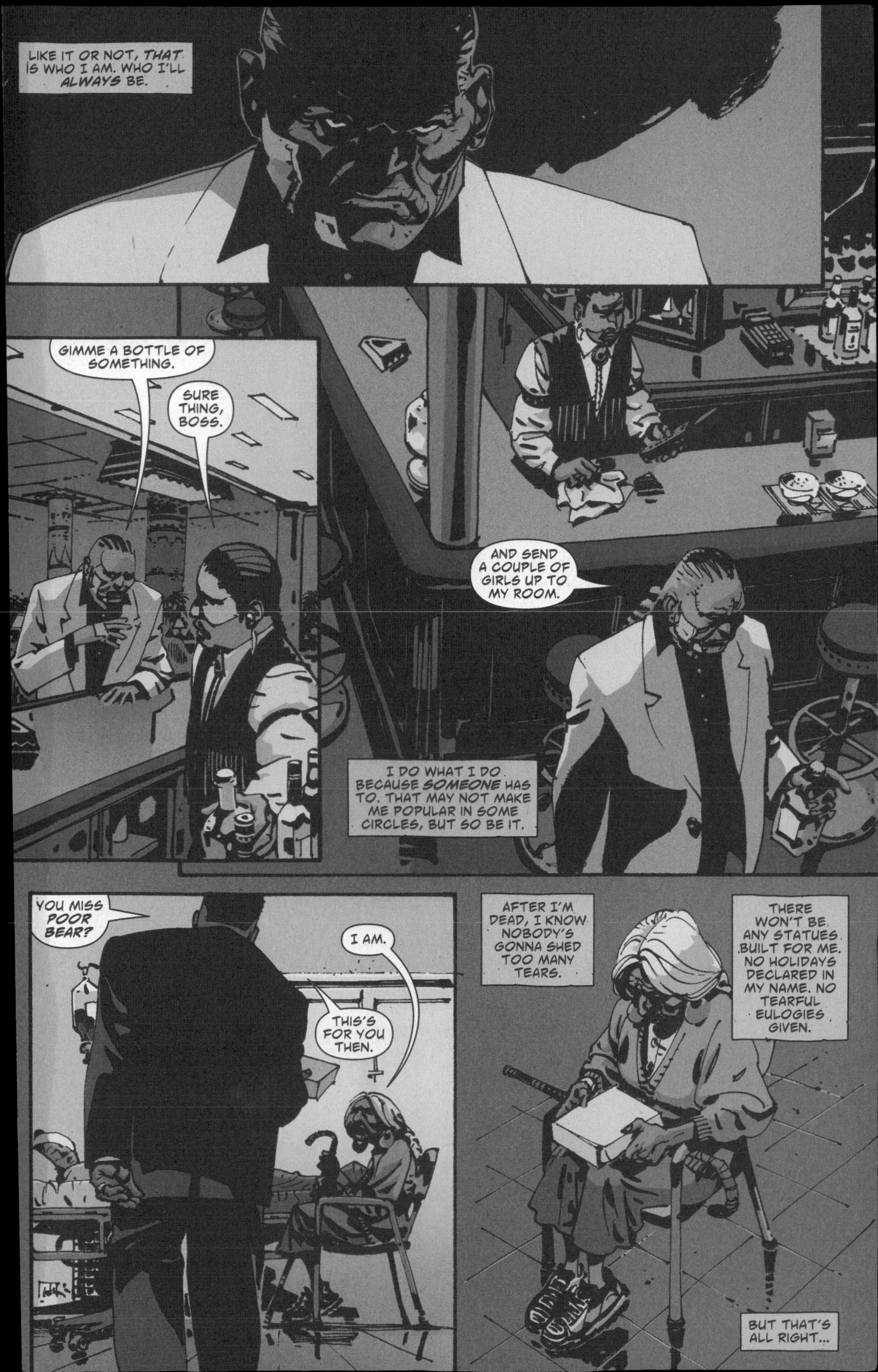

LIKE IT OR NOT, THAT IS WHO I AM. WHO I'LL ALWAYS BE.
GIMME A BOTTLE OF SOMETHING.
SURE THING, BOSS.
AND SEND A COUPLE OF GIRLS UP TO MY ROOM.
I DO WHAT I DO BECAUSE SOMEONE HAS TO. THAT MAY NOT MAKE ME POPULAR IN SOME CIRCLES, BUT SO BE IT.
YOU MISS POOR BEAR?
I AM.
THIS'S FOR YOU THEN.
AFTER I'M DEAD, I KNOW NOBODY'S GONNA SHED TOO MANY TEARS.
THERE WON'T BE ANY STATUES BUILT FOR ME. NO HOLIDAYS DECLARED IN MY NAME. NO TEARFUL EULOGIES GIVEN.
BUT THAT'S ALL RIGHT...

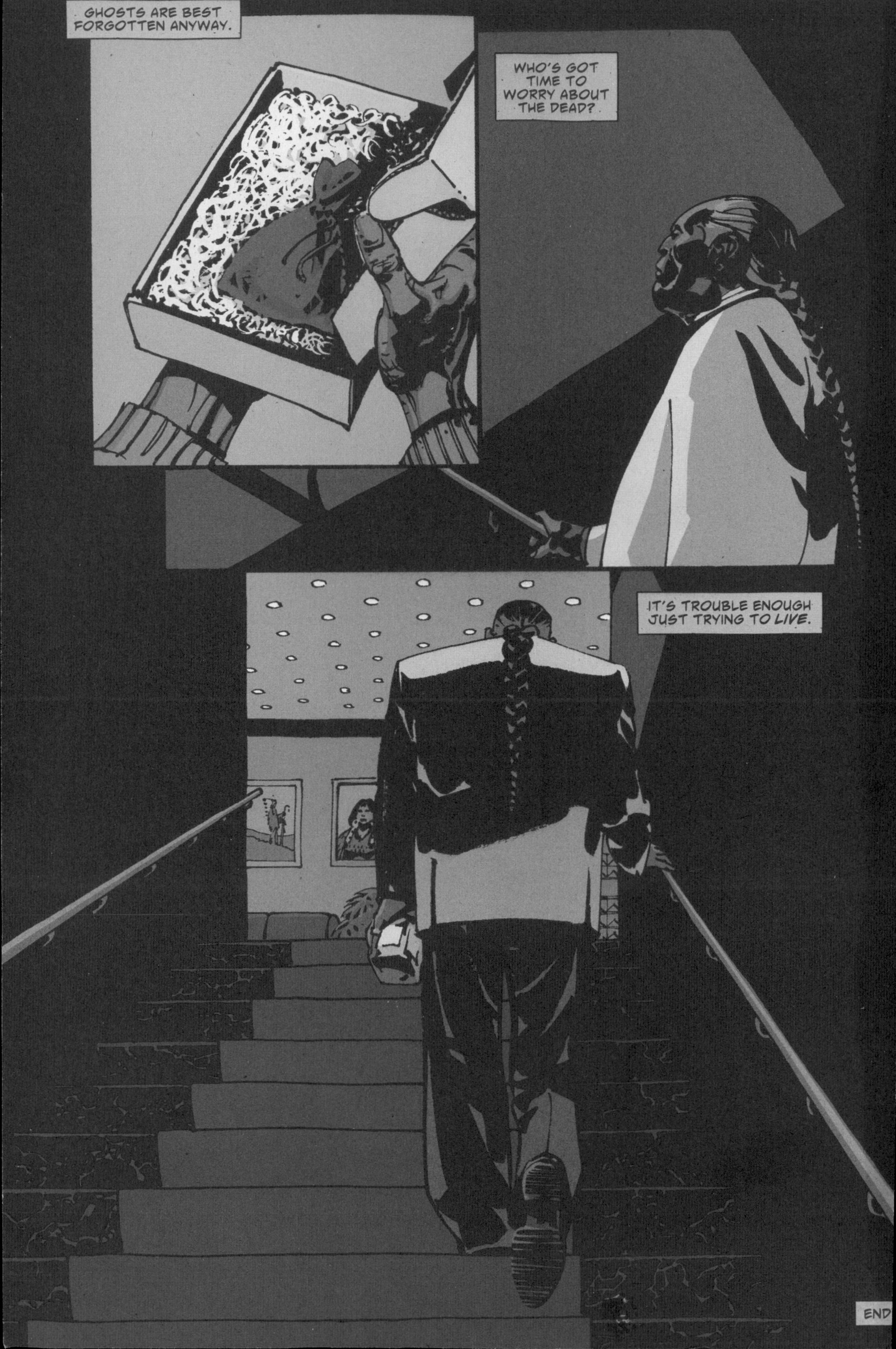
GHOSTS ARE BEST FORGOTTEN ANYWAY.
WHO'S GOT TIME TO WORRY ABOUT THE DEAD?
IT'S TROUBLE ENOUGH JUST TRYING TO *LIVE*.
END